THE WORKS OF
WILLIAM
SHAKESPEARE

VOLUME NINE

WILLIAM SHAKESPEARE

THE WORKS OF WILLIAM SHAKESPEARE

VOLUME NINE

The Tragedy of King Lear
Pericles, Prince of Tyre
The Rape of Lucrece
Sonnets

THE PEEBLES CLASSIC LIBRARY

SANDY LESBERG, *Editor*

Published by Peebles Press International
U.S.A.: 10 Columbus Circle, New York, NY 10019
U.K.: 12 Thayer Street, London W1M 5LD

Distributed by WHS Distributors

PRINTED AND BOUND IN THE U.S.A.

CONTENTS

THE TRAGEDY OF
KING LEAR

DRAMATIS PERSONÆ

LEAR, *King of Britain*
KING OF FRANCE
DUKE OF BURGUNDY
DUKE OF CORNWALL
DUKE OF ALBANY
EARL OF KENT
EARL OF GLOSTER
EDGAR, *son to Gloster*
EDMUND, *bastard son to Gloster*
CURAN, *a courtier*
OSWALD, *steward to Goneril*
Old man, tenant to Gloster
Physician
Fool
An officer, employed by Edmund
Gentleman, attendant on Cordelia
A Herald
Servants to Cornwall

GONERIL ⎫
REGAN ⎬ *daughters to Lear*
CORDELIA ⎭

Knights of Lear's Train, Officers, Messengers,
Soldiers, and Attendants

SCENE—*Britain*

THE TRAGEDY OF

KING LEAR

ACT ONE

SCENE I.—A Room of State in KING LEAR's Palace

Enter KENT, GLOSTER, *and* EDMUND

Kent. I thought, the king had more affected the Duke of Albany, than Cornwall.

Glo. It did always seem so to us: but now, in the division of the kingdom, it appears not which of the dukes he values most; for equalities are so weighed, that curiosity in neither can make choice of either's moiety.

Kent. Is not this your son, my lord?

Glo. His breeding, sir, hath been at my charge. I have so often blushed to acknowledge him, that now I am brazed to it.

Kent. I cannot conceive you.

Glo. Sir, this young fellow's mother could; whereupon she grew round-wombed, and had, indeed, sir, a son for her cradle, ere she had a husband for her bed. Do you smell a fault?

Kent. I cannot wish the fault undone, the issue of it being so proper.

Glo. But I have a son, sir, by order of law, some year elder than this, who yet is no dearer in my account, though this knave came somewhat saucily into the world, before he was sent for; yet was his mother fair, there was good sport at his making, and the whoreson must be acknowledged.—Do you know this noble gentleman, Edmund?

Edm. No, my lord.

Glo. My Lord of Kent: remember him here after as my honourable friend.

Edm. My services to your lordship.

Kent. I must love you, and sue to know you better.

Edm. Sir, I shall study deserving.

Glo. He hath been out nine years, and away he shall again.—The king is coming. *[Sennet within*

13

Enter one bearing a coronet, then LEAR, *then the* DUKES OF
   ALBANY *and* CORNWALL, *next* GONERIL, REGAN,
   CORDELIA, *with followers*

   Lear.   Attend the Lords of France and Burgundy, Gloster.
   Glo.   I shall, my liege.   [*Exeunt Gloster and Edmund*
   Lear.   Meantime we shall express our darker purpose.
Give me the map there.   Know, that we have divided
In three our kingdom; and 't is our fast intent
To shake all cares and business from our age,
Conferring them on younger strengths, while we
Unburthened crawl toward death —Our son of Cornwall,
And you, our no less loving son of Albany,
We have this hour a constant will to publish
Our daughters' several dowers, that future strife
May be prevented now. The princes, France and Burgundy,
Great rivals in our youngest daughter's love,
Long in our court have made their amorous sojourn,
And here are to be answered.   Tell me, my daughters,—
Since now we will divest us both of rule,
Interest of territory, cares of state,—
Which of you, shall we say, doth love us most?
That we our largest bounty may extend
Where nature doth with merit challenge it.
Goneril, our eldest-born, speak first.
   Gon.   Sir,
I love you more than words can wield the matter,
Dearer than eye-sight, space, and liberty,
Beyond what can be valued, rich or rare,
No less than life, with grace, health, beauty, honour;
As much as child e'er loved, or father found:
A love that makes breath poor, and speech unable,
Beyond all manner of so much, I love you.
   Cor.   [*Aside*]   What shall Cordelia do? Love, and be
         silent.
   Lear.   Of all these bounds, even from this line to this,
With shadowy forests and with champains riched,
With plenteous rivers, and wide-skirted meads,
We make thee lady: to thine and Albany's issue
Be this perpetual.—What says our second daughter?
Our dearest Regan, wife to Cornwall? Speak.
   Reg.   I am made of that self metal as my sister,
And prize me at her worth.   In my true heart
I find she names my very deed of love,
Only she comes too short; that I profess
Myself an enemy to all other joys
Which the most precious square of sense possesses,
And find, I am alone felicitate
In your dear highness' love.
   Cor.   [*Aside*]   Then, poor Cordelia!

And yet not so; since, I am sure, my love's
More richer than my tongue.
   Lear. To thee and thine, hereditary ever
Remain this ample third of our fair kingdom;
No less in space, validity, and pleasure.
Than that conferred on Goneril.—Now, our joy,
Although our last, not least; to whose young love
The vines of France and milk of Burgundy
Strive to be interessed; what can you say, to draw
A third more opulent than your sisters? Speak.
   Cor. Nothing, my lord.
   Lear. Nothing?
   Cor. Nothing.
   Lear. Nothing will come of nothing: speak again.
   Cor. Unhappy that I am, I cannot heave
My heart into my mouth: I love your majesty
According to my bond; nor more, nor less.
   Lear. How, how, Cordelia! mend your speech a little,
Lest you may mar your fortunes.
   Cor.   Good my lord
You have begot me, bred me, loved me: I
Return those duties back as are right fit,
Obey you, love you, and most honour you.
Why have my sisters husbands, if they say
They love you all? Haply, when I shall wed,
That lord whose hand must take my plight shall carry
Half my love with him, half my care, and duty:
Sure, I shall never marry like my sisters,
To love my father all.
   Lear. But goes thy heart with this?
   Cor.   Ay, my good lord.
   Lear. So young, and so untender?
   Cor. So young, my lord, and true.
   Lear. Let it be so: thy truth then be thy dower;
For, by the sacred radiance of the sun,
The mysteries of Hecate and the night,
By all the operation of the orbs
From whom we do exist and cease to be,
Here I disclaim all my paternal care,
Propinquity and property of blood,
And as a stranger to my heart and me
Hold thee, from this, for ever. The barbarous Scythian,
Or he that makes his generation messes
To gorge his appetite, shall to my bosom
Be as well neighboured, pitied, and relieved,
As thou my sometime daughter.
   Kent.   Good my liege,—
   Lear. Peace, Kent!
Come not between the dragon and his wrath.
I loved her most, and thought to set my rest

On her kind nursery.—Hence, and avoid my sight!—
So be my grave my peace, as here I give
Her father's heart from her!—Call France. Who stirs?—
Call Burgundy. Cornwall, and Albany,
With my two daughters' dowers digest the third:
Let pride, which she calls plainness, marry her.
I do invest you jointly with my power,
Pre-eminence, and all the large effects
That troop with majesty. Ourself, by monthly course,
With reservation of an hundred knights,
By you to be sustained, shall our abode
Make with you by due turn. Only we shall retain
The name and all the additions to a king;
The sway, revenue, execution of the rest,
Beloved sons, be yours: which to confirm,
This coronet part between you.
    Kent.   Royal Lear,
Whom I have ever honoured as my king,
Loved as my father, as my master followed,
As my great patron thought on in my prayers,—
    Lear.   The bow is bent and drawn; make from the shaft.
    Kent.   Let it fall rather, though the fork invade
The region of my heart.
Be Kent unmannerly when Lear is mad.
What wouldst thou do, old man?
Think'st thou that duty shall have dread to speak,
When power to flattery bows? To plainness honour's
        bound,
When majesty stoops to folly. Reverse thy doom;
And, in thy best consideration, check
This hideous rashness. Answer my life my judgment,
Thy youngest daughter does not love thee least;
Nor are those empty-hearted whose low sound
Reverbs no hollowness.
    Lear.   Kent, on thy life, no more.
    Kent.   My life I never held but as a pawn
To wage against thine enemies, nor fear to lose it,
Thy safety being the motive.
    Lear.   Out of my sight!
    Kent.   See better, Lear; and let me still remain
The true blank of thine eye.
    Lear.   Now, by Apollo,—
    Kent.   Now, by Apollo, king,
Thou swear'st thy gods in vain.
    Lear.   O, vassal! recreant!
              [*Laying his hand upon his sword*
    Alb., Corn.   Dear sir, forbear.
    Kent.   Do;
Kill thy physician, and the fee bestow
Upon the foul disease. Revoke thy gift;

16

Or, whilst I can vent clamour from my throat,
I'll tell thee, thou dost evil.
   Lear.   Hear me, recreant!
On thine allegiance, hear me!
Since thou hast sought to make us break our vow,
Which we durst never yet, and, with strained pride,
To come betwixt our sentence and our power,
Which nor our nature nor our place can bear,
Our potency made good, take thy reward.
Five days we do allot thee for provision
To shield thee from disasters of the world;
And on the sixth to turn thy hated back
Upon our kingdom: if, on the tenth day following,
Thy banished trunk be found in our dominions,
The moment is thy death. Away! By Jupiter,
This shall not be revoked.
   Kent.   Fare thee well, king: since thus thou wilt appear,
Freedom lives hence, and banishment is here.—
[*To Cordelia*] The gods to their dear shelter take thee, maid,
That justly think'st, and hast most rightly said!—
[*To Regan and Goneril*] And your large speeches may your
          deeds approve,
That good effects may spring from words of love.—
Thus Kent, O princes, bids you all adieu;
He'll shape his old course in a country new.   [*Exit*

Flourish. Re-enter GLOSTER; *with* FRANCE *and* BURGUNDY,
and Attendants

   Glo.   Here's France and Burgundy, my noble lord.
   Lear.   My Lord of Burgundy,
We first address toward you, who with this king
Hath rivalled for our daughter. What, in the least,
Will you require in present dower with her,
Or cease your quest of love?
   Bur.   Most royal majesty,
I crave no more than hath your highness offered,
Nor will you tender less.
   Lear.   Right noble Burgundy,
When she was dear to us, we did hold her so;
But now her price is fall'n. Sir, there she stands:
If aught within that little-seeming substance,
Or all of it, with our displeasure pieced,
And nothing more, may fitly like your grace,
She's there, and she is yours.
   Bur.   I know no answer.
   Lear.   Will you, with those infirmities she owes,
Unfriended, new-adopted to our hate,
Dowered with our curse, and strangered with our oath,
Take her, or leave her?

Bur.   Pardon me, royal sir;
Election makes not up on such conditions.

    Lear. Then leave her, sir; for, by the power that made
    me,
I tell you all her wealth.—[*To France*] For you, great king,
I would not from your love make such a stray,
To match you where I hate: therefore, beseech you
To avert your liking a more worthier way
Than on a wretch whom Nature is ashamed
Almost to acknowledge hers.

    France.   This is most strange,
That she who even but now was your best object,
The argument of your praise, balm of your age,
Most best, most dearest, should in this trice of time
Commit a thing so monstrous, to dismantle
So many folds of favour. Sure, her offence
Must be of such unnatural degree,
That monsters it, or your fore-vouched affection
Fall into taint, which to believe of her,
Must be a faith that reason without miracle
Could never plant in me.

    Cor.   I yet beseech your majesty
If for I want that glib and oily art,
To speak and purpose not; since what I well intend,
I'll do't before I speak; that you make known
It is no vicious blot, murder, or foulness,
No unchaste action, or dishonoured step,
That hath deprived me of your grace and favour;
But even for want of that for which I am richer,
A still-soliciting eye, and such a tongue
That I am glad I have not, though not to have it
Hath lost me in your liking.

    Lear.   Better thou
Hadst not been born, than not to have pleased me
    better.

    France. Is it but this? a tardiness in nature,
Which often leaves the history unspoke
That it intends to do?—My Lord of Burgundy,
What say you to the lady? Love's not love,
When it is mingled with regards that stand
Aloof from the entire point. Will you have her?
She is herself a dowry.

    Bur.   Royal king,
Give but that portion which yourself proposed,
And here I take Cordelia by the hand,
Duchess of Burgundy.

    Lear. Nothing. I have sworn: I am firm.

    Bur. I am sorry, then, you have so lost a father
That you must lose a husband.

    Cor.   Peace be with Burgundy!

Since that respects of fortune are his love,
I shall not be his wife.
    France. Fairest Cordelia, that art most rich, being
poor;
Most choice, forsaken; and most loved, despised;
Thee and thy virtues here I seize upon:
Be it lawful I take up what's cast away.
Gods, gods! 't is strange, that from their cold'st neglect
My love should kindle to inflamed respect.
Thy dowerless daughter, king, thrown to my chance,
Is Queen of us, of ours, and our fair France:
Not all the dukes of waterish Burgundy
Shall buy this unprized precious maid of me.
Bid them farewell, Cordelia, though unkind:
Thou losest here, a better where to find.
    Lear. Thou hast her, France: let her be thine; for we
Have no such daughter, nor shall ever see
That face of hers again. Therefore, be gone
Without our grace, our love, our benison.—
Come, noble Burgundy.
    [*Flourish. Exeunt Lear, Burgundy, Cornwall, Albany,*
                             Gloster, and Attendants
    France. Bid farewell to your sisters.
    Cor. The jewels of our father, with washed eyes
Cordelia leaves you. I know you what you are,
And, like a sister, am most loath to call
Your faults as they are named. Love well our father:
To your professéd bosoms I commit him;
But yet, alas, stood I within his grace,
I would prefer him to a better place.
So farewell to you both.
    Reg. Prescribe not us our duty.
    Gon.   Let your study
Be, to content your lord, who hath received you
At fortune's alms: you have obedience scanted,
And well are worth the want that you have wanted.
    Cor. Time shall unfold what pleated cunning hides;
Who cover faults, at last shame them derides.
Well may you prosper!
    France.   Come, my fair Cordelia.
                     [*Exeunt France and Cordelia*
    Gon. Sister, it is not little I have to say
Of what most nearly appertains to us both.
I think, our father will hence to-night.
    Reg. That's most certain, and with you; next month
with us.
    Gon. You see how full of changes his age is; the
observation we have made of it hath not been little: he
always loved our sister most; and with what poor judgment he hath now cast her off, appears too grossly.

Reg. 'T is the infirmity of his age; yet he hath ever but
slenderly known himself.

Gon. The best and soundest of his time hath been but
rash; then must we look to receive from his age not alone
the imperfections of long-ingrafted condition, but there-
withal the unruly waywardness that infirm and choleric
years bring with them.

Reg. Such unconstant starts are we like to have from
him as this of Kent's banishment.

Gon. There is further compliment of leave-taking
between France and him. Pray you, let us hit together:
if our father carry authority with such disposition as he
bears, this last surrender of his will but offend us.

Reg. We shall further think of it.

Gon. We must do something, and i' the heat. [*Exeunt*

SCENE II.—A Hall in the EARL OF GLOSTER's Castle

Enter EDMUND, *with a letter*

Edm. Thou, Nature, art my goddess; to thy law
My services are bound. Wherefore should I
Stand in the plague of custom, and permit
The calumny of nature to deprive me,
For that I am some twelve or fourteen moonshines
Lag of a brother? Why bastard? wherefore base?
When my dimensions are as well compact,
My mind as generous, and my shape as true,
As honest madam's issue? Why brand they us
With base, with baseness, bastardy, base, base,
Who in the lusty stealth of nature take
More composition and fierce quality
Than doth, within a dull, stale, tired bed,
Go to creating a whole tribe of fops
Got 'tween asleep and wake?—Well then,
Legitimate Edgar, I must have your land.
Our father's love is to the bastard Edmund,
As to the legitimate. Fine word, legitimate!
Well, my legitimate, if this letter speed
And my invention thrive, Edmund the base
Shall to the legitimate—I grow, I prosper:
Now, gods, stand up for bastards!

Enter GLOSTER

Glo. Kent banished thus, and France in choler parted,
And the king gone to-night, subscribed his power
Confined to exhibition! All this done
Upon the gad!—Edmund! How now! what news?

20

Edm.   So please your lordship, none.

                                    [Putting up the letter

Glo.   Why so earnestly seek you to put up that letter?

Edm.   I know no news, my lord.

Glo.   What paper were you reading?

Edm.   Nothing, my lord.

Glo.   No? What needs then that terrible despatch of it into your pocket? the quality of nothing hath not such need to hide itself. Let's see; come; if it be nothing, I shall not need spectacles.

Edm.   I beseech you, sir, pardon me: it is a letter from my brother, that I have not all o'erread: and for so much as I have perused, I find it not fit for your o'erlooking.

Glo.   Give me the letter, sir.

Edm.   I shall offend, either to detain or give it. The contents, as in part I understand them, are to blame.

Glo.   Let's see, let's see.

Edm.   I hope, for my brother's justification, he wrote this but as an essay or taste of my virtue.

Glo.   [*Reads*]   *This policy, and reverence of age, makes the world bitter to the best of our times; keeps our fortunes from us, till our oldness cannot relish them. I begin to find an idle and fond bondage in the oppression of aged tyranny, who sways not as it hath power, but as it is suffered. Come to me, that of this I may speak more. If our father would sleep till I waked him, you should enjoy half his revenue for ever, and live the beloved of your brother,* EDGAR. Humph!— Conspiracy?—'Sleep till I waked him,—you should enjoy half his revenue.'—My son Edgar! Had he a hand to write this? a heart and brain to breed it in?—When came this to you? Who brought it?

Edm.   It was not brought me, my lord; there's the cunning of it. I found it thrown in at the casement of my closet.

Glo.   You know the character to be your brother's?

Edm.   If the matter were good, my lord, I durst swear it were his; but, in respect of that, I would fain think it were not.

Glo.   It is his.

Edm.   It is his hand, my lord; but, I hope, his heart is not in the contents.

Glo.   Has he never before sounded you in this business?

Edm.   Never, my lord. But I have often heard him maintain it to be fit that, sons at perfect age and fathers declined, the father should be as ward to the son, and the son manage his revenue.

Glo.   O villain, villain: his very opinion in the letter.— Abhorred villain! Unnatural, detested, brutish villain! worse than brutish! Go, sirrah, seek him; I'll apprehend him. Abominable villain!—Where is he?

Edm. I do not well know, my lord. If it shall please you to suspend your indignation against my brother till you can derive from him better testimony of his intent, you shall run a certain course; where, if you violently proceed against him, mistaking his purpose, it would make a great gap in your own honour and shake in pieces the heart of his obedience. I dare pawn down my life for him, that he hath writ this to feel my affection to your honour, and to no other pretence of danger.

Glo. Think you so?

Edm. If your honour judge it meet, I will place you where you shall hear us confer of this, and by an auricular assurance have your satisfaction, and that without any further delay than this very evening.

Glo. He cannot be such a monster.

Edm. Nor is not, sure.

Glo. To his father, that so tenderly and entirely loves him. Heaven and earth! Edmund, seek him out; wind me into him, I pray you: frame the business after your own wisdom. I would unstate myself to be in a due resolution.

Edm. I will seek him, sir, presently, convey the business as I shall find means, and acquaint you withal.

Glo. These late eclipses in the sun and moon portend no good to us: though the wisdom of nature can reason it thus and thus, yet nature finds itself scourged by the sequent effects. Love cools, friendship falls off, brothers divide: in cities, mutinies; in countries, discord; in palaces, treason; and the bond cracked between son and father. This villain of mine comes under the prediction; there's son against father: the king falls from bias of nature; there's father against child. We have seen the best of our time: machinations, hollowness, treachery, and all ruinous disorders, follow us disquietly to our graves.— Find out this villain, Edmund; it shall lose thee nothing: do it carefully.—And the noble and true-hearted Kent banished! his offence, honesty!—'T is strange.   [*Exit*

Edm. This is the excellent foppery of the world, that, when we are sick in fortune, often the surfeit of our own behaviour, we make guilty of our disasters the sun, the moon, and the stars: as if we were villains by necessity; fools by heavenly compulsion; knaves, thieves, and treachers, by spherical predominance; drunkards, liars, and adulterers, by an enforced obedience of planetary influence; and all that we are evil in, by a divine thrusting on. An admirable evasion of whoremaster man, to lay his goatish disposition on the charge of a star! My father compounded with my mother under the dragon's tail; and my nativity was under *ursa major:* so that it follows, I am rough and lecherous.—Tut! I should have been that I am,

had the maidenliest star in the firmament twinkled on my
bastardising.

Enter EDGAR

Pat: he comes, like the catastrophe of the old comedy,
my cue is villainous melancholy, with a sigh like Tom o'
Bedlam.—O! these eclipses do portend these divisions.
Fa, sol, la, mi.

Edg. How now, brother Edmund, what serious con-
templation are you in?

Edm. I am thinking, brother, of a prediction I read this
other day, what should follow these eclipses.

Edg. Do you busy yourself with that?

Edm. I promise you, the effects he writes of succeed
unhappily: as of unnaturalness between the child and the
parent; death, dearth, dissolutions of ancient amities;
divisions in state; menaces and maledictions against king
and nobles; needless diffidences, banishment of friends,
dissipation of cohorts, nuptial breaches, and I know not
what.

Edg. How long have you been a sectary astronomical?

Edm. Come, come; when saw you my father last?

Edg. The night gone by.

Edm. Spake you with him?

Edg. Ay, two hours together.

Edm. Parted you in good terms? Found you no
displeasure in him, by word, or countenance?

Edg. None at all.

Edm. Bethink yourself, wherein you may have offended
him: and at my entreaty forbear his presence, till some
little time hath qualified the heat of his displeasure, which
at this instant so rageth in him, that with the mischief of
your person it would scarce allay.

Edg. Some villain hath done me wrong.

Edm. That's my fear. I pray you, have a continent
forbearance, till the speed of his rage goes slower; and, as
I say, retire with me to my lodging, from whence I will
fitly bring you to hear my lord speak. Pray you, go:
there's my key. If you do stir abroad, go armed.

Edg. Armed, brother?

Edm. Brother, I advise you to the best; I am no
honest man if there be any good meaning towards you:
I have told you what I have seen and heard, but faintly;
nothing like the image and horror of it. Pray you, away.

Edg. Shall I hear from you anon?

Edm. I do serve you in this business.— [*Exit Edgar*
A credulous father and a brother noble,
Whose nature is so far from doing harms
That he suspects none; on whose foolish honesty
My practices ride easy!—I see the business.—

Let me, if not by birth, have lands by wit:
All with me's meet, that I can fashion fit.   [*Exit*

SCENE III.—A Room in the DUKE OF ALBANY'S Palace

Enter GONERIL, *and* OSWALD, *her steward*

Gon.   Did my father strike my gentleman for chiding of
his fool?
Osw.   Ay, madam.
Gon.   By day and night he wrongs me: every hour
He flashes into one gross crime or other,
That sets us all at odds: I'll not endure it.
His knights grow riotous, and himself upbraids us
On every trifle.   When he returns from hunting,
I will not speak with him; say, I am sick.
If you come slack of former services,
You shall do well; the fault of it I'll answer.
Osw.   He's coming, madam; I hear him.
                                             [*Horns within*
Gon.   Put on what weary negligence you please,
You and your fellows; I'd have it come to question.
If he distaste it, let him to my sister,
Whose mind and mine, I know, in that are one,
Not to be over-ruled.   Idle old man,
That still would manage those authorities
That he hath given away!—Now, by my life,
Old fools are babes again; and must be used
With checks, as flatteries, when they are seen abused.
Remember what I have said.
Osw.   Well, madam.
Gon.   And let his knights have colder looks among you;
What grows of it, no matter; advise your fellows so.
I would breed from hence occasions, and I shall,
That I may speak.   I'll write straight to my sister,
To hold my very course.—Prepare for dinner.   [*Exeunt*

SCENE IV.—A Hall in the Same

Enter KENT, *disguised*

Kent.   If but as well I other accents borrow,
That can my speech defuse, my good intent
May carry through itself to that full issue
For which I razed my likeness.—Now, banished Kent,
If thou canst serve where thou dost stand condemned,
So may it come, thy master whom thou lov'st,
Shall find thee full of labours.

24

Horns within. Enter LEAR, *Knights, and Attendants*

Lear. Let me not stay a jot for dinner; go, get it ready. [*Exit an Attendant*] How now! what art thou?

Kent. A man, sir.

Lear. What dost thou profess? What wouldst thou with us?

Kent. I do profess to be no less than I seem; to serve him truly that will put me in trust; to love him that is honest; to converse with him that is wise, and says little; to fear judgment; to fight when I cannot choose; and to eat no fish.

Lear. What art thou?

Kent. A very honest-hearted fellow, and as poor as the king.

Lear. If thou be as poor for a subject, as he is for a king, thou art poor enough. What wouldst thou?

Kent. Service.

Lear. Whom wouldst thou serve?

Kent. You.

Lear. Dost thou know me, fellow?

Kent. No, sir; but you have that in your countenance which I would fain call master.

Lear. What's that?

Kent. Authority.

Lear. What services canst thou do?

Kent. I can keep honest counsel, ride, run, mar a curious tale in telling it, and deliver a plain message bluntly: that which ordinary men are fit for, I am qualified in; and the best of me is diligence.

Lear. How old art thou?

Kent. Not so young, sir, to love a woman for singing; nor so old, to dote on her for anything: I have years on my back forty-eight.

Lear. Follow me; thou shalt serve me: if I like thee no worse after dinner, I will not part from thee yet.— Dinner, ho, dinner!—Where 's my knave? my fool? Go you, and call my fool hither.   [*Exit an Attendant*

Enter OSWALD

You, you, sirrah, where's my daughter?

Osw. So please you,—   [*Exit*

Lear. What says the fellow there? Call the clotpoll back. [*Exit a Knight*]—Where 's my fool, ho?—I think the world's asleep.

Re-enter Knight

How now! where's that mongrel?

Knight. He says, my lord, your daughter is not well.

Lear. Why came not the slave back to me, when I called him?

Knight. Sir, he answered me in the roundest manner, he would not.

Lear. He would not?

Knight. My lord, I know not what the matter is; but, to my judgment, your highness is not entertained with that ceremonious affection as you were wont; there's a great abatement of kindness appears, as well in the general dependants as in the duke himself also and your daughter.

Lear. Ha! sayest thou so?

Knight. I beseech you, pardon me, my lord, if I be mistaken; for my duty cannot be silent, when I think your highness wronged.

Lear. Thou but rememberest me of mine own conception. I have perceived a most faint neglect of late; which I have rather blamed as mine own jealous curiosity than as a very pretence and purpose of unkindness; I will look further into't.—But where's my fool? I have not seen him this two days.

Knight. Since my young lady's going into France, sir, the fool hath much pined away.

Lear. No more of that; I have noted it well.—Go you, and tell my daughter, I would speak with her. [*Exit an Attendant*]—Go you, call hither my fool.

[*Exit an Attendant*

Re-enter OSWALD

O! you sir, you, come you hither, sir: Who am I, sir?

Osw. My lady's father.

Lear. My lady's father! my lord's knave: you whoreson dog! you slave! you cur!

Osw. I am none of these, my lord; I beseech your pardon.

Lear. Do you bandy looks with me, you rascal?

[*Striking him*

Osw. I'll not be struck, my lord.

Kent. Nor tripped neither, you base football player.

[*Tripping up his heels*

Lear. I thank thee, fellow; thou servest me, and I'll love thee.

Kent. Come, sir, arise, away! I'll teach you differences; away, away! If you will measure your lubber's length again, tarry; but away! Go to: have you wisdom? so. [*Pushes Oswald out*

Lear. Now, my friendly knave, I thank thee: there's earnest of thy service. [*Giving Kent money*

Enter Fool

Fool. Let me hire him too:—here's my coxcomb.
  [*Giving Kent his cap*
Lear. How now, my pretty knave? how dost thou?
Fool. Sirrah, you were best take my coxcomb.
Kent. Why, fool?
Fool. Why, for taking one's part that's out of favour.
—Nay, an thou canst not smile as the wind sits, thou'lt
catch cold shortly: there, take my coxcomb. Why, this
fellow has banished two on's daughters, and did the third
a blessing against his will: if thou follow him, thou must
needs wear my coxcomb.—How now, nuncle? 'Would I
had two coxcombs, and two daughters!
Lear. Why, my boy?
Fool. If I gave them all my living, I'd keep my
coxcombs myself. There's mine; beg another of thy
daughters.
Lear. Take heed, sirrah,—the whip.
Fool. Truth's a dog must to kennel; he must be
whipped out, when the lady brach may stand by the fire
and stink.
Lear. A pestilent gall to me!
Fool. Sirrah, I'll teach thee a speech.
Lear. Do.
Fool. Mark it, nuncle:

> Have more than thou showest,
> Speak less than thou knowest,
> Lend less than thou owest,
> Ride more than thou goest,
> Learn more than thou trowest,
> Set less than thou throwest;
> Leave thy drink and thy whore,
> And keep in-a-door,
> And thou shalt have more
> Than two tens to a score.

Kent. This is nothing, fool.
Fool. Then't is like the breath of an unfee'd lawyer,—
you gave me nothing for't.—Can you make no use of
nothing, nuncle?
Lear. Why, no, boy; nothing can be made out of
nothing.
Fool. [*To Kent*] Pr'ythee, tell him, so much the rent
of his land comes to: he will not believe a fool.
Lear. A bitter fool!
Fool. Dost thou know the difference, my boy, between
a bitter fool and a sweet fool?
Lear. No, lad; teach me.

Fool. That lord, that counselled thee
    To give away thy land,
Come place him here by me,—
    Do thou for him stand:
The sweet and bitter fool
    Will presently appear;
The one in motley here,
    The other found out there.

Lear. Dost thou call me fool, boy?

Fool. All thy other titles thou hast given away; that thou wast born with.

Kent. This is not altogether fool, my lord.

Fool. No, 'faith; lords and great men will not let me; if I had a monopoly out, they would have part on 't; and ladies too, they will not let me have all fool to myself; they'll be snatching.—Nuncle, give me an egg, and I'll give thee two crowns.

Lear. What two crowns shall they be?

Fool. Why, after I have cut the egg i' the middle, and eat up the meat, the two crowns of the egg. When thou clovest thy crown i' the middle, and gavest away both parts, thou borest thine ass on thy back o'er the dirt: thou hadst little wit in thy bald crown, when thou gavest thy golden one away. If I speak like myself in this, let him be whipped that first finds it so.   [*Singing*

    Fools had ne'er less grace in a year;
      For wise men are grown foppish,
    And know not how their wits to wear,
      Their manners are so apish.

Lear. When were you wont to be so full of songs, sirrah?

Fool. I have used it, nuncle, ever since thou madest thy daughters thy mothers: for when thou gavest them the rod and putt'st down thine own breeches,   [*Singing*

    Then they for sudden joy did weep,
      And I for sorrow sung,
    That such a king should play bo-peep,
      And go the fools among.

Pr'ythee, nuncle, keep a schoolmaster that can teach thy fool to lie: I would fain learn to lie.

Lear. An you lie, sirrah, we'll have you whipped.

Fool. I marvel, what kin thou and thy daughters are: they'll have me whipped for speaking true, thou 'lt have me whipped for lying; and sometimes I am whipped for holding my peace. I had rather be any kind o' thing than a fool; and yet I would not be thee, nuncle; thou hast

pared thy wit o' both sides, and left nothing i' the middle:
—here comes one o' the parings.

Enter GONERIL

Lear. How now, daughter! what makes that frontlet
        on?
Methinks, you are too much of late i' the frown.
  Fool. Thou wast a pretty fellow, when thou hadst no
need to care for her frowning; now thou art an O without
a figure. I am better than thou art now; I am a fool,
thou art nothing.—[*To Goneril*] Yes, forsooth, I will hold
my tongue; so your face bids me, though you say
nothing.

            Mum, Mum:
            He that keeps nor crust nor crum,
            Weary of all, shall want some.

That's a shelled peascod.
  Gon. Not only, sir, this your all-licensed fool,
But other of your insolent retinue
Do hourly carp and quarrel; breaking forth
In rank and not-to-be enduréd riots.
Sir, I had thought, by making this well known unto you,
To have found a safe redress; but now grow fearful,
By what yourself too late have spoke and done
That you protect this course, and put it on
By your allowance; which if you should, the fault
Would not 'scape censure, nor the redresses sleep,
Which, in the tender of a wholesome weal,
Might in their working do you that offence,
Which else were shame, that then necessity
Will call discreet proceeding.
  Fool. For you know, nuncle,

            The hedge-sparrow fed the cuckoo so long,
            That it had it head bit off by it young.

So, out went the candle, and we were left darkling.
  Lear. Are you our daughter?
  Gon. I would you would make use of your good wisdom,
Whereof I know you are fraught, and put away
These dispositions, which of late transport you
From what you rightly are.
  Fool. May not an ass know when the cart draws the
horse?—Whoop, Jug! I love thee.
  Lear. Does any here know me? This is not Lear:
Does Lear walk thus? speak thus? where are his eyes?
Either his notion weakens or his discernings

Are lethargied.—Ha! waking? 't is not so.—
Who is it that can tell me who I am?—
   Fool. Lear's shadow.
   Lear. I would learn that; for by the marks of
sovereignty, knowledge, and reason, I should be false persuaded I had daughters.
   Fool. Which they will make an obedient father.
   Lear. Your name, fair gentlewoman?
   Gon. This admiration, sir, is much o' the savour
Of other your new pranks. I do beseech you
To understand my purposes aright:
As you are old and reverend, should be wise.
Here do you keep a hundred knights and squires;
Men so disordered, so debauched, and bold,
That this our court, infected with their manners,
Shows like a riotous inn: epicurism and lust
Make it more like a tavern or a brothel
Than a graced palace. The shame itself doth speak
For instant remedy: be then desired,
By her that else will take the things she begs,
A little to disquantity your train;
And the remainder that shall still depend,
To be such men as may besort your age,
Which know themselves and you.
   Lear.   Darkness and devils!—
Saddle my horses; call my train together.—
Degenerate bastard! I'll not trouble thee:
Yet have I left a daughter.
   Gon. You strike my people; and your disordered rabble
Make servants of their betters.

Enter ALBANY

   Lear. Woe, that too late repents,—[*To Albany*]
O, sir, are you come?
Is it your will? Speak, sir.—Prepare my horses.—
Ingratitude, thou marble-hearted fiend,
More hideous when thou show'st thee in a child
Than the sea-monster!
   Alb.   Pray, sir, be patient.
   Lear. [*To Goneril*] Detested kite! thou liest:
My train are men of choice and rarest parts,
That all particulars of duty know,
And in the most exact regard support
The worships of their name.—O most small fault,
How ugly didst thou in Cordelia show!
Which, like an engine, wrenched my frame of nature
From the fixed place, drew from my heart all love,
And added to the gall. O Lear, Lear, Lear!
Beat at this gate, that let thy folly in,   [*Striking his head*

And thy dear judgment out!—Go, go, my people.
   Alb. My lord, I'm guiltless, as I'm ignorant
Of what hath moved you.
   Lear.   It may be so, my lord.—
Hear, Nature, hear! dear goddess, hear!
Suspend thy purpose, if thou didst intend
To make this creature fruitful!
Into her womb convey sterility!
Dry up in her the organs of increase,
And from her derogate body never spring
A babe to honour her! If she must teem,
Create her child of spleen; that it may live,
And be a thwart disnatured torment to her!
Let it stamp wrinkles in her brow of youth;
With cadent tears fret channels in her cheeks;
Turn all her mother's pains and benefits
To laughter and contempt: that she may feel
How sharper than a serpent's tooth it is
To have a thankless child!—Away, away!   *[Exit*
   Alb. Now, gods that we adore, whereof comes this?
   Gon. Never afflict yourself to know more of it;
But let his disposition have that scope
That dotage gives it.

Re-enter LEAR

   Lear. What, fifty of my followers at a clap!
Within a fortnight?
   Alb.   What's the matter, sir?
   Lear. I'll tell thee,—[*To Goneril*] Life and death! I
      am ashamed
That thou hast power to shake my manhood thus;
That these hot tears, which break from me perforce,
Should make thee worth them.—Blasts and fogs upon thee!
The untented woundings of a father's curse
Pierce every sense about thee!—Old fond eyes,
Beweep this cause again, I'll pluck ye out,
And cast you, with the waters that you lose,
To temper clay.—Yea, is it come to this!
Let it be so:—yet have I left a daughter,
Who, I am sure, is kind and comfortable:
When she shall hear this of thee, with her nails
She'll flay thy wolfish visage. Thou shalt find
That I'll resume the shape which thou dost think
I have cast off for ever.
           [Exeunt Lear, Kent, and Attendants
   Gon. Do you mark that, my lord?
   Alb. I cannot be so partial, Goneril,
To the great love I bear you,—
   Gon. Pray you, content.—What, Oswald, ho!—

[*To the Fool*] You, sir, more knave than fool, after your
    master.
    Fool. Nuncle Lear, nuncle Lear! tarry, and take the
fool with thee.

> A fox, when one has caught her,
> And such a daughter,
> Should sure to the slaughter,
> If my cap would buy a halter;
> So the fool follows after.   [*Exit*

    Gon. This man hath had counsel:—a hundred knights!
'T is politic, and safe, to let him keep
At point a hundred knights: yes, that on every dream,
Each buzz, each fancy, each complaint, dislike,
He may enguard his dotage with their powers,
And hold our lives in mercy.—Oswald, I say!—
    Alb. Well, you may fear too far.
    Gon.   Safer than trust too far:
Let me still take away the harms I fear,
Not fear still to be taken: I know his heart.
What he hath uttered I have writ my sister:
If she sustain him and his hundred knights,
When I have showed the unfitness,—

Re-enter OSWALD

                                        How now, Oswald!
What, have you writ that letter to my sister?
    Osw. Ay, madam.
    Gon. Take you some company, and away to horse:
Inform her full of my particular fear;
And thereto add such reasons of your own
As may compact it more. Get you gone,
And hasten your return. [*Exit Oswald*] No, no, my lord,
This milky gentleness and course of yours
Though I dislike not, yet, under pardon,
You are much more attasked for want of wisdom,
Than praised for harmful mildness.
    .Alb. How far your eyes may pierce, I cannot tell:
Striving to better, oft we mar what's well.
    Gon. Nay, then—
    Alb. Well, well; the event.   [*Exeunt*

SCENE V.—Court before the Same

Enter LEAR, KENT, *and* Fool

    Lear. Go you before to Gloster, with these letters.
Acquaint my daughter no further with anything you know

than comes from her demand out of the letter. **If your**
diligence be not speedy, I shall be there before you.

Kent. I will not sleep, my lord, till I have delivered your
letter.   [*Exit*

Fool. If a man's brains were in his heels, were't not in
danger of kibes?

Lear. Ay, boy.

Fool. Then, I pr'ythee, be merry; thy wit shall not go
slip-shod.

Lear. Ha, ha, ha!

Fool. Shalt see, thy other daughter will use thee kindly;
for though she's as like this as a crab is like an apple, yet
I can tell what I can tell.

Lear. What canst tell, boy?

Fool. She will taste as like this as a crab does to a crab.
Thou canst tell why one's nose stands i' the middle on's face?

Lear. No.

Fool. Why, to keep one's eyes off either side's nose;
that what a man cannot smell out, he may spy into.

Lear. I did her wrong—

Fool. Canst tell how an oyster makes his shell?

Lear. No.

Fool. Nor I neither; but I can tell why a snail has a
house.

Lear. Why?

Fool. Why, to put his head in; not to give it away to
his daughters, and leave his horns without a case.

Lear. I will forget my nature.—So kind a father!—Be
my horses ready?

Fool. Thy asses are gone about 'em. The reason why
the seven stars are no more than seven is a pretty reason.

Lear. Because they are not eight?

Fool. Yes, indeed. Thou wouldst make a good fool.

Lear. To take 't again perforce!—Monster ingratitude!

Fool. If thou wert my fool, nuncle, I'd have thee beaten
for being old before thy time.

Lear. How's that?

Fool. Thou shouldst not have been old till thou hadst
been wise.

Lear. O, let me not be mad, not mad, sweet heaven!
Keep me in temper: I would not be mad!—

Enter Gentleman

How now! Are the horses ready?

Gent. Ready, my lord.

Lear. Come, boy.

Fool. She that's a maid now, and laughs at my departure,
Shall not be a maid long, unless things be cut shorter.
                                                      [*Exeunt*

ACT TWO

Scene I.—A Court within the Castle of the Earl of Gloster

Enter EDMUND *and* CURAN, *meeting*

Edm. Save thee, Curan

Cur. And you, sir. I have been with your father, and given him notice, that the Duke of Cornwall and Regan his duchess will be here with him to-night.

Edm. How comes that?

Cur. Nay, I know not. You have heard of the news abroad? I mean, the whispered ones, for they are yet but ear-kissing arguments.

Edm. Not I: pray you, what are they?

Cur. Have you heard of no likely wars toward, 'twixt the Dukes of Cornwall and Albany?

Edm. Not a word.

Cur. You may do then, in time. Fare you well, sir.
                                                              [*Exit*

Edm. The duke be here to-night? The better! best!
This weaves itself perforce into my business.
My father hath set guard to take my brother;
And I have one thing, of a queasy question,
Which I must act.—Briefness and fortune, work!
Brother, a word;—descend:—brother, I say!

Enter EDGAR

My father watches.—O sir, fly this place;
Intelligence is given where you are hid;
You have now the good advantage of the night:—
Have you not spoken 'gainst the Duke of Cornwall?
He's coming hither; now, i' the night, i' th' haste,
And Regan with him: have you nothing said
Upon his party 'gainst the Duke of Albany?
Advise yourself.

Edg.   I'm sure on 't, not a word.

Edm. I hear my father coming.—Pardon me:
In cunning, I must draw my sword upon you:
Draw: seem to defend yourself: now quit you well.
Yield:—come before my father.—Light, ho, here!—
Fly, brother.—Torches, torches!—So farewell.
                                                        [*Exit Edgar*
Some blood drawn on me would beget opinion
Of my more fierce endeavour: I have seen drunkards
                                                        [*Wounds his arm*
Do more than this in sport.—Father, father!
Stop, stop! No help?

Enter GLOSTER, *and Servants with torches*

Glo.   Now, Edmund, where's the villain?
Edm.   Here stood he in the dark, his sharp sword out,
Mumbling of wicked charms, conjuring the moon
To stand auspicious mistress,—
    Glo.   But where is he?
Edm.   Look, sir, I bleed.
    Glo.   Where is the villain, Edmund?
Edm.   Fled this way, sir.   When by no means he
        could—
    Glo.   Pursue him, ho!—Go after.   [*Exit Servant*]—By
        no means—what?
    Edm.   Persuade me to the murder of your lordship;
But that I told him the revenging gods
'Gainst parricides did all their thunders bend;
Spoke, with how manifold and strong a bond
The child was bound to the father;—sir, in fine,
Seeing how loathly opposite I stood
To his unnatural purpose, in fell motion,
With his preparéd sword he charges home
My unprovided body, lanced my arm:
But when he saw my best alarum'd spirits,
Bold in the quarrel's right, roused to th' encounter,
Or whether ghasted by the noise I made,
Full suddenly he fled.
    Glo.   Let him fly far:
Not in this land shall he remain uncaught;
And found—despatch.—The noble duke my master,
My worthy arch and patron, comes to-night:
By his authority I will proclaim it,
That he which finds him shall deserve our thanks,
Bringing the murderous coward to the stake;
He that conceals him, death.
    Edm.   When I dissuaded him from his intent,
And found him pight to do it with curst speech
I threatened to discover him; he replied,
'Thou unpossessing bastard! dost thou think,
If I would stand against thee, would the reposal
Of any trust, virtue, or worth, in thee
Make thy words faithed?   No: what I should deny,
As this I would: ay, though thou didst produce
My very character, I'd turn it all
To thy suggestion, plot, and damnéd practice:
And thou must make a dullard of the world,
If they not thought the profits of my death
Were very pregnant and potential spurs
To make thee seek it.'
    Glo.   Strong and fastened villain
Would he deny his letter?—I never got him. [*Tucket within*
                            35

Hark, the duke's trumpets. I know not why he comes.
All ports I'll bar; the villain shall not 'scape;
The duke must grant me that: besides, his picture
I will send far and near, that all the kingdom
May have due note of him; and of my land,
Loyal and natural boy, I'll work the means
To make thee capable.

Enter CORNWALL, REGAN, *and Attendants*

    Corn. How now, my noble friend: since I came hither—
Which I can call but now—I have heard strange news.
    Reg. If it be true, all vengeance comes too short
Which can pursue the offender. How dost, my lord?
    Glo. O, madam, my old heart is cracked—it's cracked!
    Reg. What, did my father's godson seek your life?
He whom my father named? your Edgar?
    Glo. O, lady, lady, shame would have it hid.
    Reg. Was he not companion with the riotous knights
That tend upon my father?
    Glo. I know not, madam, 't is too bad, too bad.
    Edm. Yes, madam, he was of that consort.
    Reg. No marvel then, though he were ill affected:
'T is they have put him on the old man's death,
To have th' expense and waste of his revenues.
I have this present evening from my sister
Been well informed of them; and with such cautions
That if they come to sojourn at my house,
I'll not be there.
    Corn. Nor I, assure thee, Regan.—
Edmund, I hear that you have shown your father
A child-like office.
    Edm. 'T was my duty, sir.
    Glo. He did bewray his practice! and received
This hurt you see, striving to apprehend him.
    Corn. Is he pursued?
    Glo. Ay, my good lord.
    Corn. If he be taken, he shall never more
Be feared of doing harm: make your own purpose,
How in my strength you please.—For you, Edmund,
Whose virtue and obedience doth this instant
So much commend itself, you shall be ours:
Natures of such deep trust we shall much need;
You we first seize on.
    Edm. I shall serve you, sir,
Truly, however else.
    Glo. For him I thank your grace.
    Corn. You know not why we came to visit you,—
    Reg. Thus out of season, threading dark-eyed night;
Occasions, noble Gloster, of some poise,

Wherein we must have use of your advice:—
Our father he hath writ, so hath our sister,
Of differences, which I best thought it fit
To answer from our home; the several messengers
From hence attend despatch. Our good old friend,
Lay comforts to your bosom; and bestow
Your needful counsel to our business,
Which craves the instant use.

    Glo.   I serve you, madam.
Your graces are right welcome.   *[Exeunt*

Scene II.—Before Gloster's Castle

Enter Kent *and* Oswald, *severally*

  Osw. Good dawning to thee, friend: art of this house?
  Kent. Ay.
  Osw. Where may we set our horses?
  Kent. I' the mire.
  Osw. Pr'ythee, if thou lov'st me, tell me.
  Kent. I love thee not.
  Osw. Why, then I care not for thee.
  Kent. If I had thee in Lipsbury pinfold, I would make
thee care for me.
  Osw. Why dost thou use me thus? I know thee not.
  Kent. Fellow, I know thee.
  Osw. What dost thou know me for?
  Kent. A knave; a rascal; an eater of broken meats;
a base, proud, shallow, beggarly, three-suited, hundred
pound, filthy, worsted-stocking knave; a lily-livered,
action-taking knave; a whoreson, glass-gazing, super-
serviceable, finical rogue; one-trunk-inheriting slave; one
that wouldst be a bawd, in way of good service, and art
nothing but the composition of a knave, beggar, coward,
pander, and the son and heir of a mongrel bitch; one
whom I will beat into clamorous whining, if thou deniest
the least syllable of thy addition.
  Osw. Why, what a monstrous fellow art thou, thus to
rail on one that is neither known of thee nor knows thee!
  Kent. What a brazen-faced varlet art thou, to deny
thou knowest me? Is it two days since I tripped up thy
heels, and beat thee, before the king? Draw, you rogue;
for though it be night, yet the moon shines; I'll make a
sop o' the moonshine of you: *[Drawing his sword]* Draw,
you whoreson cullionly barber-monger, draw.
  Osw. Away! I have nothing to do with thee.
  Kent. Draw, you rascal; you come with letters against
the king, and take Vanity the puppet's part, against the
royalty of her father. Draw, you rogue, or I'll so carbonado
your shanks:—draw, you rascal: come your ways.

Osw. Help, ho! murder! help!

Kent. Strike, you slave: stand, rogue, stand; you neat
slave, strike.   [*Beating him*

Osw. Help, ho! murder! murder!

Enter EDMUND

Edm. How now! What's the matter?

Kent. With you, goodman boy, if you please: come
I'll flesh you, come, young master.

Enter CORNWALL, REGAN, GLOSTER, *and Servants*

Glo. Weapons! arms! What's the matter here?

Corn. Keep peace, upon your lives;
He dies that strikes again. What is the matter?

Reg. The messengers from our sister and the king.

Corn. What is your difference? speak.

Osw. Am scarce in breath, my lord.

Kent. No marvel, you have so bestirred your valour.
You cowardly rascal, nature disclaims in thee: a tailor
made thee.

Corn. Thou art a strange fellow: a tailor make a man?

Kent. Ay, a tailor, sir: a stone-cutter, or a painter,
could not have made him so ill, though they had been but
two hours o' the trade.

Corn. Speak yet, how grew your quarrel?

Osw. This ancient ruffian, sir, whose life I have spared,
At suit of his grey beard,—

Kent. Thou whoreson zed! thou unnecessary letter?—
My lord, if you will give me leave, I will tread this unbolted
villain into mortar, and daub the wall of a jakes with him.—
Spare my grey beard, you wag-tail?

Corn. Peace, sirrah!
You beastly knave, know you no reverence!

Kent. Yes, sir; but anger hath a privilege.

Corn. Why art thou angry?

Kent. That such a slave as this should wear a sword,
Who wears no honesty. Such smiling rogues as these,
Like rats, oft bite the holy cords a-twain
Which are too intrinse t' unloose; smooth every passion
That in the natures of their lords rebel;
Bring oil to fire, snow to their colder moods;
Renege, affirm, and turn their halcyon beaks
With every gale and vary of their masters,
Knowing naught, like dogs, but following.—
A plague upon your epileptic visage!
Smile you my speeches, as I were a fool?
Goose, if I had you upon Sarum plain,
I'd drive ye cackling home to Camelot.

Corn. What, art thou mad, old fellow?

38

Glo. How fell you out? say that
Kent. No contraries hold more antipathy,
Than I and such a knave.
   Corn. Why dost thou call him knave? What is his
     fault?
   Kent. His countenance likes me not.
   Corn. No more, perchance, does mine, nor his, nor hers.
   Kent. Sir, 't is my occupation to be plain:
I have seen better faces in my time
Than stands on any shoulder that I see
Before me at this instant.
   Corn.   This is some fellow,
Who, having been praised for bluntness, doth affect
A saucy roughness, and constrains the garb
Quite from his nature: he cannot flatter, he;
An honest mind and plain,—he must speak truth:
An they will take it, so; if not, he's plain.
These kind of knaves I know, which in this plainness
Harbour more craft, and more corrupter ends,
Than twenty silly ducking observants,
That stretch their duties nicely.
   Kent. Sir, in good sooth, in sincere verity,
Under the allowance of your great aspect,
Whose influence, like the wreath of radiant fire
On flickering Phœbus' front,—
   Corn.   What mean'st by this?
   Kent. To go out of my dialect, which you discommend
so much. I know, sir, I am no flatterer: he that beguiled
you in a plain accent was a plain knave; which, for my
part, I will not be, though I should win your displeasure
to entreat me to 't.
   Corn. What was the offence you gave him?
   Osw. I never gave him any:
It pleased the king, his master, very late,
To strike at me, upon his misconstruction;
When he, conjunct, and flattering his displeasure,
Tripped me behind; being down, insulted, railed,
And put upon him such a deal of man,
That worthied him, got praises of the king
For him attempting who was self-subdued;
And, in the fleshment of this dread exploit,
Drew on me here again.
   Kent. None of these rogues, and cowards
But Ajax is their fool.
   Corn.   Fetch forth the stocks!
You stubborn ancient knave, you reverend braggart,
We'll teach you.
   Kent.   Sir, I am too old to learn.
Call not your stocks for me; I serve the king,
On whose employment I was sent to you:

You shall do small respect, show too bold malice
Against the grace and person of my master,
Stocking his messenger.
   Corn.   Fetch forth the stocks!
As I have life and honour, there shall he sit till noon.
   Reg.   Till noon! till night, my lord; and all night too.
   Kent.   Why, madam, if I were your father's dog,
You should not use me so.
   Reg.   Sir, being his knave, I will.
   Corn.   This is a fellow of the selfsame colour
Our sister speaks of.—Come, bring away the stocks.
                              [Stocks brought out
   Glo.   Let me beseech your grace not to do so.
His fault is much, and the good king his master
Will check him for 't: your purposed low correction
Is such as basest and contemned'st wretches,
For pilferings and most common trespasses,
Are punished with. The king must take it ill,
That he, so slightly valued in his messenger,
Should have him thus restrained.
   Corn.   I'll answer that.
   Reg.   My sister may receive it much more worse,
To have her gentleman abused, assaulted,
For following her affairs.—Put in his legs.—
                     [Kent is put in the stocks
Come, my lord, away.   *[Exeunt all but Gloster and Kent*
   Glo.   I am sorry for thee, friend; 't is the duke's pleasure,
Whose disposition, all the world well knows,
Will not be rubbed, nor stopped: I'll entreat for thee.
   Kent.   Pray, do not, sir. I have watched, and travelled
      hard;
Some time I shall sleep out, the rest I'll whistle.
A good man's fortune may grow out at heels:
Give you good morrow!
   Glo.   The duke's to blame in this: 't will be ill taken. *[Exit*
   Kent.   Good king, that must approve the common saw,—
Thou out of heaven's benediction com'st
To the warm sun.
Approach, thou beacon to this under globe,
That by thy comfortable beams I may
Peruse this letter.—Nothing almost sees miracles
But misery:—I know, 't is from Cordelia;
Who hath most fortunately been informed
Of my obscuréd course; and shall find turn
From this injurious state, seeking to give
Losses their remedies.—All weary and o'erwatched,
Take vantage, heavy eyes, not to behold
This shameful lodging.
Fortune, good night; smile once more; turn thy wheel!
                              [He sleeps

Scene III.—A part of the Heath

Enter Edgar

Edg. I heard myself proclaimed;
And, by the happy hollow of a tree,
Escaped the hunt. No port is free; no place,
That guard and most unusual vigilance
Does not attend my taking. While I may 'scape
I will preserve myself; and am bethought
To take the basest and most poorest shape
That ever penury, in contempt of man,
Brought near to beast; my face I'll grime with filth,
Blanket my loins, elf all my hair in knots,
And with presented nakedness outface
The winds and persecutions of the sky.
The country gives me proof and precedent
Of Bedlam beggars, who, with roaring voices,
Strike in their numbed and mortified bare arms
Pins, wooden pricks, nails, sprigs of rosemary;
And with this horrible object, from low farms,
Poor pelting villages, sheep-cotes, and mills,
Sometime with lunatic bans, sometime with prayers,
Enforce their charity.—Poor Turlygood! poor Tom!
That's something yet:—Edgar I nothing am.   *[Exit*

Scene IV.—Before Gloster's Castle: Kent in the Stocks

Enter Lear, Fool, and Gentleman

Lear. 'T is strange that they should so depart from home,
And not send back my messenger.
   Gent.   As I learned,
The night before there was no purpose in them
Of this remove.
   Kent.   Hail to thee, noble master!
   Lear. Ha!
Mak'st thou this shame thy pastime?
                    No, my lord.
   Fool. Ha, ha! look; he wears cruel garters.
Horses are tied by the head, dogs and bears by the neck,
monkeys by the loins, and men by the legs: when a man's
over-lusty at legs, then he wears wooden nether-stocks.
   Lear. What's he that hath so much thy place mistook
To set thee here?
   Kent.   It is both he and she,—
Your son and daughter.

41

Lear. No.
Kent. Yes.
Lear. No, I say.
Kent. I say, yea.
Lear. No, no; they would not.
Kent. Yes, they have.
Lear. By Jupiter, I swear, no.
Kent. By Juno, I swear, ay.
Lear.   They durst not do 't;
They could not, would not do 't: 't is worse than murder,
To do upon respect such violent outrage.
Resolve me, with all modest haste, which way
Thou mightst deserve, or they impose, this usage
Coming from us.
Kent.   My lord, when at their home
I did commend your highness' letters to them,
Ere I was risen from the place that showed
My duty kneeling, came there a reeking post,
Stewed in his haste, half breathless, panting forth
From Goneril, his mistress, salutations;
Delivered letters, spite of intermission,
Which presently they read: on whose contents
They summoned up their meiny, straight took horse;
Commanded me to follow, and attend
The leisure of their answer; gave me cold looks:
And meeting here the other messenger,
Whose welcome, I perceived, had poisoned mine,—
Being the very fellow which of late
Displayed so saucily against your highness,
Having more man than wit about me, drew:
He raised the house with loud and coward cries.
Your son and daughter found this trespass worth
The shame which here it suffers.
Fool. Winter's not gone yet, if the wild-geese fly that
way.

> Fathers, that wear rags,
>   Do make their children blind;
> But fathers, that bear bags,
>   Shall see their children kind.
> Fortune, that arrant whore,
>   Ne'er turns the key to the poor.—

But, for all this, thou shalt have as many dolours for thy
daughters, as thou canst tell in a year.
Lear. O, how this mother swells up toward my heart!
Hysterica passio ! down, thou climbing sorrow,
Thy element's below.—Where is this daughter?
Kent. With the earl, sir; here, within.
Lear. Follow me not; stay here.   [*Exit*
Gent. Made you no more offence than what you speak of?

Kent.   None.
How chance the king comes with so small a number?
Fool.   An thou had been set i' the stocks for that question,
thou hadst well deserved it.
Kent.   Why fool?
Fool.   We'll set thee to school to an ant, to teach thee
there's no labouring i' the winter. All that follow their
noses are led by their eyes, but blind men; and there's
not a nose among twenty but can smell him that's
stinking. Let go thy hold, when a great wheel runs down a
hill, lest it break thy neck with following it; but the great
one that goes up the hill, let him draw thee after. When
a wise man gives thee better counsel, give me mine again;
I would have none but knaves follow it, since a fool gives it.

> That sir, which serves and seeks for gain,
>   And follows but for form,
> Will pack when it begins to rain,
>   And leave thee in the storm.
> But I will tarry; the fool will stay,
>   And let the wise man fly:
> The knave turns fool that runs away;
>   The fool no knave, perdy.

Kent.   Where learned you this, fool?
Fool.   Not i' the stocks, fool.

Re-enter LEAR, *with* GLOSTER

Lear.   Deny to speak with me? They are sick? they
        are weary?
They have travelled all the night? Mere fetches,
The images of revolt and flying off!
Fetch me a better answer.
Glo.   My dear lord,
You know the fiery quality of the duke;
How unremovable and fixed he is
In his own course.
Lear.   Vengeance! plague! death! confusion!
Fiery? what quality? Why, Gloster, Gloster,
I'd speak with the Duke of Cornwall and his wife.
Glo.   Well, my good lord, I have informed them so.
Lear.   Informed them! Dost thou understand me,
        man?
Glo.   Ay, my good lord.
Lear.   The king would speak with Cornwall; the dear
        father
Would with his daughter speak, commands her service:
Are they 'informed' of this? My breath and blood!—
Fiery? the fiery duke?—Tell the hot duke, that—

43

No, but not yet:—may be, he is not well:
Infirmity doth still neglect all office
Whereto our health is bound; we are not ourselves,
When nature, being oppressed, commands the mind
To suffer with the body. I'll forbear;
And am fallen out with my more headier will,
To take the indisposed and sickly fit
For the sound man.—Death on my state! wherefore
[Looking on Kent
Should he sit here? This act persuades me
That this remotion of the duke and her
Is practice only. Give me my servant forth.
Go, tell the duke and 's wife, I'd speak with them,
Now, presently: bid them come forth and hear me,
Or at their chamber-door I'll beat the drum,
Till it cry, sleep to death.
   Glo. I would have all well betwixt you.   [*Exit*
   Lear. O me, my heart, my rising heart!—but, down.
   Fool. Cry to it, nuncle, as the cockney did to the eels,
when she put them i' the paste alive; she knapp'd 'em o'
the coxcombs with a stick, and cried, 'Down, wantons,
down!' 'T was her brother that, in pure kindness to his
horse, buttered his hay.

    Enter CORNWALL, REGAN, GLOSTER, *and Servants*

   Lear. Good morrow to you both.
   Corn.
Hail to your grace!
[*Kent is set at liberty*
   Reg. I am glad to see your highness.
   Lear. Regan, I think you are; I know what reason
I have to think so: if thou shouldst not be glad,
I would divorce me from thy mother's tomb,
Sepulchring an adult'ress.—[*To Kent*] O! are you free?
Some other time for that.—Belovéd Regan,
Thy sister's naught: O Regan, she hath tied
Sharp-toothed unkindness, like a vulture, here.—
[*Points to his heart*
I can scarce speak to thee; thou'lt not believe,
With how depraved a quality—O Regan!
   Reg. I pray you, sir, take patience. I have hope,
You less know how to value her desert
Than she to scant her duty.
   Lear.   Say, how is that?
   Reg. I cannot think my sister in the least
Would fail her obligation: if, sir, perchance,
She have restrained the riots of your followers,
'T is on such ground, and to such wholesome end,
As clears her from all blame.
   Lear. My curses on her!

Reg.   O, sir! you are old;
Nature in you stands on the very verge
Of her confine: you should be ruled and led
By some discretion that concerns your state
Better than you yourself. ·Therefore, I pray you
That to our sister you do make return:
Say, you have wronged her, sir.
    Lear.   Ask her forgiveness?
Do you but mark how this becomes the house:
'Dear daughter, I confess that I am old;
Age is unnecessary: on my knees I beg,   [*Kneeling*
That you'll vouchsafe me raiment, bed, and food.'
    Reg.   Good sir, no more: these are unsightly tricks.
Return you to my sister.
    Lear. [*Rising*]   Never, Regan.
She hath abated me of half my train;
Looked black upon me; struck me with her tongue,
Most serpent-like, upon the very heart.—
All the stored vengeances of heaven fall
On her ungrateful top! Strike her young bones,
You taking airs, with lameness!
    Corn.   Fie, sir, fie!
    Lear.   You nimble lightnings, dart your blinding flames
Into her scornful eyes! Infect her beauty,
You fen-sucked fogs, drawn by the powerful sun
To fall and blast her pride!
    Reg.   O the blest gods! so will you wish on me,
When the rash mood is on.
    Lear.   No, Regan, thou shalt never have my curse:
Thy tender-hefted nature shall not give
Thee o'er to harshness: her eyes are fierce; but thine
Do comfort, and not burn. 'T is not in thee
To grudge my pleasures, to cut off my train,
To bandy hasty words, to scant my sizes,
And, in conclusion, to oppose the bolt
Against my coming in: thou better know'st
The offices of nature, bond of childhood,
Effects of courtesy, dues of gratitude;
Thy half o' the kingdom hast thou not forgot,
Wherein I thee endowed.
    Reg.   Good sir, to the purpose.
    Lear.   Who put my man i' the stocks? [*Tucket within*
    Corn.   What trumpet's that?
    Reg.   I know 't, my sister's: this approves her letter,
That she would soon be here.

Enter OSWALD

                  Is your lady come?
    Lear.   This is a slave, whose easy-borrow'd pride
Dwells in the fickle grace of her he follows.—

Out, varlet, from my sight!
    Corn.   What means your grace?
    Lear.   Who stocked my servant? Regan, I have good hope
Thou didst not know on't.—Who comes here? O heavens,

Enter GONERIL

If you do love old men, if your sweet sway
Allow obedience, if yourselves are old,
Make it your cause; send down, and take my part!—
[*To Goneril*] Art not ashamed to look upon this beard?
O Regan, wilt thou take her by the hand?
    Gon. Why not by the hand, sir? How have I offended?
All's not offence that indiscretion finds
And dotage terms so.
    Lear.   O sides, you are too tough:
Will you get hold?—How came my man i' the stocks?
    Corn. I set him there, sir; but his own disorders
Deserved much less advancement.
    Lear.   You! did you?
    Reg. I pray you, father, being weak, seem so.
If, till the expiration of your month,
You will return and sojourn with my sister,
Dismissing half your train, come then to me:
I am now from home, and out of that provision
Which shall be needful for your entertainment.
    Lear. Return to her? and fifty men dismissed?
No, rather I abjure all roofs, and choose
To wage against the enmity o' the air;
To be a comrade with the wolf and owl,—
Necessity's sharp pinch!—Return with her?
Why, the hot-blooded France, that dowerless took
Our youngest-born, I could as well be brought
To knee his throne, and, squire-like, pension beg
To keep base life afoot.—Return with her?
Persuade me rather to be slave and sumpter
To this detested groom   [*Pointing at Oswald*
    Gon.   At your choice, sir.
    Lear. I pr'ythee, daughter, do not make me mad:
I will not trouble thee, my child; farewell.
We'll no more meet, no more see one another:—
But yet thou art my flesh, my blood, my daughter;
Or, rather, a disease that's in my flesh,
Which I must needs call mine: thou art a boil,
A plague-sore, an embosséd carbuncle,
In my corrupted blood. But I'll not chide thee;
Let shame come when it will, I do not call it:
I do not bid the thunder-bearer shoot,
Nor tell tales of thee to high-judging Jove:

Mend, when thou canst; be better, at thy leisure:
I can be patient; I can stay with Regan,
I, and my hundred knights.
    Reg.   Not altogether so:
I looked not for you yet, nor am provided
For your fit welcome. Give ear, sir, to my sister;
For those that mingle reason with your passion,
Must be content to think you old, and so—
But she knows what she does.
    Lear.   Is this well spoken?
    Reg.   I dare avouch it, sir. What, fifty followers?
Is it not well? What should you need of more?
Yea, or so many, sith that both charge and danger
Speak 'gainst so great a number? How, in one house,
Should many people, under two commands,
Hold amity? 'T is hard; almost impossible.
    Gon. Why might not you, my lord, receive attendance
From those that she calls servants, or from mine?
    Reg. Why not, my lord? If then they chanced to slack
      you,
We could control them. If you will come to me—
For now I spy a danger.—I entreat you
To bring but five-and-twenty: to no more
Will I give place, or notice.
    Lear. I gave you all—
    Reg.   And in good time you gave it.
    Lear. Made you my guardians, my depositaries;
But kept a reservation, to be followed
With such a number. What, must I come to you
With five-and-twenty? Regan, said you so?
    Reg. And speak't again, my lord; no more with me.
    Lear. Those wicked creatures yet do look well-favoured
When others are more wicked; not being the worst
Stands in some rank of praise.—[*To Goneril*] I'll go with
      thee:
Thy fifty yet doth double five-and twenty,
And thou art twice her love.
    Gon.   Hear me, my lord:
What need you five-and twenty, ten, or five,
To follow in a house where twice so many
Have a command to tend you?
    Reg.   What need one?
    Lear. O, reason not the need; our basest beggars
Are in the poorest thing superfluous:
Allow not nature more than nature needs,
Man's life is cheap as beast's. Thou art a lady;
If only to go warm were gorgeous,
Why, nature needs not what thou gorgeous wear'st,
Which scarcely keeps thee warm. But, for true need,—
You heavens, give me that patience, patience I need!

You see me here, you gods, a poor old man,
As full of grief as age; wretched in both:
If it be you that stir these daughters' hearts
Against their father, fool me not so much
To bear it tamely; touch me with noble anger.
O, let not women's weapons, water-drops,
Stain my man's cheeks.—No, you unnatural hags,
I will have such revenges on you both
That all the world shall—I will do such things,—
What they are, yet I know not; but they shall be
The terrors of the earth.   You think, I'll weep;
No, I'll not weep:—
I have full cause of weeping; but this heart
Shall break into a hundred thousand flaws,
Or ere I'll weep.—O fool, I shall go mad!
                          [*Exeunt Lear, Gloster, Kent, and Fool*
   Corn.   Let us withdraw, 't will be a storm.
                             [*Storm heard at a distance*
   Reg.   This house is little: the old man and his people
Cannot be well bestowed.
   Gon.   'T is his own blame; hath put himself from rest,
And must needs taste his folly.
   Reg.   For his particular, I'll receive him very gladly,
But not one follower.
   Gon.   So am I purposed.
Where is my Lord of Gloster?

Re-enter GLOSTER

   Corn.   Followed the old man forth.—He is returned.
   Glo.   The king is in high rage.
   Corn.   Whither is he going?
   Glo.   He calls to horse; but will I know not whither.
   Corn.   'T is best to give him way; he leads himself.
   Gon.   My lord, entreat him by no means to stay.
   Glo.   Alack! the night comes on, and the high winds
Do sorely ruffle; for many miles about
There's scarce a bush.
   Reg.   O, sir, to wilful men,
The injuries that they themselves procure
Must be their schoolmasters.   Shut up your doors:
He is attended with a desperate train;
And what they may incense him to, being apt
To have his ears abused, wisdom bids fear.
   Corn.   Shut up your doors, my lord; 't is a wild night:
My Regan counsels well.   Come out o' the storm.   [*Exeunt*

ACT THREE

SCENE I.—A Heath.   A storm, with thunder and lightning

Enter KENT *and a Gentleman, meeting*

Kent.   Who's there, beside foul weather?
Gent.   One minded like the weather, most unquietly.
Kent.   I know you.   Where's the king?
Gent.   Contending with the fretful elements;
Bids the wind blow the earth into the sea,
Or swell the curléd waters 'bove the main,
That things might change or cease; tears his white hair,
Which the impetuous blasts, with eyeless rage,
Catch in their fury, and make nothing of;
Strives in his little world of man to out-scorn
The to-and-fro conflicting wind and rain.
This night, wherein the cub-drawn bear would couch,
The lion and the belly-pinchéd wolf
Keep their fur dry, unbonneted he runs,
And bids what will take all.
Kent.   But who is with him?
Gent.   None but the fool, who labours to outjest
His heart-struck injuries.
Kent.   Sir, I do know you;
And dare, upon the warrant of my note,
Commend a dear thing to you.   There is division,
Although as yet the face of it be covered
With mutual cunning, 'twixt Albany and Cornwall;
Who have—as who have not, that their great stars
Throned and set high?—servants, who seem no less,
Which are to France the spies and speculations
Intelligent of our state; what hath been seen,
Either in snuffs and packings of the dukes,
Or the hard rein which both of them have borne
Against the old kind king; or something deeper,
Whereof, perchance, these are but furnishings;—
But, true it is, from France there comes a power
Into this scattered kingdom; who already,
Wise in our negligence, have secret feet
In some of our best ports, and are at point
To show their open banner.—Now to you:
If on my credit you dare build so far
To make your speed to Dover, you shall find
Some that will thank you, making just report
Of how unnatural and bemadding sorrow
The king hath cause to plain.
I am a gentleman of blood and breeding,
And, from some knowledge and assurance, offer

This office to you.
    Gent.   I will talk further with you.
    Kent.   No, do not.
For confirmation that I am much more
Than my out-wall, open this purse, and take
What it contains.   If you shall see Cordelia,—
As fear not but you shall,—show her this ring,
And she will tell you who your fellow is
That yet you do not know.   Fie on this storm!
I will go seek the king.
    Gent.   Give me your hand:—have you no more to say?
    Kent.   Few words, but, to effect, more than all yet,—
That, when we have found the king,—in which your pain
That way, I'll this,—he that first lights on him
Holla the other.   *[Exeunt severally*

SCENE II.—Another part of the Heath.   Storm continues

Enter LEAR *and Fool*

    Lear.   Blow, winds, and crack your cheeks! rage! blow!
You cataracts and hurricanoes, spout
Till you have drenched our steeples, drowned the cocks!
You sulphurous and thought-executing fires,
Vaunt-couriers of oak-cleaving thunderbolts,
Singe my white head!   And thou, all shaking thunder,
Strike flat the thick rotundity o' the world!
Crack nature's moulds, all germens spill at once,
That make ingrateful man!
    Fool.   O nuncle, court holy-water in a dry house is better
than this rain-water out o' door.   Good nuncle, in, ask thy
daughters' blessing: here's a night pities neither wise men
nor fools.
    Lear.   Rumble thy bellyful! spit, fire! spout, rain!
Nor rain, wind, thunder, fire, are my daughters:
I tax not you, you elements, with unkindness;
I never gave you kingdom, called you children,
You owe me no subscription: then let fall
Your horrible pleasure; here I stand, your slave,
A poor, infirm, weak, and despised old man—
But yet I call you servile ministers,
That will with two pernicious daughters join
Your high-engendered battles 'gainst a head
So old and white as this.   O! O! 't is foul!
    Fool.   He that has a house to put's head in has a good
head-piece.

            The cod-piece that will house
              Before the head has any,
            The head and he shall louse;—
              So beggars marry many.

    The man that makes his toe
     What he his heart should make,
    Shall of a corn cry woe,
     And turn his sleep to wake

For there was never yet fair woman but she made mouths
in a glass.
 Lear. No, I will be the pattern of all patience; I will say
nothing.

     Enter KENT

 Kent. Who's there?
 Fool. Marry, here's grace and a cod-piece; that's a
wise man, and a fool.
 Kent. Alas, sir, are you here? things that love
   night
Love not such nights as these; the wrathful skies
Gallow the very wanderers of the dark,
And make them keep their caves. Since I was man,
Such sheets of fire, such bursts of horrid thunder,
Such groans of roaring wind and rain, I never
Remember to have heard: man's nature cannot carry
The affliction, nor the fear.
 Lear.   Let the great gods,
That keep this dreadful pother o'er our heads,
Find out their enemies now. Tremble, thou wretch,
That hast within thee undivulgéd crimes,
Unwhipped of justice: hide thee, thou bloody hand;
Thou perjured, and thou simular of virtue
That art incestuous: caitiff, to pieces shake,
That under covert and convenient seeming
Hast practised on man's life: close pent-up guilts,
Rive your concealing continents, and cry
These dreadful summoners grace.—I am a man
More sinned against than sinning.
 Kent.   Alack, bare-headed!
Gracious my lord, hard by here is a hovel;
Some friendship will it lend you 'gainst the tempest:
Repose you there, while I to this hard house—
More harder than the stones whereof 't is raised,
Which even but now, demanding after you,
Denied me to come in—return, and force
Their scanted courtesy.
 Lear.   My wits begin to turn.—
Come on, my boy. How dost, my boy? Art cold?
I am cold myself.—Where is this straw, my fellow?
The art of our necessities is strange,
That can make vile things precious. Come, your hovel.
Poor fool and knave, I have one part in my heart
That's sorry yet for thee.

Fool. [*Sings*] *He that has a little tiny wit,—*
　　　With heigh, ho, the wind and the rain,
Must make content with his fortunes fit,
　　Though the rain it raineth every day.

　Lear. True, my good boy.—Come, bring us to this hovel.
　　　　　　　　　　　　　　[*Exeunt Lear and Kent*
　Fool. This is a brave night to cool a courtesan.—
I'll speak a prophecy ere I go:

When priests are more in word than matter;
When brewers mar their malt with water;
When nobles are their tailor's tutors;
No heretics burned but wenches' suitors;
When every case in law is right;
No squire in debt, nor no poor knight;
When slanders do not live in tongues;
Nor cutpurses come not to throngs;
When usurers tell their gold i' the field;
And bawds and whores do churches build;
Then shall the realm of Albion
Come to great confusion:
Then comes the time, who lives to see't,
That going shall be used with feet.

This prophecy Merlin shall make; for I live before his time.
　　　　　　　　　　　　　　　　　　　　[*Exit*

SCENE III.—A Room in GLOSTER'S Castle

Enter GLOSTER *and* EDMUND

　Glo. Alack, alack! Edmund, I like not this unnatural dealing. When I desired their leave that I might pity him, they took from me the use of mine own house, charged me, on pain of perpetual displeasure, neither to speak of him, entreat for him, nor any way sustain him.
　Edm. Most savage and unnatural!
　Glo. Go to; say you nothing. There is division between the dukes, and a worse matter than that. I have received a letter this night;—'t is dangerous to be spoken;—I have locked the letter in my closet. These injuries the king now bears will be revenged home; there is part of a power already footed; we must incline to the king. I will seek him, and privily relieve him: go, you, and maintain talk with the duke, that my charity be not of him perceived: if he ask for me, I am ill, and gone to bed. If I die for it, as no less is threatened me, the king, my old master, must be relieved. There is some strange thing toward, Edmund; pray you, be careful.
　　　　　　　　　　　　　　　　　　　　[*Exit*

Edm.   This courtesy, forbid thee, shall the duke
Instantly know; and of that letter too.
This seems a fair deserving, and must draw me
That which my father loses,—no less than all:
The younger rises when the old doth fall.   [*Exit*

SCENE IV.—A part of the Heath, with a Hovel.   Storm
continues

Enter LEAR, KENT, *and Fool*

Kent.   Here is the place, my lord; good my lord, enter:
The tyranny of the open night's too rough
For nature to endure.   Let me alone.
Lear.
Kent.   Good my lord, enter here.
Lear.   Wilt break my heart?
Kent.   I'd rather break mine own.   Good my lord,
          enter.
Lear.   Thou think'st 't is much, that this contentious
          storm
Invades us to the skin: so 't is to thee;
But where the greater malady is fixed,
The lesser is scarce felt.   Thou'dst shun a bear;
But if thy flight lay toward the roaring sea,
Thou'dst meet the bear i' the mouth.   When the mind's
          free,
The body's delicate: the tempest in my mind
Doth from my senses take all feeling else
Save what beats there.   Filial ingratitude!
Is it not as this mouth should tear this hand
For lifting food to 't?—But I will punish home:—
No, I will weep no more.—In such a night
To shut me out!—Pour on; I will endure:—
In such a night as this!   O Regan, Goneril!—
Your old kind father, whose frank heart gave all,—
O, that way madness lies; let me shun that;
No more of that.
Kent.   Good my lord, enter here.
Lear.   Pr'ythee, go in thyself; seek thine own ease:
This tempest will not give me leave to ponder
On things would hurt me more.—But I'll go in.
[*To the Fool*]   In, boy; go first.   You houseless poverty,—
Nay, get thee in.   I'll pray, and then I'll sleep.—
                                              [*Fool goes in*

Poor naked wretches, wheresoe'er you are,
That bide the pelting of this pitiless storm,
How shall your houseless heads and unfed sides,
Your looped and windowed raggedness, defend you

From seasons such as these?   O, I have ta'en
Too little care of this!   Take physic, pomp;
Expose thyself to feel what wretches feel,
That thou may'st shake the superflux to them,
And show the heavens more just.
   Edg. [*Within*] Fathom and half, fathom and half!
Poor Tom!   [*The Fool runs out from the hovel*
   Fool. Come not in here, nuncle; here's a spirit.   Help
me! help me!
   Kent. Give me thy hand.—Who's there?
   Fool. A spirit, a spirit: he says his name's poor Tom.
   Kent. What art thou that dost grumble there i' the
      straw?
Come forth.

Enter EDGAR, *disguised as a madman*

   Edg. Away! the foul fiend follows me!—
Through the sharp hawthorn blows the cold wind.—
Humh! Go to thy cold bed, and warm thee.
   Lear. Didst thou give all to thy daughters?   And art
thou come to this?
   Edg. Who gives anything to poor Tom? whom the
foul fiend hath led through fire and through flame, through
ford and whirlpool, o'er bog and quagmire; that hath
laid knives under his pillow, and halters in his pew; set
ratsbane by his porridge; made him proud of heart, to
ride on a bay trotting-horse over four-inched bridges, to
course his own shadow for a traitor.—Bless thy five wits!
Tom's a-cold.—O! do de, do de, do de.—Bless thee from
whirlwinds, star-blasting, and taking! Do poor Tom
some charity, whom the foul fiend vexes.—There could I
have him now,—and there,—and there,—and there again,
and there.   [*Storm continues*
   Lear. What, have his daughters brought him to this
      pass?—
Couldst thou save nothing?   Didst thou give them all?
   Fool. Nay, he reserved a blanket, else we had been all
shamed.
   Lear. Now, all the plagues that in the pendulous air
Hang fated o'er men's faults, light on thy daughters!
   Kent. He hath no daughters, sir.
   Lear. Death, traitor! nothing could have subdued
      nature
To such a lowness, but his unkind daughters.—
Is it the fashion, that discarded fathers
Should have thus little mercy on their flesh?
Judicious punishment! 't was this flesh begot
Those pelican daughters.
   Edg. Pillicock sat on Pillicock-hill:—
Halloo, halloo, loo, loo!

Fool. This cold night will turn us all to fools and madmen.

Edg. Take heed o' the foul fiend. Obey thy parents; keep thy word justly; swear not; commit not with man's sworn spouse; set not thy sweet heart on proud array. Tom's a-cold.

Lear. What hast thou been?

Edg. A serving-man, proud in heart and mind; that curled my hair, wore gloves in my cap, served the lust of my mistress's heart, and did the act of darkness with her; swore as many oaths as I spake words, and broke them in the sweet face of heaven: one that slept in the contriving of lust, and waked to do it. Wine loved I deeply; dice dearly; and in woman, out-paramoured the Turk: false of heart, light of ear, bloody of hand; hog in sloth, fox in stealth, wolf in greediness, dog in madness, lion in prey. Let not the creaking of shoes nor the rustling of silks betray thy poor heart to woman; keep thy foot out of brothels, thy hand out of plackets, thy pen from lenders' books, and defy the foul fiend.—Still through the hawthorn blows the cold wind, says suum, mun, hay no nonny. Dolphin my boy, my boy; sessa! let him trot by.

[Storm still continues

Lear. Why, thou wert better in thy grave, than to answer with thy uncovered body this extremity of the skies. Is man no more than this? Consider him well. Thou owest the worm no silk, the beast no hide, the sheep no wool, the cat no perfume.—Ha! here's three on's are sophisticated: thou art the thing itself: unaccommodated man is no more but such a poor, bare, forked animal as thou art.—Off, off, you lendings.—Come; unbutton here.— *[Tearing off his clothes*

Fool. Pr'ythee, nuncle, be contented; 't is a naughty night to swim in.—Now, a little fire in a wild field were like an old lecher's heart; a small spark, all the rest on's body cold.—Look, here comes a walking fire.

Edg. This is the foul fiend Flibbertigibbet: he begins at curfew, and walks till the first cock; he gives the web and the pin, squints the eye, and makes the hare-lip; mildews the white wheat, and hurts the poor creature of earth.

> *Swithold footed thrice the wold;*
> *He met the night-mare, and her nine-fold;*
> > *Bid her alight,*
> > *And her troth plight,*
> *And aroint thee, witch, aroint thee!*

Kent. How fares your grace?

Enter GLOSTER, *with a torch*

Lear. What's he?

55

Kent. Who's there? What is't you seek?

Glo. What are you there? Your names?

Edg. Poor Tom; that eats the swimming frog, the toad, the tadpole, the wall-newt, and the water; that in the fury of his heart, when the foul fiend rages, eats cowdung for sallets; swallows the old rat, and the ditch-dog; drinks the green mantle of the standing pool; who is whipped from tithing to tithing, and stock-punished, and imprisoned; who hath had three suits to his back, six shirts to his body, horse to ride, and weapon to wear,—

> *But mice, and rats, and such small deer,*
> *Have been Tom's food for seven long year.*

Beware my follower.—Peace, Smulkin; peace, thou fiend!

Glo. What, hath your grace no better company?

Edg. The prince of darkness is a gentleman;
Modo he's called, and Mahu.

Glo. Our flesh and blood, my lord, is grown so vile,
That it doth hate what gets it.

Edg. Poor Tom's a-cold.

Glo. Go in with me. My duty cannot suffer
To obey in all your daughters' hard commands:
Though their injunction be to bar my doors,
And let this tyrannous night take hold upon you,
Yet have I ventured to come seek you out,
And bring you where both fire and food is ready.

Lear. First let me talk with this philosopher.—
What is the cause of thunder?

Kent. Good my lord, take his offer: go into th'
house.

Lear. I'll take a word with this same learned Theban.
What is your study?

Edg. How to prevent the fiend, and to kill vermin.

Lear. Let me ask you one word in private.

Kent. Importune him once more to go, my lord;
His wits begin to unsettle.

Glo.   Canst thou blame him?
His daughters seek his death.—Ah, that good Kent!—
He said it would be thus,—poor banished man!—
Thou say'st, the king grows mad: I'll tell thee, friend,
I am almost mad myself. I had a son,
Now outlawed from my blood; he sought my life,
But lately, very late: I loved him, friend,—
No father his son dearer: true to tell thee,
The grief hath crazed my wits. What a night's this?
                                              [*Storm continues*
I do beseech your grace,—

Lear.   O! cry you mercy, sir.—
Noble philosopher, your company.

Edg Tom's a-cold.

Glo. In, fellow, there, into the hovel: keep thee warm.
Lear. Come, let's in all.
Kent.   This way, my lord.
Lear.   With him;
I will keep still with my philosopher.
Kent. Good my lord, soothe him; let him take the
fellow.
Glo. Take him you on.
Kent. Sirrah, come on; go along with us.
Lear. Come, good Athenian.
Glo. No words, no words: hush.

Edg. *Child Rowland to the dark tower came,*
         His word was still,—Fie, foh, and fum,
         I smell the blood of a British man.   [*Exeunt*

Scene V.—A Room in Gloster's Castle

Enter Cornwall *and* Edmund

Corn. I will have my revenge ere I depart this house.
Edm. How, my lord, I may be censured, that nature
thus gives way to loyalty, something fears me to think of.
Corn. I now perceive, it was not altogether your
brother's evil disposition make him seek his death; but a
provoking merit, set a-work by a reprovable badness in
himself.
Edm. How malicious is my fortune, that I must repent
to be just! This is the letter he spoke of, which approves
him an intelligent party to the advantages of France. O
heavens, that this treason were not, or not I the detector!
Corn. Go with me to the duchess.
Edm. If the matter of this paper be certain, you have
mighty business in hand.
Corn. True, or false, it hath made thee Earl of Gloster.
Seek out where thy father is, that he may be ready for our
apprehension.
Edm. [*Aside*] If I find him comforting the king, it
will stuff his suspicion more fully.—I will persever in my
course of loyalty, though the conflict be sore between that
and my blood.
Corn. I will lay trust upon thee; and thou shalt find a
dearer father in my love.   [*Exeunt*

SCENE VI.—A Chamber in a Farm-house, adjoining
GLOSTER'S Castle

Enter GLOSTER, LEAR, KENT, *Fool, and* EDGAR

Glo. Here is better than the open air; take it thankfully. I will piece out the comfort with what addition I
can: I will not be long from you.
Kent. All the power of his wits have given way to his
impatience.—The gods reward your kindness.
                                              [*Exit Gloster*
Edg. Frateretto calls me, and tells me, Nero is an
angler in the lake of darkness. Pray, innocent, and
beware the foul fiend.
Fool. Pr'ythee, nuncle, tell me, whether a madman be
a gentleman, or a yeoman?
Lear. A king, a king!
Fool. No: he's a yeoman, that has a gentleman to his
son; for he's a mad yeoman that sees his son a gentleman
before him.
Lear. To have a thousand with red burning spits
Come hissing in upon 'em,—
Edg. The foul fiend bites my back.
Fool. He's mad that trusts in the tameness of a wolf,
a horse's health, a boy's love, or a whore's oath.
Lear. It shall be done; I will arraign them straight.—
[*To Edgar*] Come, sit thou here, most learned justicer;—
[*To the Fool*] Thou, sapient sir, sit here.—Now, you she-
         foxes!—
Edg. Look, where he stands and glares!
Wantest thou eyes at trial, madam?

       Come o'er the bourn, Bessie, to me:—
Fool. *Her boat hath a leak,*
       And she must not speak
       Why she dares not come over to thee.

Edg. The foul fiend haunts poor Tom in the voice of a
nightingale. Hopdance cries in Tom's belly for two white
herring. Croak not, black angel; I have no food for
thee.
Kent. How do you, sir? Stand you not so amazed:
Will you lie down and rest upon the cushions?
Lear. I'll see their trial first.—Bring in the evidence.—
[*To Edgar*] Thou robèd man of justice, take thy place;—
[*To the Fool*] And thou, his yoke-fellow of equity,
Bench by his side:—
[*To Kent*] You are of the commission, sit you too.
Edg. Let us deal justly.

> *Sleepest, or wakest thou, jolly shepherd?*
> *Thy sheep be in the corn;*
> *And for one blast of thy minikin mouth,*
> *Thy sheep shall take no harm.*

Pur! the cat is grey.

Lear. Arraign her first; 't is Goneril. I here take my oath before this honourable assembly, she kicked the poor king her father.

Fool. Come hither, mistress. Is your name Goneril?

Lear. She cannot deny it.

Fool. Cry you mercy, I took you for a joint-stool.

Lear. And here's another, whose warped looks proclaim

What store her heart is made of.—Stop her there!
Arms, arms, sword, fire!—corruption in the place!
False justicer, why hast thou let her 'scape?

Edg. Bless thy five wits!

Kent. O pity!—Sir, where is the patience now,
That you so oft have boasted to retain?

Edg. [*Aside*] My tears begin to take his part so much,
They'll mar my counterfeiting.

Lear. The little dogs and all,
Tray, Blanch, and Sweet-heart, see, they bark at me.

Edg. Tom will throw his head at them.—
Avaunt, you curs!

> Be thy mouth or black or white,
> Tooth that poisons if it bite;
> Mastiff, greyhound, mongrel, grim,
> Hound or spaniel, brach or lym;
> Or bobtail tike or trundle-tail,—
> Tom will make them weep and wail;
> For, with throwing thus my head,
> Dogs leap the hatch, and all are fled.

Do, de, de, de. Sessa! Come, march to wakes and fairs, and market-towns.—Poor Tom, thy horn is dry.

Lear. Then let them anatomise Regan, see what breeds about her heart. Is there any cause in nature, that makes these hard hearts?—[*To Edgar*] You, sir, I entertain you for one of my hundred; only, I do not like the fashion of your garments: you will say, they are Persian attire; but let them be changed.

Kent. Now, good my lord, lie here, and rest awhile.

Lear. Make no noise, make no noise; draw the curtains: so, so, so. We'll go to supper i' the morning: so, so, so.

Fool. And I'll go to bed at noon.

Re-enter GLOSTER

Glo. Come hither, friend: where is the king my master?
Kent. Here, sir; but trouble him not—his wits are
    gone.
Glo. Good friend, I pr'ythee, take him in thy arms;
I have o'erheard a plot of death upon him.
There is a litter ready; lay him in't,
And drive toward Dover, friend, where thou shalt meet
Both welcome and protection.   Take up thy master:
If thou shouldst dally half an hour, his life,
With thine, and all that offer to defend him,
Stand in assuréd loss; take up, take up;
And follow me, that will to some provision
Give thee quick conduct.
Kent.   Oppressed nature sleeps:—·
This rest might yet have balmed thy broken sinews,
Which, if convenience will not allow,
Stand in hard cure.—[*To the Fool*]   Come, help to bear
    thy master;
Thou must not stay behind.
Glo.   Come, come, away.
    [*Exeunt Kent, Gloster, and the Fool, bearing off the King*
Edg.   When we our betters see bearing our woes,
We scarcely think our miseries our foes.
Who alone suffers, suffers most i' the mind,
Leaving free things and happy shows behind;
But then the mind much sufferance doth o'erskip,
When grief hath mates, and bearing-fellowship.
How light and portable my pain seems now,
When that which makes me bend makes the king bow:
He childed, as I fathered!—Tom, away!
Mark the high noises, and thyself bewray
When false opinion, whose wrong thought defiles thee,
In thy just proof repeals and reconciles thee.
What will hap more to-night, safe 'scape the king!
Lurk, lurk.
                                          [*Exit*

SCENE VII.—A Room in GLOSTER's Castle

Enter CORNWALL, REGAN, GONERIL, EDMUND, *and Servants*

Corn.   Post speedily to my lord your husband; show
him this letter:—The army of France is landed.—Seek
out the traitor Gloster.   [*Exeunt some of the Servants*
Reg.   Hang him instantly.
Gon.   Pluck out his eyes.
Corn.   Leave him to my displeasure.—Edmund, keep
you our sister company: the revenges we are bound to

take upon your traitorous father are not fit for your beholding. Advise the duke, where you are going, to a most
festinate preparation: we are bound to the like. Our
posts shall be swift and intelligent betwixt us. Farewell,
dear sister:—farewell, my Lord of Gloster.

Enter OSWALD

How now! Where's the king?
  Osw. My lord of Gloster hath conveyed him hence:
Some five or six and thirty of his knights,
Hot questrists after him, met him at gate;
Who, with some other of the lord's dependants,
Are gone with him towards Dover, where they boast
To have well-arméd friends.   Get horses for your mistress.
  Corn.
  Gon. Farewell, sweet lord, and sister.
               [Exeunt Goneril, Edmund, and Oswald
  Corn. Edmund, farewell.—Go, seek the traitor Gloster,
Pinion him like a thief, bring him before us.
               [Exeunt other Servants
Though well we may not pass upon his life
Without the form of justice, yet our power
Shall do a courtesy to our wrath, which men
May blame, but not control. Who's there? The traitor?

Re-enter Servants with GLOSTER

  Reg. Ingrateful fox! 't is he.
  Corn. Bind fast his corky arms.
  Glo. What mean your graces?—Good my friends,
      consider
You are my guests: do me no foul play, friends.
  Corn. Bind him, I say.   *[Servants bind him*
  Reg.   Hard, hard.—O filthy traitor!
  Glo. Unmerciful lady as you are, I'm none.
  Corn. To this chair bind him.—Villain, thou shalt
    find—   *[Regan plucks his beard*
  Glo. By the kind gods, 't is most ignobly done
To pluck me by the beard.
  Reg. So white, and such a traitor!
  Glo.   Naughty lady,
These hairs, which thou dost ravish from my chin,
Will quicken, and accuse thee. I am your host:
With robbers' hands my hospitable favours
You should not ruffle thus. What will you do?
  Corn. Come sir, what letters had you late from France?
  Reg. Be simple-answered, for we know the truth.
  Corn. And what confederacy have you with the traitors
Late footed in the kingdom?

Reg.   To whose hands have you sent the lunatic king?
Speak.
Glo.   I have a letter guessingly set down,
Which came from one that's of a neutral heart,
And not from one opposed.
Corn.   Cunning.
Reg.   And false.
Corn.   Where hast thou sent the king?
Glo.   To Dover.
Reg.   Wherefore to Dover? Wast thou not charged at
          peril—
Corn.   Wherefore to Dover? Let him answer that.
Glo.   I am tied to the stake, and I must stand the course.
Reg.   Wherefore to Dover?
Glo.   Because I would not see thy cruel nails
Pluck out his poor old eyes; nor thy fierce sister
In his anointed flesh stick boarish fangs.
The sea, with such a storm as his bare head
In hell-black night endured, would have buoyed up,
And quenched the stelléd fires;
Yet, poor old heart, he holp the heavens to rain.
If wolves had at thy gate howled that stern time,
Thou shouldst have said, 'Good porter, turn the key,'
All cruels else subscribed:—but I shall see
The wingéd vengeance overtake such children.
Corn.   See't shalt thou never.—Fellows, hold the chair.—
Upon those eyes of thine I'll set my foot.
Glo.   He, that will think to live till he be old,
Give me some help!—O cruel, O ye gods!
Reg.   One side will mock another; the other too.
Corn.   If you see vengeance,—
First Serv.   Hold your hand, my lord.
I have served you ever since I was a child;
But better service have I never done you
Than now to bid you hold.
Reg.   How now, you dog!
First Serv.   If you did wear a beard upon your chin,
I'd shake it on this quarrel. What do you mean?
Corn.   My villain!   [*Draws and runs at him*
First Serv.   Nay then, come on, and take the chance of
          anger.   [*Draws. Cornwall is wounded*
Reg.   Give me thy sword. A peasant stand up thus!
First Serv.   O, I am slain!—My lord, you have one eye
          left
To see some mischief on him.—O!   [*Dies*
Corn.   Lest it see more, prevent it.—Out, vile jelly!
Where is thy lustre now?
Glo.   All dark and comfortless.—Where's my son
          Edmund?
Edmund, enkindle all the sparks of nature,

To quit this horrid act.
   Reg.   Out, treacherous villain!
Thou call'st on him that hates thee: it was he
That made the ovérture of thy treasons to us,
Who is too good to pity thee.
   Glo.   O my follies!
Then Edgar was abused.—
Kind gods, forgive me that, and prosper him!
   Reg. Go, thrust him out at gates, and let him smell
His way to Dover.—How is 't, my lord? How look you?
   Corn. I have received a hurt.—Follow me, lady.
Turn out that eyeless villain;—throw this slave
Upon the dunghill.—Regan, I bleed apace:
Untimely comes this hurt: give me your arm.
        [Exit Cornwall, led by Regan:—Servants unbind
                  Gloster, and lead him out
   Sec. Serv. I'll never care what wickedness I do,
If this man come to good.
   Third Serv.   If she live long,
And in the end meet the old course of death,
Women will all turn monsters.
   Sec. Serv. Let's follow the old earl, and get the Bedlam
To lead him where he would: his roguish madness
Allows itself to anything.
   Third Serv. Go thou; I'll fetch some flax, and whites of
      eggs,
To apply to his bleeding face. Now, heaven help him!
                       [Exeunt severally

ACT FOUR

Scene I.—The Heath

Enter EDGAR

   Edgar. Yet better thus, and known to be contemned,
Than still contemned and flattered. To be worst,
The lowest and most dejected thing of fortune,
Stands still in esperance, lives not in fear:
The lamentable change is from the best;
The worst returns to laughter. Welcome, then,
Thou unsubstantial air that I embrace:
The wretch that thou hast blown unto the worst
Owes nothing to thy blasts.—But who comes here?—

Enter GLOSTER, *led by an Old Man*

My father, poorly led?—World, world, O world!
But that thy strange mutations make us hate thee,

Life would not yield to age.

   Old Man. O my good lord! I have been your tenant, and your father's tenant, these fourscore years.

   Glo. Away, get thee away; good friend, be gone:
Thy comforts can do me no good at all;
Thee they may hurt.

   Old Man.   You cannot see your way.

   Glo. I have no way, and therefore want no eyes;
I stumbled when I saw: full oft 't is seen,
Our means secure us, and our mere defects
Prove our commodities.—Ah, dear son Edgar,
The food of thy abuséd father's wrath!
Might I but live to see thee in my touch,
I'd say I had eyes again!

   Old Man.   How now! who's there?

   Edg. [*Aside*] O gods! Who is 't can say 'I am at the
         worst?'
I am worse than e'er I was.

   Old Man.   'T is poor mad Tom.

   Edg. [*Aside*] And worse I may be yet: the worst is
         not,
So long as we can say, 'This is the worst.'

   Old Man. Fellow, where goest?

   Glo.   Is it a beggar-man?

   Old Man. Madman and beggar too.

   Glo. He has some reason, else he could not beg.
I' the last night's storm I such a fellow saw,
Which made me think a man a worm: my son
Came then into my mind; and yet my mind
Was then scarce friends with him: I have heard more since.
As flies to wanton boys, are we to the gods,—
They kill us for their sport.

   Edg. [*Aside*]   How should this be?—
Bad is the trade that must play fool to sorrow,
Angering itself and others:—Bless thee, master!

   Glo. Is that the naked fellow?

   Old Man.   Ay, my lord.

   Glo. Then, pr'ythee, get thee gone. If, for my sake,
Thou wilt o'ertake us, hence a mile or twain,
I' the way toward Dover, do it for ancient love;
And bring some covering for this naked soul,
Which I'll entreat to lead me.

   Old Man.   Alack, sir, he is bad.

   Glo. 'T is the times' plague, when madmen lead the
         blind.
Do as I bid thee, or rather do thy pleasure;
Above the rest, be gone.

   Old Man. I'll bring him the best 'parel that I have,
Come on 't what will.   [*Exit*

   Glo. Sirrah, naked fellow.

Edg.   Poor Tom's a-cold.—[*Aside*]   I cannot daub it
   further.
Glo.   Come hither, fellow.
Edg.   [*Aside*]   And yet I must.—Bless thy sweet eyes,
   they bleed.
Glo.   Know'st thou the way to Dover?
Edg.   Both stile and gate, horse-way and foot-path.
Poor Tom hath been scared out of his good wits: bless thee,
good man's son, from the foul fiend!   Five fiends have been
in poor Tom at once; of lust, as Obidicut; Hobbididance,
prince of dumbness; Mahu, of stealing; Modo, of murder;
Flibbertigibbet, of mopping and mowing; who since pos-
sesses chambermaids and waiting-women.   So, bless thee,
master!
Glo.   Here, take this purse, thou whom the heavens'
   plagues
Have humbled to all strokes: that I am wretched
Makes thee the happier:—heavens, deal so still!
Let the superfluous and lust-dieted man
That slaves your ordinance, that will not see
Because he doth not feel, feel your power quickly;
So distribution should undo excess,
And each man have enough.—Dost thou know Dover?
Edg.   Ay, master.
Glo.   There is a cliff, whose high and bending head
Looks fearfully in the confinéd deep:
Bring me but to the very brim of it,
And I'll repair the misery thou dost bear
With something rich about me: from that place
I shall no leading need.
Edg.   Give me thy arm:
Poor Tom shall lead thee.   [*Exeunt*

SCENE II.—Before the DUKE OF ALBANY's Palace

Enter GONERIL *and* EDMUND; OSWALD *meeting them*

Gon.   Welcome, my lord: I marvel, our mild husband
Not met us on the way.—Now, where's your master?
Osw.   Madam, within; but never man so changed.
I told him of the army that was landed;
He smiled at it: I told him, you were coming;
His answer was, 'The worse:' of Gloster's treachery,
And of the loyal service of his son,
When I informed him, then he called me sot,
And told me I had turned the wrong side out.
What most he should dislike, seems pleasant to him;
What like, offensive.
Gon.   [*To Edmund*]   Then shall you go no further.

It is the cowish terror of his spirit,
That dares not undertake: he'll not feel wrongs
Which tie him to an answer. Our wishes on the way
May prove effects. Back, Edmund, to my brother;
Hasten his musters and conduct his powers:
I must change arms at home, and give the distaff
Into my husband's hands. This trusty servant
Shall pass between us: ere long you are like to hear,
If you dare venture in your own behalf,
A mistress's command. Wear this; spare speech;

          [Giving a favour
Decline your head: this kiss, if it durst speak,
Would stretch thy spirits up into the air:—
Conceive, and fare thee well.
 Edm. Yours in the ranks of death.
 Gon.   My most dear Gloster!

          [Exit Edmund

O, the difference of man and man!
To thee a woman's services are due:
A fool usurps my bed.
 Osw.   Madam, here comes my lord. *[Exit*

Enter ALBANY

 Gon. I have been worth the whistle.
 Alb.   O Goneril
You are not worth the dust which the rude wind
Blows in your face.—I fear your disposition:
That nature which contemns its origin
Cannot be bordered certain in itself;
She that herself will sliver and disbranch
From her material sap, perforce must wither
And come to deadly use.
 Gon. No more; the text is foolish.
 Alb. Wisdom and goodness to the vile seem vile;
Filths savour but themselves. What have you done?
Tigers, not daughters, what have you performed?
A father, and a gracious agéd man,
Whose reverence the head-lugged bear would lick,—
Most barbarous, most degenerate!—have you madded.
Could my good brother suffer you to do it?
A man, a prince, by him so benefited;
If that the heavens do not their visible spirits
Send quickly down to tame these vile offences,
'T will come, perforce, humanity must prey
Upon itself, like monsters of the deep.
 Gon.   Milk-livered man!
That bear'st a cheek for blows, a head for wrongs;
Who hast not in thy brows an eye discerning
Thine honour from thy suffering; that not know'st

Fools do those villains pity who are punished
Ere they have done their mischief.   Where's thy drum?
France spreads his banners in our noiseless land;
With pluméd helm thy slayer begins threats;
Whilst thou, a moral fool, sitt'st still, and criest,
'Alack! why does he so?'
    Alb.   See thyself, devil!
Proper deformity seems not in the fiend
So horrid as in woman.
    Gon.   O vain fool!
    Alb.   Thou changéd and self-covered thing, for shame,
Be-monster not thy feature.   Were it my fitness
To let these hands obey my blood,
They are apt enough to dislocate and tear
Thy flesh and bones:—howe'er thou art a fiend,
A woman's shape doth shield thee.
    Gon.   Marry, your manhood now!—

Enter a Messenger

    Alb.   What news?
    Mess.   O, my good lord, the Duke of Cornwall's dead;
Slain by his servant, going to put out
The other eye of Gloster.
    Alb.   Gloster's eyes!
    Mess.   A servant that he bred, thrilled with remorse,
Opposed against the act, bending his sword
To this great master; who, thereat enraged,
Flew on him, and amongst them felled him dead;
But not without that harmful stroke, which since
Hath plucked him after.
    Alb.   This shows you are above,
You justicers, that these are nether crimes
So speedily can venge!—But, O poor Gloster!
Lost he his other eye?
    Mess.   Both, both, my lord.—
This letter, madam, craves a speedy answer;
'T is from your sister.
    Gon.   [*Aside*]   One way I like this well;
But being widow, and my Gloster with her,
May all the building in my fancy pluck
Upon my hateful life: another way,
The news is not so tart.—I'll read, and answer.   [*Exit*
    Alb.   Where was his son when they did take his eyes?
    Mess.   Come with my lady hither.
    Alb.   He's not here.
    Mess.   No, my good lord; I met him back again.
    Alb.   Knows he the wickedness?
    Mess.   Ay, my good lord; 't was he informed against him,
And quit the house on purpose, that their punishment
Might have the freer course.

Alb.   Gloster, I live
To thank thee for the love thou showd'st the king.
And to revenge thine eyes.—Come hither, friend:
Tell me what more thou know'st.   [*Exeunt*

SCENE III.—The French Camp near Dover

Enter KENT *and a gentleman*

Kent.   Why the king of France is so suddenly gone back,
know you the reason?
Gent.   Something he left imperfect in the state, which
since his coming forth is thought of; which imports to the
kingdom so much fear and danger that his personal return
was most required and necessary.
Kent.   Who hath he left behind him general?
Gent.   The Marshal of France, Monsieur La Far.
Kent.   Did your letters pierce the queen to any demon-
stration of grief?
Gent.   Ay, sir; she took them, read them in my presence;
And now and then an ample tear trilled down
Her delicate cheek: it seemed, she was a queen
Over her passion, who, most rebel-like,
Sought to be king o'er her.
Kent.   O, then it moved her.
Gent.   Not to a rage: patience and sorrow strove
Who should express her goodliest.   You have seen
Sunshine and rain at once; her smiles and tears
Were like a better May: those happy smilets
That played on her ripe lip, seemed not to know
What guests were in her eyes, which parted thence
As pearls from diamonds dropped.—In brief,
Sorrow would be a rarity most beloved,
If all could so become it.
Kent.   Made she no verbal question?
Gent.   'Faith, once, or twice, she heav'd the name of
'father'
Pantingly forth, as if it pressed her heart;
Cried, 'Sisters! sisters!   Shame of ladies! sisters!
Kent! father! sisters!   What? i' the storm? i' the night?
Let pity not be believéd!'—There she shook
The holy water from her heavenly eyes,
And clamour moistened: then away she started
To deal with grief alone.
Kent.   It is the stars,
The stars above us, govern our conditions;
Else one self mate and mate could not beget
Such different issues.   You spoke not with her since?
Gent.   No.

Kent.   Was this before the king returned?
Gent.   No, since.
Kent.   Well, sir; the poor distressed Lear's i' the town;
Who sometime, in his better tune, remembers
What we are come about, and by no means
Will yield to see his daughter.
Gent.   Why, good sir?
Kent.   A sovereign shame shows him his own unkindness,
That stripped her from his benediction, turned her
To foreign casualties; gave her dear rights
To his dog-hearted daughters: these things sting
His mind so venomously, that burning shame
Detains him from Cordelia.
Gent.   Alack, poor gentleman!
Kent.   Of Albany's and Cornwall's powers you heard
                                not?
Gent.   'T is so, they are afoot.
Kent.   Well, sir, I'll bring you to our master Lear,
And leave you to attend him.   Some dear cause
Will in concealment wrap me up awhile:
When I am known aright, you shall not grieve
Lending me this acquaintance.
I pray you, go along with me.   [*Exeunt*

SCENE IV.—The Same.   A Camp

Enter CORDELIA, *Physician, and Soldiers*

Cor.   Alack! 't is he: why, he was met even now
As mad as the vexed sea: singing aloud;
Crowned with rank fumiter, and furrow-weeds,
With burdocks, hemlocks, nettles, cuckoo-flowers,
Darnel, and all the idle weeds that grow
In our sustaining corn.—A century send forth;
Search every acre in the high-grown field,
And bring him to our eye.   [*Exit an Officer*
                                —What can man's wisdom
In the restoring his bereavéd sense?
He that helps him, take all my outward worth.
Phy.   There is means, madam;
Our foster-nurse of nature is repose,
The which he lacks; that to provoke in him
Are many simples operative, whose power
Will close the eye of anguish.
Cor.   All blest secrets,
All you unpublished virtues of the earth,
Spring with my tears! be aidant, and remediate,
In the good man's distress!—Seek, seek for him;
Lest his ungoverned rage dissolve the life

That wants the means to lead it.

Enter a Messenger

Mess.   News, madam:
The British powers are marching hitherward.
  Cor.   'T is known before; our preparation stands
In expectation of them.—O dear father,
It is thy business that I go about;
Therefore great France
My mourning and importunate tears hath pitied.
No blown ambition doth our arms incite,
But love, dear love, and our aged father's right:
Soon may I hear and see him!   [*Exeunt*

SCENE V.—A Room in GLOSTER's Castle

Enter REGAN *and* OSWALD

Reg.   But are my brother's powers set forth?
Osw.   Ay, madam.
Reg.   Himself in person there?
Osw.   Madam, with much ado:
Your sister is the better soldier.
  Reg.   Lord Edmund spake not with your lord at home?
Osw.   No, madam.
Reg.   What might import my sister's letter to him?
Osw.   I know not, lady.
  Reg.   'Faith, he is posted hence on serious matter.
It was great ignorance, Gloster's eyes being out,
To let him live: where he arrives, he moves
All hearts against us: Edmund, I think, is gone,
In pity on his misery, to despatch
His nighted life; moreover, to descry
The strength o' the enemy.
  Osw.   I must needs after him, madam, with my letter.
Reg.   Our troops set forth to-morrow: stay with us;
The ways are dangerous.
  Osw.   I may not, madam;
My lady charged my duty in this business.
  Reg.   Why should she write to Edmund? Might not
                         you
Transport her purposes by word? Belike,
Something—I know not what.—I'll love thee much;
Let me unseal the letter.
  Osw.   Madam, I had rather—
Reg.   I know your lady does not love her husband;
I am sure of that: and, at her late being here,
She gave strange œiliads, and most speaking looks
To noble Edmund. I know, you are of her bosom.

70

Osw. I, madam?
Reg. I speak in understanding; you are, I know 't:
Therefore, I do advise you, take this note:
My lord is dead; Edmund and I have talked;
And more convenient is he for my hand
Than for your lady's:—You may gather more.
If you do find him, pray you, give him this;
And when your mistress hears thus much from you,
I pray, desire her call her wisdom to her.
So, fare you well.
If you do chance to hear of that blind traitor,
Preferment falls on him that cuts him off.
Osw. 'Would I could meet him, madam: I would show
What party I do follow.
Reg.   Fare thee well.   [*Exeunt*

Scene VI.—The Country near Dover

Enter Gloster, *and* Edgar *dressed like a peasant*

Glo. When shall I come to the top of that same hill?
Edg. You do climb up it now: look how we labour.
Glo. Methinks the ground is even.
Edg.   Horrible steep.
Hark, do you hear the sea?
Glo.   No, truly.
Edg. Why, then your other senses grow imperfect
By your eyes' anguish.
Glo.   So may it be, indeed.
Methinks, thy voice is altered; and thou speak'st
In better phrase and matter than thou didst.
Edg. You're much deceived: in nothing am I changed
But in my garments.
Glo. Methinks, you're better spoken.
Edg. Come on, sir; here's the place: stand still.—
How fearful
And dizzy 't is, to cast one's eyes so low!
The crows, and choughs, that wing the midway air
Show scarce so gross as beetles: half way down
Hangs one that gathers samphire,—dreadful trade:
Methinks, he seems no bigger than his head.
The fishermen that walk upon the beach
Appear like mice, and yond tall anchoring bark
Diminished to her cock,—her cock, a buoy
Almost too small for sight. The murmuring surge,
That on the unnumbered idle pebbles chafes,
Cannot be heard so high.—I'll look no more;
Lest my brain turn, and the deficient sight
Topple down headlong.

71

Glo.   Set me where you stand.
Edg.   Give me your hand; you are now within a foot
Of the extreme verge: for all beneath the moon
Would I not leap upright.
Glo.   Let go my hand.
Here, friend, 's another purse; in it, a jewel
Well worth a poor man's taking: fairies and gods
Prosper it with thee! Go thou further off;
Bid me farewell, and let me hear thee going.
Edg.   Now fare you well, good sir.
Glo.   With all my heart.
Edg.   [*Aside*] Why I do trifle thus with his despair,
Is done to cure it.
Glo.   O you mighty gods!
This world I do renounce, and in your sights
Shake patiently my great affliction off;
If I could bear it longer, and not fall
To quarrel with your great opposeless wills,
My snuff and loathéd part of nature should
Burn itself out. If Edgar live, O, bless him!—
Now, fellow, fare thee well.
Edg.   Gone, sir: farewell.—
[*Aside*] And yet I know not how conceit may rob
The treasury of life, when life itself
Yields to the theft.—Had he been where he thought,
By this had thought been past.—Alive, or dead?
Ho, you sir! friend!—Hear you, sir?—speak!—
Thus might he pass indeed,—yet he revives.—
What are you, sir?
Glo.   Away, and let me die.
Edg.   Hadst thou been aught but gossamer, feather, air,
So many fathom down precipitating
Thou 'dst shivered like an egg; but thou dost breathe;
Hast heavy substance; bleed'st not; speak'st; art sound.
Ten masts at each make not the altitude
Which thou hast perpendicularly fell:
Thy life's a miracle. Speak yet again.
Glo. But have I fallen, or no?
Edg.   From the dread summit of this chalky bourn.
Look up a-height; the shrill-gorged lark so far
Cannot be seen or heard: do but look up.
Glo. Alack! I have no eyes.—
Is wretchedness deprived that benefit
To end itself by death? 'T was yet some comfort,
When misery could beguile the tyrant's rage
And frustrate his proud will.
Edg.   Give me your arm:
Up:—so; how is 't? Feel you your legs? You stand.
Glo. Too well, too well.
Edg.   This is above all strangeness.

Upon the crown o' the cliff, what thing was that
Which parted from you?
 Glo.   A poor unfortunate beggar.
 Edg. As I stood here below, methought, his eyes
Were two full moons; he had a thousand noses,
Horns whelked and waved like the enridgéd sea:
It was some fiend; therefore, thou happy father,
Think that the clearest gods, who make them honours
Of men's impossibilities, have preserved thee.
 Glo. I do remember now: henceforth I'll bear
Affliction, till it do cry out itself
'Enough, enough,' and 'die.' That thing you speak of,
I took it for a man; often 't would say,
'The fiend, the fiend:' he led me to that place.
 Edg. Bear free and patient thoughts.—But who comes
   here?

Enter LEAR, *fantastically dressed with wild flowers*

The safer sense will ne'er accommodate
His master thus.
 Lear. No, they cannot touch me for coining; I am the
   king himself.
 Edg. O thou side-piercing sight!
 Lear. Nature 's above art in that respect.—There's your
press-money. That fellow handles his bow like a crow-
keeper: draw me a clothier's yard.—Look, look, a mouse.
Peace, peace; this piece of toasted cheese will do 't.—
There's my gauntlet, I'll prove it on a giant.—Bring up
the brown-bills.—O, well flown, bird!—i' the clout, i' the
clout: hewgh!—Give the word.
 Edg. Sweet marjoram.
 Lear. Pass.
 Glo. I know that voice.
 Lear. Ha! Goneril,—with a white beard!—They
flatter'd me like a dog; and told me, I had white hairs in
my beard, ere the black ones were there. To say 'ay' and
'no' to everything I say!—'Ay' and 'no' too was no
good divinity. When the rain came to wet me once, and
the wind to make me chatter; when the thunder would not
peace at my bidding; there I found 'em, there I smelt 'em
out. Go to, they are not men o' their words: they told
me I was everything; 't is a lie, I am not ague-proof.
 Glo. The trick of that voice I do well remember:
Is 't not the king?
 Lear.   Ay, every inch a king.
When I do stare, see, how the subject quakes.
I pardon that man's life. What was thy cause?—
Adultery?—
Thou shalt not die: die for adultery! No:

The wren goes to 't, and the small gilded fly
Does lecher in my sight.
Let copulation thrive; for Gloster's bastard son
Was kinder to his father than my daughters
Got 'tween the lawful sheets.
To 't, luxury, pell-mell! for I lack soldiers.—
Beyond yond simpering dame,
Whose face between her forks presages snow;—
That minces virtue, and does shake the head
To hear of pleasure's name,—
The fitchew, nor the soiléd horse goes to 't
With a more riotous appetite.
Down from the waist they are centaurs
Though women all above:
But to the girdle do the gods inherit,
Beneath is all the fiend's: there's hell, there's darkness,
there is the sulphurous pit, burning, scalding, stench, con-
sumption;—fie, fie, fie! pah, pah! Give me an ounce of
civet, good apothecary, to sweeten my imagination: there's
money for thee.

Glo. O, let me kiss that hand!

Lear. Let me wipe it first; it smells of mortality.

Glo. O ruined piece of nature! This great world
Shall so wear out to nought.—Dost thou know me?

Lear. I remember thine eyes well enough. Dost thou
squiny at me? No, do thy worst, blind Cupid; I'll not
love.—Read thou this challenge; mark but the penning
of it.

Glo. Were all thy letters suns, I could not see one.

Edg. I would not take this from report; it is,
And my heart breaks at it.

Lear. Read.

Glo. What! with the case of eyes?

Lear. O, ho! are you there with me? No eyes in
your head, nor no money in your purse? Your eyes are
in a heavy case, your purse in a light: yet you see how
this world goes.

Glo. I see it feelingly.

Lear. What, art mad? A man may see how this world
goes, with no eyes. Look with thine ears: see how yond
justice rails upon yond simple thief. Hark, in thine ear:
change places; and, handy-dandy, which is the justice,
which is the thief?—Thou hast seen a farmer's dog bark at
a beggar?

Glo. Ay, sir.

Lear. And the creature run from the cur?
There thou mightst behold the great image of authority: a
       dog 's obeyed in office.—
Thou rascal beadle, hold thy bloody hand!
Why dost thou lash that whore? Strip thine own back:

Thou hotly lust'st to use her in that kind
For which thou whipp'st her. The usurer hangs the
      cozener.
Through tattered clothes small vices do appear:
Robes and furred gowns hide all. Plate sin with gold,
And the strong lance of justice hurtless breaks;
Arm it with rags, a pigmy's straw doth pierce it.
None does offend, none, I say, none; I'll able 'em:
Take that of me, my friend, who have the power
To seal the accuser's lips. Get thee glass eyes;
And, like a scurvy politician, seem
To see the things thou dost not.—Now, now, now, now,
Pull off my boots:—harder, harder;—so.
   Edg. O, matter and impertinency mixed!
Reason in madness!
   Lear. If thou wilt weep my fortunes, take my eyes.
I know thee well enough; thy name is Gloster:
Thou must be patient. We came crying hither:
Thou know'st, the first time that we smell the air,
We wawl and cry. I will preach to thee: mark me.
   Glo. Alack, alack the day!
   Lear. When we are born, we cry that we are come
To this great stage of fools.—This a good block!—
It were a delicate stratagem to shoe
A troop of horse with felt: I'll put 't in proof;
And when I've stol'n upon these sons-in-law
Then, kill, kill, kill, kill, kill, kill!

Enter a Gentleman with Attendants

   Gent. O, here he is: lay hand upon him.—Sir,
Your most dear daughter—
   Lear. No rescue? What, a prisoner? I am even
The natural fool of fortune.—Use me well;
You shall have ransom. Let me have a surgeon;
I am cut to the brains.
   Gent.   You shall have anything.
   Lear. No seconds? All myself?
Why, this would make a man a man of salt,
To use his eyes for garden water-pots,
Ay, and for laying autumn's dust.
   Gent.   Good sir,—
   Lear. I will die bravely, like a smug bridegroom.
      What!
I will be jovial; come, come; I am a king,
My masters, know you that?
   Gent. You are a royal one, and we obey you.
   Lear. Then there's life in it. Nay, an you get it, you
shall get it by running. Sa, sa, sa, sa.
                         [Exit; Attendants follow

Gent. A sight most pitiful in the meanest wretch,
Past speaking of in a king!—Thou hast one daughter
Who redeems nature from the general curse
Which twain have brought her to.

Edg. Hail, gentle sir!

Gent. Sir, speed you: what's your will?

Edg. Do you hear aught, sir, of a battle toward?

Gent. Most sure, and vulgar; every one hears that,
Which can distinguish sound.

Edg. But, by your favour,
How near's the other army?

Gent. Near, and on speedy foot; the main descry
Stands on the hourly thought.

Edg. I thank you, sir: that's all.

Gent. Though that the queen on special cause is here,
Her army is moved on.

Edg. I thank you, sir. [*Exit Gentleman*

Glo. You ever-gentle gods, take my breath from me;
Let not my worser spirit tempt me again
To die before you please!

Edg. Well pray you, father.

Glo. Now, good sir, what are you?

Edg. A most poor man, made tame to fortune's blows;
Who, by the art of known and feeling sorrows,
Am pregnant to good pity. Give me you hand,
I'll lead you to some biding.

Glo. Hearty thanks:
The bounty and the benison of heaven
To boot, and boot!

Enter Oswald

Osw. I proclaimed prize! Most happy!
That eyeless head of thine was first framed flesh
To raise my fortunes.—Thou old unhappy traitor,
Briefly thyself remember:—thy sword is out
That must destroy thee.

Glo. Now let thy friendly hand
Put strength enough to it. [*Edgar interposes*

Osw. Wherefore, bold peasant,
Dar'st thou support a published traitor? Hence;
Lest that the infection of his fortune take
Like hold on thee. Let go his arm.

Edg. Ch'ill not let go, zir, without vurther 'casion.

Osw. Let go, slave, or thou diest.

Edg. Good gentleman, go your gait, and let poor volk
pass. An ch'ud ha' been zwagger'd out of my life, 't
would not ha' been zo long as 't is by a vortnight. Nay,
come not near the old man: keep out, che vor'ye, or ise
try whether your costard or my ballow be the harder.
Ch'ill be plain with you.

Osw.   Out, dunghill!
Edg.   Ch'ill pick your teeth, zir.   Come; no matter vor
your foins.   [*They fight, and Edgar knocks him down*
Osw.   Slave, thou hast slain me.—Villain, take my
        purse.
If ever thou wilt thrive, bury my body;
And give the letters which thou find'st about me
To Edmund Earl of Gloster: seek him out
Upon the English party;—O, untimely death!   [*Dies*
Edg.   I know thee well: a serviceable villain;
As duteous to the vices of thy mistress
As badness would desire.
                Glo.   What! is he dead?
Edg.   Sit you down, father; rest you.—
Let's see his pockets: these letters that he speaks of
May be my friends.—He's dead: I am only sorry
He had no other death's-man.—Let us see:—
Leave, gentle wax; and, manners, blame us not:
To know our enemies' minds, we'd rip their hearts.
Their papers, is more lawful.
   [*Reads*]   'Let our reciprocal vows be remembered.
You have many opportunities to cut him off; if your will
want not, time and place will be fruitfully offered.   There
is nothing done, if he return the conqueror; then am I
the prisoner, and his bed my gaol; from the loathed
warmth whereof deliver me, and supply the place for your
labour.
                Your (wife, so I would say)
                    Affectionate servant,
                        GONERIL.'

O undistinguished space of woman's will!
A plot upon her virtuous husband's life;
And the exchange, my brother!—Here, in the sands,
Thee I'll rake up, the post unsanctified
Of murderous lechers; and, in the mature time,
With this ungracious paper strike the sight
Of the death-practised duke.   For him 't is well,
That of thy death and business I can tell.
   Glo.   The king is mad: how stiff is my vile sense,
That I stand up, and have ingenious feeling
Of my huge sorrows!   Better I were distract:
So should my thoughts be severed from my griefs;
And woes, by wrong imaginations, lose
The knowledge of themselves.   [*Drums afar off*
   Edg.   Give me you hand:
Far off, methinks, I hear the beaten drum.
Come, father, I'll bestow you with a friend.   [*Exeunt*

SCENE VII.—A Tent in the French Camp

LEAR *on a bed asleep, soft music playing.* *Enter* CORDELIA, *and* KENT, *Doctor, Gentleman, and others, watching*

Cor. O thou good Kent! how shall I live and work,
To match thy goodness? My life will be too short,
And every measure fail me.
Kent. To be acknowledged, madam, is o'er-paid.
All my reports go with the modest truth;
Nor more, nor clipped, but so.
Cor. Be better suited:
These weeds are memories of those worser hours:
I pr'ythee, put them off.
Kent. Pardon, dear madam;
Yet to be known shortens my made intent:
My boon I make it, that you know me not
Till time and I think meet.
Cor. Then be't so, my good lord.—[*To the Doctor*]
How does the king?
Doct. Madam, sleeps still.
Cor. O you kind gods,
Cure this great breach in his abused nature!
The untuned and jarring senses, O, wind up
Of this child-changéd father!
Doct. So please your majesty,
That we may wake the king: he hath slept long.
Cor. Be governed by your knowledge, and proceed
I' the sway of your own will. Is he arrayed?
Doct. Ay, madam; in the heaviness of sleep,
We put fresh garments on him.
Kent. Be by, good madam, when we do awake him;
I doubt not of his temperance.
Cor. Very well. [*Music*
Doct. Please you, draw near.—Louder the music there!
Cor. O my dear father! Restoration hang
Thy medicine on my lips; and let this kiss
Repair those violent harms that my two sisters
Have in thy reverence made!
Kent. Kind and dear princess!
Cor. Had you been their father, these white flakes
Had challenged pity of them. Was this a face
To be opposed against the warring winds?
To stand against the deep dread-bolted thunder?
In the most terrible and nimble stroke
Of quick cross lightning? to watch—poor perdu!—
With this thin helm? Mine enemy's dog,
Though he had bit me, should have stood that night
Against my fire. And wast thou fain, poor father,

To hovel thee with swine, and rogues forlorn,
In short and musty straw?   Alack, alack!
'T is wonder, that thy life and wits at once
Had not concluded all.—He wakes; speak to him.
    Doct.   Madam, do you; 't is fittest.
    Cor.   How does my royal lord?   How fares your
        majesty?
    Lear.   You do me wrong, to take me out o' the grave:—
Thou art a soul in bliss; but I am bound
Upon a wheel of fire, that mine own tears,
Do scald like molten lead.
    Cor.   Sir, do you know me?
    Lear.   You are a spirit, I know.   When did you die?
    Cor.   Still, still, far wide.
    Doct.   He's scarce awake: let him alone awhile.
    Lear.   Where have I been!   Where am I?—Fair day-
        light?—
I am mightily abused.—I should even die with pity,
To see another thus.—I know not what to say.—
I will not swear these are my hands:—let's see;
I feel this pin prick.   'Would I were assured
Of my condition.
    Cor.   O, look upon me, sir,
And hold your hands in benediction o'er me.—
No, sir, you must not kneel.
    Lear.   Pray, do not mock me:
I am a very foolish fond old man,
Fourscore and upward, not an hour more nor less;
And, to deal plainly,
I fear, I am not in my perfect mind.
Methinks, I should know you, and know this man;
Yet I am doubtful, for I am mainly ignorant
What place is this; and all the skill I have
Remember not these garments; nor I know not
Where I did lodge last night.   Do not laugh at me;
For, as I am a man, I think this lady
To be my child Cordelia.
    Cor.   And so I am, I am.
    Lear.   Be your tears wet?   Yes, 'faith.   I pray, weep
        not;
If you have poison for me, I will drink it.
I know, you do not love me; for your sisters
Have, as I do remember, done me wrong:
You have some cause, they have not.
    Cor.   No cause, no cause.
    Lear.   Am I in France?
    Kent.   In your own kingdom, sir.
    Lear.   Do not abuse me.
    Doct.   Be comforted, good madam: the great rage,
You see, is killed in him; and yet it is danger

To make him even o'er the time he has lost.
Desire him to go in; trouble him no more,
Till further settling.

Cor. Will 't please your highness walk?

Lear. You must bear with me.
Pray you now, forget and forgive: I am old and foolish.

        [Exeunt Lear, Cordelia, Doctor, and Attendants

Gent. Holds it true, sir, that the Duke of Cornwall was
so slain?

Kent. Most certain, sir.

Gent. Who is conductor of his people?

Kent. As 't is said, the bastard son of Gloster.

Gent. They say, Edgar, his banished son, is with the Earl
of Kent in Germany.

Kent. Report is changeable. 'T is time to look about;
the powers of the kingdom approach apace.

Gent. The arbitrement is like to be bloody. Fare you
well, sir. *[Exit*

Kent. My point and period will be throughly wrought,
Or well or ill, as this day's battle's fought. *[Exit*

ACT FIVE

Scene I.—The Camp of the British Forces, near Dover

Enter with drums and colours, Edmund, Regan, *Officers,
Soldiers, and others*

Edm. Know of the Duke, if his last purpose hold,
Or whether, since, he is advised by aught
To change the course. He's full of alteration,
And self-reproving:—bring his constant pleasure.

        [To an Officer, who goes out

Reg. Our sister's man is certainly miscarried.

Edm. 'T is to be doubted, madam.

Reg. Now, sweet lord,
You know the goodness I intend upon you:
Tell me,—but truly,—but then speak the truth,—
Do you not love my sister?

Edm. In honoured love.

Reg. But have you never found my brother's way
To the forfended place?

Edm. That thought abuses you.

Reg. I am doubtful that you have been conjunct
And bosomed with her, as far as we call hers.

Edm. No, by mine honour, madam.

Reg. I never shall endure her: dear my lord,
Be not familiar with her.

Edm.   Fear me not.—
She, and the duke her husband!

Enter ALBANY, GONERIL, *and Soldiers*

Gon. [*Aside*] I had rather lose the battle, than that sister
Should loosen him and me.
   Alb.   Our very loving sister, well be-met.—
Sir, this I heard,—the king is come to his daughter,
With others whom the rigour of our state
Forced to cry out.   Where I could not be honest,
I never yet was valiant: for this business,
It toucheth us, as France invades our land;
Not bolds the king, with others whom, I fear,
Most just and heavy causes make oppose.
   Edm.   Sir, you speak nobly.
   Reg.   Why is this reasoned?
   Gon.   Combine together 'gainst the enemy:
For these domestic and particular broils
Are not the question here.   Let us then determine
   Alb.
With the ancient of war on our proceeding.
   Edm.   I shall attend you presently at your tent.
   Reg.   Sister, you'll go with us?
   Gon.   No.
   Reg.   'T is most convenient; pray you, go with us.
   Gon.   [*Aside*]   O, ho! I know the riddle.—
I will go.

Enter EDGAR, *disguised*

Edg.   If e'er your grace had speech with man so poor,
Hear me one word.
   Alb.   I'll overtake you.—Speak.
          [*Exeunt all but Albany and Edgar*
   Edg.   Before you fight the battle, ope this letter,
If you have victory, let the trumpet sound
For him that brought it: wretched though I seem,
I can produce a champion, that will prove
What is avouchéd there.   If you miscarry,
Your business of the world hath so an end,
And machination ceases.   Fortune love you!
   Alb.   Stay till I have read the letter.
   Edg.   I was forbid it.
When time shall serve, let but the herald cry,
And I'll appear again.
   Alb.   Why, fare thee well: I will o'erlook thy paper.
          [*Exit Edgar*

Re-enter EDMUND

Edm.   The enemy's in view; draw up your powers.

Here is the guess of their true strength and forces
By diligent discovery;—but your haste
Is now urged on you.
 Alb.   We will greet the time.   [*Exit*
 Edm. To both these sisters have I sworn my love;
Each jealous of the other, as the stung
Are of the adder. Which of them shall I take?
Both? one? or neither? Neither can be enjoyed,
If both remain alive: to take the widow
Exasperates, makes mad, her sister Goneril:
And hardly shall I carry out my side,
Her husband being alive. Now then, we'll use
His countenance for the battle; which being done,
Let her who would be rid of him devise
His speedy taking-off. As for the mercy
Which he intends to Lear and to Cordelia,—
The battle done, and they within our power,
Shall never see his pardon; for my state
Stands on me to defend, not to debate.   [*Exit*

SCENE II.—A Field between the two Camps

Alarum within. Enter, with drum and colours, LEAR,
CORDELIA, and their Forces ; and exeunt

Enter EDGAR and GLOSTER

 Edg. Here, father, take the shadow of this tree
For your good host; pray that the right may thrive.
If ever I return to you again,
I'll bring you comfort.
 Glo.   Grace go with you, sir!
               [*Exit Edgar*

Alarum ; afterwards a Retreat. Re-enter EDGAR

 Edg. Away, old man! give me thy hand: away!
King Lear hath lost, he and his daughter ta'en.
Give me thy hand; come on.
 Glo. No further, sir; a man may rot even here.
 Edg. What, in ill thoughts again? Men must endure
Their going hence, even as their coming hither:
Ripeness is all. Come on.
 Glo.   And that's true too. [*Exeunt*

SCENE III.—The British Camp near Dover

Enter in conquest, with drums and colours, EDMUND; LEAR,
and CORDELIA, as Prisoners ; Captain, Officers, Soldiers,
etc.

  Edm. Some officers take them away: good guard,
Until their greater pleasures first be known,
That are to censure them.   We are not the first,
  Cor.
Who, with best meaning, have incurred the worst.
For thee, oppressèd king, am I cast down;
Myself could else out-frown false fortune's frown.
Shall we not see these daughters, and these sisters?
  Lear. No, no, no, no! Come, let's away to prison;
We two alone will sing like birds i' the cage:
When thou dost ask me blessing, I'll kneel down,
And ask of thee forgiveness: so we'll live,
And pray, and sing, and tell old tales, and laugh
At gilded butterflies, and hear poor rogues
Talk of court news; and we'll talk with them too,—
Who loses, and who wins; who's in, who's out;
And take upon's the mystery of things,
As if we were God's spies: and we'll wear out,
In a walled prison, packs and sects of great ones
That ebb and flow by the moon.   Take them away.
  Edm.
  Lear. Upon such sacrifices, my Cordelia,
The gods themselves throw incense. Have I caught thee?
He that parts us shall bring a brand from heaven,
And fire us hence like foxes. Wipe thine eyes;
The goujeers shall devour them, flesh and fell,
Ere they shall make us weep: we'll see them starve first.
Come.   *[Exeunt Lear and Cordelia, guarded*
  Edm. Come hither, captain; hark.
Take thou this note *[giving a paper]*; go, follow them to
        prison.
One step I have advanced thee; if thou dost
As this instructs thee, thou dost make thy way
To noble fortunes. Know thou this, that men
Are as the time is: to be tender-minded
Does not become a sword. Thy great employment
Will not bear question; either say, thou'lt do't,
Or thrive by other means.
  Capt.   I'll do't, my lord.
  Edm. About it; and write happy when thou hast done.
Mark,—I say, instantly; and carry it so
As I have set it down.
  Capt. I cannot draw a cart, nor eat dried oats:
If 't be man's work, I'll do't.   *[Exit*

Flourish. *Enter* ALBANY, GONERIL, REGAN, *Officers, and Attendants*

Alb. Sir, you have shown to-day your valiant strain,
And fortune led you well. You have the captives
Who were the opposites of this day's strife:
We do require them of you, so to use them
As we shall find our merits and our safety
May equally determine.
  Edm.   Sir, I thought it fit
To send the old and miserable king
To some retention and appointed guard;
Whose age has charms in it, whose title more,
To pluck the common bosom on his side,
And turn our impressed lances in our eyes
Which do command them. With him I sent the queen;
My reason all the same; and they are ready
To-morrow, or at further space, to appear
Where you shall hold your session. At this time
We sweat and bleed: the friend hath lost his friend;
And the best quarrels, in the heat, are cursed
By those that feel their sharpness.—
The question of Cordelia and her father
Requires a fitter place.
  Alb.   Sir, by your patience,
I hold you but a subject of this war,
Not as a brother.
  Reg.   That's as we list to grace him.
Methinks our pleasure might have been demanded
Ere you had spoke so far. He led our powers,
Bore the commission of my place and person;
The which immediacy may well stand up
And call itself your brother.
  Gon.   Not so hot:
In his own grace he doth exalt himself
More than in your addition.
  Reg.   In my rights,
By me invested, he compeers the best.
  Alb. That were the most, if he should husband you.
  Reg. Jesters do oft prove prophets.
  Gon.   Holla, holla!
That eye that told you so looked but a-squint.
  Reg. Lady, I am not well; else I should answer
From a full-flowing stomach.—General,
Take thou my soldiers, prisoners, patrimony;
Dispose of them, of me; the walls are thine.
Witness the world, that I create thee here
My lord and master.
  Gon.   Mean you to enjoy him?
  Alb. The let-alone lies not in your good will.

Edm.   Nor in thine, lord.
Alb.   Half-blooded fellow, yes.
Reg.   [*To Edmund*]   Let the drum strike, and prove my
                    title thine.
Alb.   Stay yet; hear reason.—Edmund, I arrest thee
On capital treason; and, in thy arrest,
This gilded serpent [*pointing to Goneril*].—For your claim,
                    fair sister,
I bar it in the interest of my wife;
'T is she is sub-contracted to this lord,
And I, her husband, contradict your bans.
If you will marry, make your loves to me;
My lady is bespoke.
Gon.   An interlude!
Alb.   Thou art armed, Gloster:—let the trumpet sound:
If none appear to prove upon thy person
Thy heinous, manifest, and many treasons,
There is my pledge [*throwing down a glove*]; I'll make it
                    on thy heart,
Ere I taste bread, thou art in nothing else
Than I have here proclaimed thee.
Reg.   Sick, O, sick!
Gon.   [*Aside*]   If not, I'll ne'er trust medicine.
Edm.   There's my exchange [*throwing down a glove*]:
                    what in the world he is
That names me traitor, villain-like he lies.
Call by thy trumpet: he that dares approach,
On him, on you, who not?   I will maintain
My truth and honour firmly.
Alb.   A herald, ho!
Edm.   A herald, ho, a herald!
Alb.   Trust to thy single virtue; for thy soldiers,
All levied in my name, have in my name
Took their discharge.
Reg.   My sickness grows upon me.
Alb.   She is not well; convey her to my tent.
                                        [*Exit Regan, led*

Enter a Herald

Come hither, herald.—Let the trumpet sound,
And read out this.
Capt.   Sound, trumpet!   [*A trumpet sounds*

Herald reads

'If any man of quality, or degree, within the lists of
the army, will maintain upon Edmund, supposed Earl of
Gloster, that he is a manifold traitor, let him appear by
the third sound of the trumpet.   He is bold in his defence.'
Edm.   Sound!   [*First trumpet*
Her.   Again!   [*Sec. trumpet*

85

Her. Again!

Enter EDGAR, *armed, preceded by a trumpet*

Alb. Ask him his purposes, why he appears
Upon this call o' the trumpet.
Her.   What are you?
Your name? your quality? and why you answer
This present summons?
Edg.   Know, my name is lost;
By treason's tooth bare-gnawn, and canker-bit:
Yet am I noble as the adversary
I come to cope.
Alb.   Which is that adversary?
Edg. What's he that speaks for Edmund Earl of
        Gloster?
Edm. Himself: what say'st thou to him?
Edg.   Draw thy sword,
That, if my speech offend a noble heart,
Thy arm may do thee justice; here is mine:
Behold, it is the privilege of mine honours,
My oath, and my profession: I protest,—
Maugre thy strength, youth, place, and eminence,
Despite thy victor sword, and fire-new fortune,
Thy valour, and thy heart,—thou art a traitor:
False to thy gods, thy brother, and thy father;
Conspirant 'gainst this high illustrious prince;
And, from the extremest upward of thy head
To the descent and dust below thy foot,
A most toad-spotted traitor. Say thou, 'No,'
This sword, this arm, and my best spirits, are bent
To prove upon thy heart, whereto I speak,
Thou liest.
Edm. In wisdom, I should ask thy name;
But, since thy outside looks so fair and warlike,
And that thy tongue some say of breeding breathes,
What safe and nicely I might well delay
By rule of knighthood, I disdain and spurn.
Back do I toss these treasons to thy head;
With the hell-hated lie o'erwhelm thy heart;
Which,—for they yet glance by, and scarcely bruise—
This sword of mine shall give them instant way,
Where they shall rest for ever.—Trumpets, speak!
                [*Alarums.   They fight.   Edmund falls*
Alb. Save him, save him!
Gon.   This is practice, Gloster;
By the law of arms, thou wast not bound to answer
An unknown opposite; thou art not vanquished,
But cozened and beguiled.

86

Alb.   Shut your mouth, dame;
Or with this paper shall I stop it?—Hold, sir;
Thou worse than any name, read thine own evil:—
No tearing, lady; I perceive, you know it.
                              [Gives the letter to Edmund

Gon.   Say, if I do, the laws are mine, not thine:
Who can arraign me for 't?
Alb.   Most monstrous!
Know'st thou this paper?
Gon.   Ask me not what I know.   *[Exit*
Alb.   Go after her: she's desperate; govern her.
                              [Exit an Officer

Edm.   What you have charged me with, that have I
                done,
And more, much more; the time will bring it out:
'T is past, and so am I.—But what art thou,
That hast this fortune on me? If thou art noble,
I do forgive thee.
Edg.   Let's exchange charity.
I am no less in blood than thou art, Edmund;
If more, the more thou hast wronged me.
My name is Edgar, and thy father's son.
The gods are just, and of our pleasant vices
Make instruments to plague us:
The dark and vicious place where thee he got
Cost him his eyes.
Edm.   Thou hast spoken right, 't is true
The wheel is come full circle; I am here.
Alb.   Methought, thy very gait did prophesy
A royal nobleness. I must embrace thee:
Let sorrow split my heart, if ever I
Did have thee or thy father.
Edg.   Worthy prince,
I know 't.
Alb.   Where have you hid yourself?
How have you known the miseries of your father?
Edg.   By nursing them, my lord.—List a brief tale;
And when 't is told, O, that my heart would burst!—
The bloody proclamation to escape,
That followed me so near,—O, our lives' sweetness!
That we the pain of death would hourly die,
Rather than die at once!—taught me to shift
Into a madman's rags, to assume a semblance
That very dogs disdained: and in this habit
Met I my father with his bleeding rings,
Their precious stones new lost; became his guide,
Led him, begged for him, saved him from despair;
Never—O fault!—revealed myself unto him,
Until some half-hour past, when I was armed;
Not sure, though hoping, of this good success,

I asked his blessing, and from first to last
Told him my pilgrimage: but his flawed heart,—
Alack, too weak the conflict to support!—
'Twixt two extremes of passion, joy and grief,
Burst smilingly.
    Edm.   This speech of yours hath moved me,
And shall, perchance, do good: but speak you on;
You look as you had something more to say.
    Alb.   If there be more, more woful, hold it in;
For I am almost ready to dissolve,
Hearing of this.
    Edg.   This would have seemed a period
To such as love not sorrow; but another,
To amplify too much, would make much more,
And top extremity.
Whilst I was big in clamour, came there a man,
Who, having seen me in my worst estate,
Shunned my abhorred society; but then, finding
Who 't was that so endured, with his strong arms
He fastened on my neck, and bellowed out
As he'd burst heaven; threw him on my father;
Told the most piteous tale of Lear and him
That ever ear received; which in recounting,
His grief grew puissant, and the strings of life
Began to crack: twice then the trumpets sounded,
And there I left him tranced.
    Alb.   But who was this?
    Edg.   Kent, sir, the banished Kent; who in disguise
Followed his enemy king, and did him service
Improper for a slave.

Enter a Gentleman, with a bloody knife

    Gent.   Help, help, O, help!
    Edg.   What kind of help?
    Alb.   Speak, man.
    Edg.   What means that bloody knife?
    Gent.   'T is hot, it smokes;
It came even from the heart of—O, she's dead!
    Alb.   Who dead? speak, man.
    Gent.   Your lady, sir, your lady: and her sister
By her is poisonéd; she has confessed it.
    Edm.   I was contracted to them both: all three
Now marry in an instant.
    Edg.   Here comes Kent.
    Alb.   Produce their bodies, be they alive or dead:—
This judgment of the heavens, that makes us tremble,
Touches us not with pity.   [*Exit Gentleman*

Enter KENT

O, is this he?
The time will not allow the compliment,
Which very manners urges.
    Kent.   I am come
To bid my king and master aye good night:
Is he not here?
    Alb.   Great thing of us forgot!—
Speak, Edmund, where's the king? and where's
           Cordelia?—
Seest thou this object, Kent?
          [The bodies of Goneril and Regan are brought in
    Kent. Alack! why thus?
    Edm.   Yet Edmund was beloved:
The one the other poisoned for my sake,
And after slew herself.
    Alb. Even so.—Cover their faces.
    Edm. I pant for life:—some good I mean to do,
Despite of mine own nature. Quickly send—
Be brief in it—to the castle; for my writ
Is on the life of Lear, and on Cordelia:—
Nay, send in time.
    Alb.   Run, run, O, run!
    Edg. To who, my lord?—Who has the office? send
Thy token of reprieve.
    Edm. Well thought on: take my sword,
Give it the captain.
    Alb.   Haste thee, for thy life. *[Exit Edgar*
    Edm. He hath commission from thy wife and me
To hang Cordelia in the prison, and
To lay the blame upon her own despair,
That she fordid herself.
    Alb. The gods defend her!—Bear him hence awhile.
          [Edmund is borne off

Re-enter LEAR, *with* CORDELIA *dead in his arms;* EDGAR,
Officers, and others

    Lear. Howl, howl, howl, howl!—O? you are men of
        stone:
Had I your tongues and eyes, I'd use them so
That heaven's vault should crack.—She's gone for ever.—
I know when one is dead, and when one lives;
She's dead as earth.—Lend me a looking-glass;
If that her breath will mist or stain the stone,
Why, then she lives.
    Kent.   Is this the promised end?
    Edg. Or image of that horror?
    Alb.   Fall, and cease!

Lear.　This feather stirs; she lives! if it be so,
It is a chance which does redeem all sorrows
That ever I have felt.
　Kent.　　　　　　O my good master!　　　[*Kneeling*
　Lear.　Pr'ythee, away.
　Edg.　　　　　　'T is noble Kent, your friend.
　Lear.　A plague upon you, murderers, traitors all!
I might have saved her; now, she's gone for ever!—
Cordelia, Cordelia! stay a little. Ha!
What is 't thou say'st?—Her voice was ever soft,
Gentle, and low,—an excellent thing in woman.—
I killed the slave that was a-hanging thee.
　Off.　'T is true, my lords, he did.
　Lear.　　　　　　　Did I not, fellow?
I have seen the day, with my good biting falchion
I would have made them skip: I am old now,
And these same crosses spoil me.—Who are you?
Mine eyes are not o' the best:—I'll tell you straight.
　Kent.　If fortune brag of two she loved and hated,
One of them we behold.
　Lear.　This is a dull sight.—Are you not Kent?
　Kent.　　　　　　　The same;
Your servant Kent. Where is your servant Caius?
　Lear.　He's a good fellow, I can tell you that;
He'll strike, and quickly too.—He's dead and rotten.
　Kent.　No, my good lord; I am the very man,—
　Lear.　I'll see that straight.
　Kent.　That from your first of difference and decay
Have followed your sad steps—
　Lear.　　　　　You are welcome hither.
　Kent.　Nor no man else.—All's cheerless, dark, and
　　　　deadly:
Your eldest daughters have fordone themselves,
And desperately are dead.
　Lear.　　　　　Ay, so I think.
　Alb.　He knows not what he says, and vain is it,
That we present us to him.
　Edg.　　　　　Very bootless.

Enter an Officer

　Off.　Edmund is dead, my lord.
　Alb.　　　　　　That's but a trifle here.—
You lords and noble friends, know our intent.
What comfort to this great decay may come,
Shall be applied: for us, we will resign,
During the life of this old majesty.
To him our absolute power.—[*To Edgar and Kent*]　You,
　　　　to your rights,
With boot, and such addition as your honours

Have more than merited.—All friends shall taste
The wages of their virtue, and all foes
The cup of their deservings.—O! see, see!
   Lear. And my poor fool is hanged! No, no, no life!
Why should a dog, a horse, a rat, have life,
And thou no breath at all? Thou 'lt come no more,
Never, never, never, never, never!—
Pray you, undo this button:—thank you, sir.—
Do you see this? Look on her,—look,—her lips,—
Look there, look there!—   [*Dies*
   Edg. He faints!—My lord, my lord!—
   Kent. Break, heart; I pr'ythee, break!
   Edg.   Look up, my lord.
   Kent. Vex not his ghost: O, let him pass! he hates
      him
That would upon the rack of this tough world
Stretch him out longer.
   Edg.   He is gone, indeed.
   Kent. The wonder is, he hath endured so long:
He but usurped his life.
   Alb. Bear them hence.—Our present business
Is general woe.—[*To Kent and Edgar*] Friends of my
      soul, you twain
Rule in this realm, and the gored state sustain.
   Kent. I have a journey, sir, shortly to go:
My master calls me,—I must not say, no.
   Edg. The weight of this sad time we must obey;
Speak what we feel, not what we ought to say.
The oldest hath borne most: we, that are young
Shall never see so much, nor live so long.
                  [*Exeunt, with a dead march*

PERICLES

DRAMATIS PERSONÆ

ANTIOCHUS, *king of Antioch*
PERICLES, *prince of Tyre*
HELICANUS
ESCANES } *two lords of Tyre*
SIMONIDES, *king of Pentapolis*
CLEON, *governor of Tarsus*
LYSIMACHUS, *governor of Mitylene*
CERIMON, *a lord of Ephesus*
THALIARD, *a lord of Antioch*
PHILEMON, *servant to Cerimon*
LEONINE, *servant to Dionyza*
Marshal
A Pander. BOULT, *his servant*

The daughter of Antiochus
DIONYZA, *wife to Cleon*
THAISA, *daughter to Simonides*
MARINA, *daughter to Pericles and Thaisa*
LYCHORIDA, *nurse to Marina*
A Bawd

DIANA
GOWER, *as Chorus*

Lords, Ladies, Knights, Gentlemen, Sailors,
Pirates, Fishermen, and Messengers

SCENE.—*Dispersedly in various Countries*

94

PERICLES

ACT ONE

Enter GOWER

Before the Palace of Antioch

To sing a song that old was sung,
From ashes ancient Gower is come,
Assuming man's infirmities,
To glad your ear and please your eyes.
It hath been sung at festivals,
On ember-eves, and holy-ales;
And lords and ladies in their lives
Have read it for restoratives:
The purchase is to make men glorious;
Et bonum quo antiquius, eo melius.
If you, born in these latter times,
When wit's more ripe, accept my rhymes,
And that to hear an old man sing
May to your wishes pleasure bring,
I life would wish, and that I might
Waste it for you, like taper-light.—
This Antioch, then, Antiochus the Great
Built up, this city, for his chiefest seat;
The fairest in all Syria,—
I tell you what my authors say:
This king unto him took a fere,
Who died and left a female heir,
So buxom, blithe, and full of face,
As heaven had lent her all his grace;
With whom the father liking took,
And her to incest did provoke:—
Bad child, worse father! to entice his own
To evil should be done by none.
By custom what they did begin
Was, with long use, account no sin.
The beauty of this sinful dame
Made many princes thither frame,
To seek her as a bed-fellow,
In marriage-pleasures playfellow:
Which to prevent he made a law,—

95

To keep her still, and men in awe,—
That whoso asked her for his wife,
His riddle told not, lost his life:
So for her many a wight did die,
As yon grim looks do testify.
What now ensues, to the judgment of your eye
I give, my cause who best can justify.   [*Exit*

SCENE I.—Antioch. A Room in the Palace

Enter ANTIOCHUS, PERICLES, *and Attendants*

Ant.   Young Prince of Tyre, you have at large received
The danger of the task you undertake.
Per.   I have, Antiochus, and with a soul
Emboldened with the glory of her praise,
Think death no hazard in this enterprise.
Ant.   Bring in our daughter, clothéd like a bride,
For the embracements even of Jove himself;
At whose conception, till Lucina reigned,
Nature this dowry gave, to glad her presence,
The senate-house of planets all did sit
To knit in her their best perfections.

Music.   Enter the Daughter of ANTIOCHUS

Per.   See where she comes, apparelled like the spring,
Graces her subjects, and her thoughts the ring
Of every virtue gives renown to men!
Her face the book of praises, where is read
Nothing but curious pleasures, as from thence
Sorrow were ever razed, and testy wrath
Could never be her mild companion.
You gods, that made me man, and sway in love,
That have inflamed desire in my breast
To taste the fruit of yon celestial tree
Or die in the adventure, be my helps,
As I am son and servant to your will,
To compass such a boundless happiness!
Ant.   Prince Pericles,—
Per.   That would be son to great Antiochus.
Ant.   Before thee stands this fair Hesperides,
With golden fruit, but dangerous to be touched;
For death-like dragons here affright thee hard:
Her face, like heaven, enticeth thee to view
Her countless glory, which desert must gain;
And which, without desert, because thine eye
Presumes to reach, all thy whole heap must die.
Yon sometime famous princes, like thyself,

Drawn by report, adventurous by desire,
Tell thee with speechless tongues and semblance pale
That without covering save yon field of stars,
They here stand martyrs, slain in Cupid's wars;
And with dead cheeks advise thee to desist,
For going on death's net, whom none resist.
    Per.   Antiochus, I thank thee, who hath taught
My frail mortality to know itself,
And by those tearful objects to prepare
This body, like to them, to what I must:
For death remembered should be like a mirror
Who tells us life 's but breath, to trust it, error.
I 'll make my will then; and, as sick men do,
Who know the world, see heaven, but, feeling woe,
Gripe not at earthly joys as erst they did:
So, I bequeath a happy peace to you
And all good men, as every prince should do;
My riches to the earth from whence they came,
[*To the Daughter of Antiochus*]   But my unspotted fire of
            love to you.
Thus, ready for the way of life or death,
I wait the sharpest blow.
    Ant.   Scorning advice,—read the conclusion then;
Which read and not expounded, 't is decreed,
As these before thee, thou thyself shalt bleed.
    Daugh.   Of all 'sayed yet, may'st thou prove prosperous!
Of all 'sayed yet, I wish thee happiness.
    Per.   Like a bold champion, I assume the lists,
Nor ask advice of any other thought
But faithfulness, and courage.   [*Reads the riddle*

> *I am no viper, yet I feed*
> *On mother's flesh which did me breed;*
> *I sought a husband, in which labour*
> *I found that kindness in a father.*
> *He 's father, son, and husband mild;*
> *I mother, wife, and yet his child.*
> *How they may be, and yet in two,*
> *As you will live, resolve it you.*

Sharp physic is the last: but, O you powers
That give heaven countless eyes to view men's acts,
Why cloud they not their sights perpetually,
If this be true, which makes me pale to read it?
Fair glass of light, I loved you, and could still,
Were not this glorious casket stored with ill:
But I must tell you,—now, my thoughts revolt;
For he 's no man on whom perfections wait,
That, knowing sin within, will touch the gate.
You 're a fair viol, and your sense the strings,

Who, fingered to make man his lawful music,
Would draw heaven down and all the gods to hearken;
But being played upon before your time,
Hell only danceth at so harsh a chime.
Good sooth, I care not for you.
    Ant. Prince Pericles, touch not, upon thy life,
For that's an article within our law
As dangerous as the rest. Your time's expired:
Either expound now, or receive your sentence.
    Per. Great king,
Few love to hear the sins they love to act;
'T would braid yourself too near for me to tell it.
Who has a book of all that monarchs do,
He 's more secure to keep it shut, than shown;
For vice repeated 's like the wandering wind,
Blows dust in other's eyes to spread itself;
And yet the end of all is bought thus dear,
The breath is gone, and the sore eyes see clear—
To stop the air would hurt them. The blind mole casts
Copped hills towards heaven, to tell the earth is thronged
By man's oppression; and the poor worm doth die for 't.
Kings are earth's gods; in vice their law 's their will;
And if Jove stray, who dares say Jove doth ill?
It is enough you know; and it is fit,
What being more known grows worse, to smother it.
All love the womb that their first being bred,
Then give my tongue like leave to love my head.
    Ant. [*Aside*] Heaven, that I had thy head! he has
        found the meaning;
But I will gloze with him.—Young Prince of Tyre,
Though by the tenor of our strict edict,
Your exposition misinterpreting,
We might proceed to cancel of your days;
Yet hope, succeeding from so fair a tree
As your fair self, doth tune us otherwise.
Forty days longer we do respite you;
If by which time our secret be undone,
This mercy shows we 'll joy in such a son:
And until then your entertain shall be
As doth befit our honour, and your worth.
                         [*Exeunt all but Pericles*
    Per. How courtesy would seem to cover sin,
When what is done is like an hypocrite,
The which is good in nothing but in sight!
If it be true that I interpret false,
Then were it certain you were not so bad
As with foul incest to abuse your soul;
Where now you 're both a father and a son,
By your untimely claspings with your child
(Which pleasure fits a husband, not a father),

And she an eater of her mother's flesh
By the defiling of her parent's bed;
And both like serpents are, who though they feed
On sweetest flowers, yeet they poison breed.
Antioch, farewell! for wisdom sees, where men
Blush not in actions blacker than the night,
They 'll shun no course to keep them from the light:
One sin, I know, another doth provoke;
Murder 's as near to lust as flame to smoke;
Poison and treason are the hands of sin,
Ay, and the targets, to put off the shame:
Then, lest my life be cropped to keep you clear,
By flight I 'll shun the danger which I fear.   *[Exit*

Re-enter ANTIOCHUS

Ant. He hath found the meaning; for the which we mean
To have his head.
He must not live to trumpet forth my infamy,
Nor tell the world, Antiochus doth sin
In such a loathéd manner:
And therefore instantly this prince must die;
For by his fall my honour must keep high.
Who attends us there?

Enter THALIARD

Thal.   Doth your highness call?
Ant. Thaliard!
You 're of our chamber, and our mind partakes
Her private actions to your secrecy;
And for your faithfulness we will advance you.
Thaliard, behold, here 's poison, and here 's gold;
We hate the Prince of Tyre, and thou must kill him:
It fits thee not to ask the reason why,
Because we bid it. Say, is it done?
Thal. My lord, 't is done.
Ant. Enough.—

Enter a Messenger

Let your breath cool yourself, telling your haste.
Mess. My lord, Prince Pericles is fled.   *[Exit*
Ant.   As thou
Wilt live, fly after: and, as an arrow, shot
From a well-experienced archer, hits the mark
His eye doth level at, so ne'er return
Unless thou say, "Prince Pericles is dead."
Thal. My lord,
If I get him within my pistol's length,
I 'll make him sure enough: farewell to your highness.
Ant. Thaliard, adieu. *[Exit Thaliard]*—Till Pericles
be dead,
My heart can lend no succour to my head.   *[Exit*

Scene II.—Tyre. A Room in the Palace

Enter Pericles

Per. [*To those without*] Let none disturb us.—Why
    should this charge of thoughts,
The sad companion, dull-eyed melancholy,
Be my so used a guest, as not an hour
In the day's glorious walk or peaceful night—
The tomb where grief should sleep—can breed me quiet?
Here pleasures court mine eyes, and mine eyes shun them,
And danger which I feared 's at Antioch,
Whose aims seems far too short to hit me here;
Yet neither pleasure's art can joy my spirits,
Nor yet the other's distance comfort me.
Then it is thus: the passions of the mind,
That have their first conception by mis-dread,
Have after-nourishment and life by care;
And what was first but fear what might be done,
Grows elder now and cares it be not done.
And so with me:—the great Antiochus—
'Gainst whom I am too little to contend,
Since he 's so great, can make his will his act—
Will think me speaking, though I swear to silence;
Nor boots it me to say, I honour him,
If he suspect I may dishonour him:
And what may make him blush in being known,
He 'll stop the course by which it might be known.
With hostile forces he 'll o'erspread the land,
And with the ostent of war will look so huge,
Amazement shall drive courage from the state,
Our men be vanquished ere they do resist,
And subjects punished that ne'er thought offence:
Which care of them, not pity of myself,—
Who am no more but as the tops of trees
Which fence the roots they grow by and defend them,—
Makes both my body pine and soul to languish,
And punish that before, that he would punish.

Enter Helicanus *and other Lords*

First Lord. Joy and all comfort in your sacred breast!
Sec. Lord. And keep your mind, till you return to us,
Peaceful and comfortable!
Hel. Peace, peace, and give experience a tongue.
They do abuse the king that flatter him,
For flattery is the bellows blows up sin;
The thing the which is flattered, but a spark,
To which that blast gives heat and stronger glowing;

Whereas reproof, obedient and in order,
Fits kings, as they are men, for they may err.
When Signior Sooth here does proclaim a peace,
He flatters you, makes war upon your life.
Prince, pardon me, or strike me, if you please;
I cannot be much lower than my knees.
   Per. All leave us else; but let your cares o'erlook
What shipping and what lading 's in our haven,
And then return to us. [*Exeunt Lords*]—Helicanus, thou
Hast movéd us: what seest thou in our looks?
   Hel. An angry brow, dread lord.
   Per. If there be such a dart in princes' frowns,
How durst thy tongue move anger to our face?
   Hel. How dare the plants look up to heaven, from
     whence
They have their nourishment?
   Per.   Thou know'st I 've power
To take thy life from thee.
   Hel. [*Kneeling*] I 've ground the axe;
Do you but strike the blow.
   Per.   Rise, prithee, rise;
Sit down; I thank thee for 't, thou art no flatterer,
And Heaven forbid but kings should let their ears
Hear their faults chid!
Fit counsellor, and servant for a prince,
Who by thy wisdom mak'st a prince thy servant,
What wouldst thou have me do?
   Hel.   To bear with patience
Such griefs as you do lay upon yourself.
   Per. Thou speak'st like a physician, Helicanus,
That minister'st a potion unto me
That thou wouldst tremble to receive thyself.
Attend me then: I went to Antioch,
Where, as thou know'st, against the face of death
I sought the purchase of a glorious beauty
From whence an issue I might propagate
As arms to princes that bring joys to subjects.
Her face was to mine eye beyond all wonder;
The rest—hark in thine ear—as black as incest:
Which by my knowledge found, the sinful father
Seemed not to strike, but smooth; but thou know'st this,
'T is time to fear when tyrants seem to kiss;
Which fear so grew in me, I hither fled,
Under the covering of a careful night
Who seemed my good protector: and, being here,
Bethought me what was past, what might succeed.
I knew him tyrannous; and tyrants' fears
Decrease not, but grow faster than their years.
And should he doubt it—as no doubt he doth—
That I should open to the listening air

How many worthy princes' bloods were shed
To keep his bed of blackness unlaid ope,—
To lop that doubt he 'll fill this land with arms,
And make pretence of wrong that I have done him;
When all for mine, if I may call 't, offence,
Must feel war's blow who spares not innocence:
Which love to all,—of which thyself art one,
Who now reprov'dst me for it,—

    Hel.   Alas, sir!

    Per.   Drew sleep out of mine eyes, blood from my cheeks,
Musings into my mind, a thousand doubts
How I might stop this tempest ere it came;
And finding little comfort to relieve them,
I thought it princely charity to grieve them.

    Hel.   My lord, since you have given me leave to speak,
Freely I'll speak. Antiochus you fear,
And justly too, I think, you fear the tyrant,
Who either by public war or private treason
Will take away your life.
Therefore, my lord, go travel for a while,
Till that his rage and anger be forgot,
Or till the Fates do cut his thread of life.
Your rule direct to any; if to me,
Day serves not light more faithful than I'll be.

    Per.   I do not doubt thy faith; but should he wrong
My liberties in my absence?

    Hel.   We'll mingle our bloods together in the earth
From whence we had our being and our birth.

    Per.   Tyre, I now look from thee then, and to Tarsus
Intend my travel, where I'll hear from thee,
And by whose letters I'll dispose myself.
The care I had, and have, of subjects' good,
On thee I lay, whose wisdom's strength can bear it.
I'll take thy word for faith, not ask thine oath:
Who shuns not to break one, will sure crack both.
But in our orbs we'll live so round and safe,
That time of both this truth shall ne'er convince,
Thou show'dst a subject's shine, I a true prince.   [*Exeunt*

SCENE III.—Tyre. An Ante-chamber in the Palace

Enter THALIARD

    Thal.   So, this is Tyre, and this is the court. Here must
I kill King Pericles; and if I do not, I am sure to be hanged
at home: 't is dangerous.—Well, I perceive he was a wise
fellow and had good discretion, that, being bid to ask what
he would of the king, desired he might know none of his
secrets: now do I see he had some reason for 't; for if a
king bid a man be a villain, he is bound by the indenture
of his oath to be one.—Hush! here come the lords of Tyre.

Enter HELICANUS, ESCANES, *and other Lords*

Hel. You shall not need, my fellow peers of Tyre,
Further to question me of your king's departure:
His sealed commission, left in trust with me,
Doth speak sufficiently, he 's gone to travel.
    Thal. [*Aside*] How! the king gone?
    Hel. If further yet you will be satisfied
Why, as it were unlicensed of your loves,
He would depart, I 'll give some light unto you.
Being at Antioch—
    Thal. [*Aside*] What from Antioch?
    Hel. Royal Antiochus—on what cause I know not—
Took some displeasure at him: at least, he judged so;
And doubting lest that he had erred or sinned,
To show his sorrow he 'd correct himself;
So puts himself unto the shipman's toil,
With whom each minute threatens life or death.
    Thal. [*Aside*] Well, I perceive
I shall not be hanged now, although I would;
But since he 's gone, the king it sure must please,
He scaped the land, to perish on the seas.—
Now I 'll present myself.—[*To them*] Peace to the lords of
    Tyre!
    Hel. Lord Thaliard from Antiochus is welcome.
    Thal. From him I come,
With message unto princely Pericles;
But since my landing I have understood
Your lord 's betook himself to unknown travels,
My message must return from whence it came.
    Hel. We have no reason to desire it,
Commended to our master, not to us:
Yet, ere you shall depart, this we desire,—
As friends to Antioch, we may feast in Tyre.   [*Exeunt*

SCENE IV.—Tarsus. A Room in the Governor's House

Enter CLEON, DIONYZA, *and Attendants*

    Cle. My Dionyza, shall we rest us here,
And by relating tales of others' griefs,
See if 't will teach us to forget our own?
    Dio. That were to blow at fire in hope to quench it;
For who digs hills because they do aspire
Throws down one mountain to cast up a higher.
O my distressèd lord, even such our griefs are;
Here they 're but felt and seen with mischief's eyes,
But like to groves, being topped, they higher rise.
    Cle. O Dionyza,
Who wanteth food and will not say he wants it,

Or can conceal his hunger till he famish?
Our tongues and sorrows do sound deep our woes
Into the air; our eyes do weep till lungs
Fetch breath that may proclaim them louder; that
If heaven slumber while their creatures want,
They make awake their helps to comfort them.
I 'll then discourse our woes, felt several years,
And, wanting breath to speak, help me with tears.
    Dio.   I 'll do my best, sir.
    Cle.   This Tarsus, o'er which I 've the government,
A city, on whom plenty held full hand,
For Riches strewed herself even in the street;
Whose towers bore heads so high, they kissed the clouds,
And strangers ne'er beheld, but wondered at:
Whose men and dames so jetted and adorned,
Like one another's glass to trim them by:
Their tables were stored full to glad the sight,
And not so much to feed on as delight;
All poverty was scorned, and pride so great,
The name of help grew odious to repeat.
    Dio.   O, 't is too true.
    Cle.   But see what heaven can do! By this our change,
These mouths whom but of late, earth, sea, and air,
Were all too little to content and please,
Although they gave their creatures in abundance,
As houses are defiled for want of use,
They are now starved for want of exercise:
Those palates, who, not yet two summers younger,
Must have inventions to delight the taste,
Would now be glad of bread, and beg for it:
Those mothers, who, to nousle up their babes,
Thought nought too curious, are ready now
To eat those little darlings whom they loved.
So sharp are hunger's teeth, that man and wife
Draw lots, who first shall die to lengthen life.
Here stands a lord, and there a lady weeping;
Here many sink, yet those which see them fall,
Have scarce strength left to give them burial.
Is not this true?
    Dio.   Our cheeks and hollow eyes do witness it.
    Cle.   O, let those cities that of plenty's cup
And her prosperities so largely taste
With their superfluous riots, hear these tears:
The misery of Tarsus may be theirs.

Enter a Lord

    Lord.   Where 's the lord governor?
    Cle.   Here.
Speak out thy sorrows which thou bring'st, in haste,
For comfort is too far for us to expect.

  Lord. We have descried, upon our neighbouring shore,
A portly sail of ships make hitherward.
  Cle. I thought as much.
One sorrow never comes but brings an heir
That may succeed as his inheritor;
And so in ours. Some neighbouring nation,
Taking advantage of our misery,
Hath stuffed these hollow vessels with their power,
To beat us down, the which are down already;
And make a conquest of unhappy me,
Whereas no glory 's got to overcome.
  Lord. That 's the least fear; for, by the semblance
Of their white flags displayed, they bring us peace,
And come to us as favourers, not as foes.
  Cle. Thou speak'st like him 's untutored to repeat:
Who makes the fairest show means most deceit.
But bring they what they will, and what they can,
What need we fear?
The ground 's the lowest, and we 're half way there.
Go, tell their general we attend him here
To know for what he comes, and whence he comes
And what he craves.
  Lord. I go, my lord.   *[Exit*
  Cle. Welcome is peace, if he on peace consist;
If wars, we are unable to resist.

    Enter PERICLES, *with Attendants*

  Per. Lord governor, for so we hear you are,
Let not our ships and number of our men
Be, like a beacon fired, to amaze your eyes.
We have heard your miseries as far as Tyre,
And seen the desolation of your streets;
Nor come we to add sorrow to your tears,
But to relieve them of their heavy load:
And these our ships you happily may think
Are like the Trojan horse was stuffed within
With bloody veins, expecting overthrow,
Are stored with corn to make your needy bread,
And give them life whom hunger starved half dead.
  All. The gods of Greece protect you!
And we will pray for you.
  Per.   Rise, pray you rise:
We do not look for reverence, but for love,
And harbourage for ourself, our ships, and men.
  Cle. The which when any shall not gratify,
Or pay you with unthankfulness in thought,—
Be it our wives, our children, or ourselves,—
The curse of heaven and men succeed their evils!
Till when,—the which, I hope, shall ne'er be seen,—
Your grace is welcome to our town and us.

Per. Which welcome we 'll accept; feast here awhile,
Until our stars that frown lend us a smile.   [*Exeunt*

ACT TWO

Enter GOWER

Gower. Here have you seen a mighty king
His child, iwis, to incest bring;
A better prince and benign lord
That will prove awful both in deed and word:
Be quiet, then, as men should be,
Till he has passed Necessity:
I 'll show you, those in trouble's reign
Losing a mite a mountain gain.
The good in conversation—
To whom I give my benison—
Is still at Tarsus, where each man
Thinks all is writ he speken can;
And, to remember what he does,
Build his statue to make him glorious:
But tidings to the contrary
Are brought your eyes; what need speak I?

DUMB-SHOW

Enter at one door, PERICLES, *talking with* CLEON; *their
Trains with them. Enter at another door, a Gentleman,
with a letter to* PERICLES; *who shows the letter to* CLEON;
*then gives the Messenger a reward, and knights him.
Exeunt* PERICLES *and* CLEON, *with their Trains.*

Gow. Good Helicane, that stayed at home
Not to eat honey like a drone
From others' labours; though he strive
To killen bad, keep good alive;
And, to fulfil his prince' desire,
Sends word of all that haps in Tyre:
How Thaliard came full bent with sin
And hid intent to murder him;
And that in Tarsus was not best
Longer for him to make his rest.
He, doing so, put forth to seas,
Where when men ben there 's seldom ease:
For now the wind begins to blow;
Thunder above, and deeps below,
Make such unquiet, that the ship
Should house him safe is wracked and split;
And he, good prince, all having lost,
By waves from coast to coast is tost.

All perishen, of man, of pelf,
Ne aught escapen but himself;
Till Fortune, tired with doing bad,
Threw him ashore, to give him glad:
And here he comes. What shall be next,
Pardon old Gower;—this longs the text.   [*Exit*

SCENE I.—Pentapolis. An Open Place by the Sea-side

Enter PERICLES, *wet*

Per. Yet cease your ire, you angry stars of heaven!
Wind, rain, and thunder, remember, earthly man
Is but a substance that must yield to you;
And I, as fits my nature, do obey you.
Alas, the sea hath cast me on the rocks,
Washed me from shore to shore, and left me breath
Nothing to think on but ensuing death:
Let it suffice the greatness of your powers
To have bereft a prince of all his fortunes;
And having thrown him from your watery grave,
Here to have death in peace is all he 'll crave.

Enter three Fishermen

First Fish. What, ho, Pilch!
Sec. Fish. Ho, come, and bring away the nets.
First Fish. What, Patch-breech, I say!
Third Fish. What say you, master?
First Fish. Look how thou stirrest now! come away,
or I 'll fetch thee with a wanion.
Third Fish. Faith, master, I am thinking of the poor
men that were cast away before us even now.
First Fish. Alas, poor souls! it grieved my heart to
hear what pitiful cries they made to us to help them, when,
well-a-day, we could scarce help ourselves.
Third Fish. Nay, master, said not I as much, when I
saw the porpus, how he bounced and tumbled? they say,
they're half fish, half flesh: a plague on them, they ne'er
come, but I look to be washed. Master, I marvel how the
fishes live in the sea.
First Fish. Why, as men do a-land—the great ones eat
up the little ones. I can compare our rich misers to nothing
so fitly as to a whale; 'a plays and tumbles, driving the
poor fry before him, and at last devours them all at a mouth-
ful. Such whales have I heard on o' the land, who never
leave gaping till they 've swallowed the whole parish,
church, steeple, bells, and all.
Per. [*Aside*] A pretty moral.
Third Fish. But, master, if I had been the sexton, I
would have been that day in the belfry.

Sec. Fish. Why, man?

Third Fish. Because he should have swallowed me too; and when I had been in his belly, I would have kept such a jangling of the bells, that he should never have left, till he cast bells, steeple, church, and parish, up again. But if the good King Simonides were of my mind—

Per. [*Aside*] Simonides?

Third Fish. We would purge the land of these drones, that rob the bee of her honey.

Per. [*Aside*] How from the finny subject of the sea
These fishers tell the infirmities of men;
And from their watery empire recollect
All that may men approve or men detect !—
Peace be at your labour, honest fishermen.

Sec. Fish. Honest ! good fellow, what 's that ? if it be a day fits you, search out of the calendar, and nobody look after it.

Per. Y' may see, the sea hath cast upon your coast—

Sec. Fish. What a drunken knave was the sea, to cast thee in our way !—

Per. A man whom both the waters and the wind,
In that vast tennis-court, hath made the ball
For them to play upon, entreats you pity him;
He asks of you, that never used to beg.

First Fish. No, friend, cannot you beg ? Here 's them in our country of Greece, gets more with begging than we can do with working.

Sec. Fish. Canst thou catch any fishes then ?

Per. I never practised it.

Sec. Fish. Nay, then thou wilt starve, sure; for here 's nothing to be got now-a-days, unless thou canst fish for 't.

Per. What I have been, I have forgot to know;
But what I am, want teaches me to think on:
A man thronged up with cold; my veins are chill,
And have no more of life than may suffice
To give my tongue that heat to ask your help;
Which if you shall refuse, when I am dead,
For that I am a man, pray see me buried.

First Fish. Die, quoth-a ? Now, gods forbid it ! I have a gown here; come, put it on; keep thee warm. Now, afore me, a handsome fellow ! Come, thou shalt go home, and we 'll have flesh for holidays, fish for fasting days, and moreo'er puddings and flapjacks ; and thou shalt be welcome.

Per. I thank you, sir.

Sec. Fish. Hark you, my friend,—you said you could not beg.

Per. I did but crave.

Sec. Fish. But crave? Then I 'll turn craver too, and so I shall scape whipping.

Per. Why, are all your beggars whipped then?

Sec. Fish. O, not all, my friend, not all: for if all your beggars were whipped, I would wish no better office than to be a beadle. But, master, I 'll go draw up the net.

[Exeunt two of the Fishermen

Per. [*Aside*] How well this honest mirth becomes their labour!

First Fish. Hark you, sir,—do you know where you are ?

Per. Not well.

First Fish. Why, I 'll tell you: this is called Pentapolis, and our king, the good Simonides.

Per. The good King Simonides, do you call him ?

First Fish. Ay, sir; and he deserves to be so called, for his peaceable reign and good government.

Per. He is a happy king, since he gains from his subjects the name of good by his government. How far is his court distant from this shore ?

First Fish. Marry, sir, half a day's journey: and I 'll tell you, he hath a fair daughter, and to-morrow is her birthday; and there are princes and knights come from all parts of the world to joust and tourney for her love.

Per. Were my fortunes equal to my desires, I could wish to make one there.

First Fish. O, sir, things must be as they may; and what a man cannot get, he may lawfully deal for his wife's soul.

Re-enter the two Fishermen, drawing up a net

Sec. Fish. Help, master, help! here 's a fish hangs in the net, like a poor man's right in the law; 't will hardly come out. Ha! bots on 't; 't is come at last, and 't is turned to a rusty armour.

Per. An armour, friends! I pray you, let me see 't.
Thanks, Fortune, yet, that after all thy crosses
Thou giv'st me somewhat to repair myself,
And though it was mine own; part of mine heritage
Which my dead father did bequeath to me
With this strict charge, even as he left his life,
"Keep it, my Pericles, it hath been a shield
'Twixt me and death"—and pointed to this brace;
"For that it saved me, keep it; in like need—
From which the gods protect thee!—it may defend thee."
It kept where I kept, I so dearly loved it,
Till the rough seas that spare not any man
Took it in rage, though calmed have given 't again.
I thank thee for 't: my shipwreck now 's no ill,
Since I have here my father's gift in 's will.

First Fish. What mean you, sir?

Per. To beg of you, kind friends, this coat of worth,
For it was sometime target to a king;

I know it by this mark. He loved me dearly,
And for his sake I wish the having of it;
And that you 'd guide me to your sovereign's court,
Where with 't I may appear a gentleman:
And if that ever my low fortunes better,
I 'll pay your bounties; till then, rest your debtor.
    First Fish.   Why, wilt thou tourney for the lady?
    Per.   I 'll show the virtue I have borne in arms.
    First Fish.   Why, do ye take it; and the gods give thee
good on 't.
    Sec. Fish.   Ay, but hark you, my friend; 't was we that
made up this garment through the rough seams of the
waters: there are certain condolements, certain vails. I
hope, sir, if you thrive, you 'll remember from whence you
had it.
    Per.   Believe 't, I will.
By your furtherance I am clothed in steel;
And spite of all the rapture of the sea,
This jewel holds his gilding on my arm:
Unto thy value will I mount myself
Upon a courser, whose delightful steps
Shall make the gazer joy to see him tread.—
Only, my friends, I yet am unprovided
Of a pair of bases.
    Sec. Fish.   We 'll sure provide: thou shalt have my best
gown to make thee a pair, and I 'll bring thee to the court
myself.
    Per.   Then honour be but equal to my will!
This day I 'll rise, or else add ill to ill.   *[Exeunt*

SCENE II.—Pentapolis. A public Way or Platform leading
    to the Lists. A Pavilion near it, for the reception of
    the KING, PRINCESS, Ladies, Lords, etc.

Enter SIMONIDES, THAISA, *Lords, and Attendants*

    Sim.   Are the knights ready to begin the triumph?
    First Lord.   They are, my liege;
And stay your coming to present themselves.
    Sim.   Return them, we are ready; and our daughter,
In honour of whose birth these triumphs are,
Sits here, like beauty's child, whom nature gat
For men to see, and seeing wonder at.   *[Exit a Lord*
    Thai.   It pleaseth you, my father, to express
My commendations great, whose merit's less.
    Sim.   'T is fit it should be so; for princes are
A model, which heaven makes like to itself:
As jewels lose their glory if neglected,
So princes their renown, if not respected.

'T is now your honour, daughter, to explain
The labour of each knight in his device.
 Thai. Which, to preserve mine honour, I'll perform.

*Enter a Knight: he passes over the stage, and his Squire
presents his shield to the Princess*

 Sim. Who is the first that doth prefer himself?
 Thai. A knight of Sparta, my renownèd father;
And the device he bears upon his shield
Is the black Ethiop, reaching at the sun;
The word, *Lux tua vita mihi.*
 Sim. He loves you well that holds his life of you.
        [*The second Knight passes over*
Who is the second that presents himself?
 Thai. A prince of Macedon, my royal father;
And the device he bears upon his shield
Is an armed knight, that's conquered by a lady;
The motto thus, in Spanish, *Piu por dulzura que por fuerza.*
        [*The third Knight passes over*
 Sim. And what's the third?
 Thai.   The third of Antioch;
And his device, a wreath of chivalry;
The word, *Me pompæ provexit apex.*
        [*The fourth Knight passes over*
 Sim. What is the fourth?
 Thai. A burning torch, that's turnèd upside down;
The word, *Quod me alit, me extinguit.*
 Sim. Which shows that beauty hath his power and will,
Which can as well inflame as it can kill.
        [*The fifth Knight passes over*
 Thai. The fifth, a hand environèd with clouds,
Holding out gold that's by the touchstone tried;
The motto thus, *Sic spectanda fides.*
       [*The sixth Knight (Pericles) passes over*
 Sim. And what's
The sixth and last, the which the knight himself
With such a graceful courtesy delivered?
 Thai. He seems to be a stranger; but his present's
A withered branch, that's only green at top;
The motto, *In hac spe vivo.*
 Sim. A pretty moral:
From the dejected state wherein he is,
He hopes by you his fortunes yet may flourish.
 First Lord. He hath need mean better than his outward
   show
Can any way speak in his just commend;
For by his rusty outside he appears
To have practised more the whipstock than the lance.
 Sec. Lord. He well may be a stranger, for he comes
To an honoured triumph strangely furnishèd.

Third Lord. And on set purpose let his armour rust
Until this day, to scour it in the dust.
Sim. Opinion 's but a fool, that makes us scan
The outward habit for the inward man.
But stay, the knights are coming; we 'll withdraw
Into the gallery. [*Exeunt*
[*Great shouts within, all crying,* "The mean Knight!"

SCENE III.—Pentapolis. A Hall of State.—A Banquet
prepared

Enter SIMONIDES, THAISA, *Ladies, Lords, Knights, and
Attendants*

Sim. Knights,
To say you 're welcome were superfluous.
To place upon the volume of your deeds,
As in a title-page, your worth in arms,
Were more than you expect, or more than 's fit,
Since every worth in show commends itself.
Prepare for mirth, for mirth becomes a feast:
You are princes, and my guests.
Thai. But you, my knight and guest;
To whom this wreath of victory I give
And crown you king of this day's happiness.
Per. 'T is more by fortune, lady, than by merit.
Sim. Call it by what you will, the day is yours;
And here, I hope, is none that envies it.
In framing an artist art hath thus decreed,
To make some good but others to exceed;
And you 're her laboured scholar.—Come, queen o' the
feast,—
For, daughter, so you are,—here take your place:
Marshal the rest as they deserve their grace.
Knights. We are honoured much by good Simonides.
Sim. Your presence glads our days: honour we love,
For who hates honour hates the gods above.
Marshal. Sir, yonder is your place.
Per. Some other is more fit.
First Knight. Contend not, sir; for we are gentlemen
That neither in our hearts nor outward eyes
Envy the great, nor do the low despise.
Per. You are right courteous knights.
Sim. Sit, sir; sit.
Per. [*Aside*] By Jove, I wonder, that is king of thoughts,
These cates resist me, she but thought upon.
Thai. [*Aside*] By Juno, that is queen
Of marriage, all viands that I eat
Do seem unsavoury, wishing him my meat.
Sure, he 's a gallant gentleman.

Sim. [*Aside*]   He 's but a country gentleman:
Has done no more than other knights have done,
Has broken a staff, or so; so let it pass.
   Thai. [*Aside*]   To me he seems like diamond to glass.
   Per. [*Aside*] Yon king 's to me like to my father's
         picture,
Which tells me in that glory once he was,
Had princes sit, like stars, about his throne,
And he the sun for them to reverence;
None that beheld him but like lesser lights
Did vail their crowns to his supremacy;
Where now his son 's a glow-worm in the night,
The which hath fire in darkness, none in light:
Whereby I see that Time 's the king of men;
He 's both their parent, and he is their grave.
And gives them what he will, not what they crave.
   Sim.   What, are you merry, knights?
   First Knight.   Who can be other in this royal presence?
   Sim.   Here, with a cup that 's stored unto the brim,—
As you do love, fill to your mistress' lips,—
We drink this health to you.
   Knights.   We thank your grace.
   Sim.   Yet pause awhile;
Yon knight doth sit with us too melancholy,
As if the entertainment in our court
Had not a show might countervail his worth.
Note it not you, Thaisa?
   Thai.   What is it
To me, my father?
   Sim.   O, attend, my daughter:
Princes, in this, should live like gods above,
Who freely give to every one that comes
To honour them;
And princes, not doing so, are like to gnats
Which make a sound, but killed are wondered at.
Therefore, to make his entrance more sweet,
Here say, we drink this standing-bowl to him.
   Thai.   Alas, my father, it befits not me
Unto a stranger knight to be so bold:
He may my proffer take for an offence,
Since men take women's gifts for impudence.
   Sim.   How!
Do as I bid you. or you 'll move me else.
   Thai. [*Aside*]   Now, by the gods, he could not please me
         better.
   Sim.   Furthermore tell him, we desire to know
Of whence he is, his name, and parentage.
   Thai.   The king my father, sir, has drunk to you.
   Per.   I thank him.
   Thai.   Wishing it so much blood unto your life.

                           113

Per.   I thank both him and you, and pledge him freely.

Thai.   And further he desires to know of you,
Of whence you are, your name, and parentage.

Per.   A gentleman of Tyre,—my name, Pericles,
My education been in arts and arms,—
Who, looking for adventures in the world,
Was by the rough seas reft of ships and men,
And after shipwreck driven upon this shore.

Thai.   He thanks your grace; names himself Pericles,
A gentleman of Tyre,
Who only by misfortune of the seas
Bereft of ships and men, cast on this shore.

Sim.   Now, by the gods, I pity his misfortune,
And will awake him from his melancholy.
Come, gentlemen, we sit too long on trifles,
And waste the time which looks for other revels.
Even in your armours, as you are addressed,
Will very well become a soldier's dance.
I will not have excuse, with saying this
Loud music is too harsh for ladies' heads,
Since they love men in arms as well as beds.
                 [*The Knights dance*
So this was well asked, 't was so well performed.
Come, sir;
Here is a lady that wants breathing too:
And I have often heard, you knights of Tyre
Are excellent in making ladies trip,
And that their measures are as excellent.

Per.   In those that practise them, they are, my lord.

Sim.   O, that 's as much as you would be denied
Of your fair courtesy.   [*The Knights and Ladies dance.*
                 Unclasp, unclasp:
Thanks, gentlemen, to all; all have done well,
[*To Pericles*] But you the best.—Pages and lights, to
     conduct
These knights unto their several lodgings!—Yours, sir,
We have given order to be next our own.

Per.   I am at your grace's pleasure.

Sim.   Princes, it is too late to talk of love,
And that 's the mark I know you level at:
Therefore, each one betake him to his rest;
To-morrow all for speeding do their best.   [*Exeunt*

SCENE IV.—Tyre.   A Room in the Governor's House

Enter HELICANUS *and* ESCANES

Hel.   No, Escanes, know this of me,
Antiochus from incest lived not free:

For which, the most high gods not minding longer
To withhold the vengeance that they had in store,
Due to his heinous capital offence,
Even in the height and pride of all his glory,
When he was seated in a chariot
Of priceless value, and his daughter with him,
A fire from heaven came, and shrivelled up
Their bodies, even to loathing; they so stunk,
That those whose eyes adored them ere their fall,
Scorn now their hand should give them burial.

Esca. 'T was very strange.
Hel.   And yet but just; for though
This king were great, his greatness was no guard
To bar heaven's shaft; but sin had his reward.

Esca. 'T is very true.

Enter two or three Lords

First Lord. See, not a man in private conference
Or council has respect with him but he.

Sec. Lord. It shall no longer grieve without reproof.

Third Lord. And cursed be he that will not second it.

First Lord. Follow me then.—Lord Helicane, a word.

Hel. With me? and welcome.—Happy day, my lords.

First Lord. Know, that our griefs are risen to the top,
And now at length they overflow their banks.

Hel. Your griefs! for what? wrong not the prince you
love.

First Lord. Wrong not yourself then, noble Helicane;
But if the prince do live, let us salute him,
Or know what ground 's made happy by his breath.
If in the world he live, we 'll seek him out;
If in his grave he rest, we 'll find him there;
And be resolved, he lives to govern us,
Or dead, gives cause to mourn his funeral
And leaves us to our free election.

Sec. Lord. Whose death 's, indeed, the strongest in our
censure:
And knowing this kingdom is without a head,—
As goodly buildings left without a roof
Soon fall to ruin,—your most noble self,
That best know how to rule, and how to reign,
We thus submit unto, our sovereign.

All. Live, noble Helicane!

Hel. For honour's cause forbear your suffrages:
If that you love Prince Pericles, forbear.
Take I your wish, I leap into the seas,
Where 's hourly trouble for a minute's ease.
A twelvemonth longer, let me still entreat
You to forbear the absence of your king;
If in which time expired he not return,

115

I shall with agéd patience bear your yoke.
But if I cannot win you to this love,
Go search like nobles, like his noble subjects,
And in your search spend your adventurous worth;
Whom if you find and win unto return
You shall like diamonds sit about his crown.
 First Lord. To wisdom he 's a fool that will not yield:
And since Lord Helicane enjoineth us,
We with our travels will endeavour it.
 Hel. Then you love us, we you, and we 'll clasp hands:
When peers thus knit, a kingdom ever stands. [*Exeunt*

 Scene V.—Pentapolis. A Room in the Palace

Enter Simonides, *reading a letter : the Knights meet him*

 First Knight. Good morrow to the good Simonides.
 Sim. Knights, from my daughter this I let you know,
That for this twelvemonth she 'll not undertake
A married life.
Her reason to herself is only known,
Which yet from her by no means can I get.
 Sec. Knight. May we not get access to her, my lord?
 Sim. Faith, by no means; she hath so strictly tied her
To her chamber, that it is impossible.
One twelve moons more she 'll wear Diana's livery;
This by the eye of Cynthia hath she vowed,
And on her virgin honour will not break it.
 Third Knight. Loth to bid farewell, we take our leaves.
             [*Exeunt Knights*
 Sim. So,
They 're well dispatched; now to my daughter's letter.
She tells me here, she'll wed the stranger knight,
Or never more to view nor day nor light.
'T is well, mistress; your choice agrees with mine;
I like that well:—how absolute she 's in 't.
Not minding whether I dislike or no!
Well, I commend her choice,
And will no longer have it be delayed.
Soft, here he comes: I must dissemble it.

      Enter Pericles

 Per. All fortune to the good Simonides!
 Sim. To you as much, sir! I 'm beholding to you
For your sweet music this last night: I do
Protest, my ears were never better fed
With such delightful pleasing harmony.
 Per. It is your grace's pleasure to commend,
Not my desert.

Sim.   Sir, you are music's master.
Per.   The worst of all her scholars, my good lord.
Sim.   Let me ask one thing.
What do you think of my daughter, sir?
   Per.   A most virtuous princess.
   Sim.   And she is fair too, is she not?
   Per.   As a fair day in summer; wondrous fair.
   Sim.   My daughter, sir, thinks very well of you;
Ay, so well, sir, that you must be her master,
And she will be your scholar: therefore, look to it.
   Per.   I am unworthy for her schoolmaster.
   Sim.   She thinks not so; peruse this writing else.
   Per.   [*Aside*] What 's here?
A letter, that she loves the knight of Tyre?
'T is the king's subtilty, to have my life.—
O, seek not to entrap me, gracious lord,
A stranger and distresséd gentleman,
That never aimed so high to love your daughter,
But bent all offices to honour her.
   Sim.   Thou hast bewitched my daughter, and thou art
A villain.
   Per.   By the gods, I have not:
Never did thought of mine levy offence;
Nor never act of mine did yet commence
A deed might gain her love, or your displeasure.
   Sim.   Traitor, thou liest.
   Per.   Traitor!
   Sim.   Ay, traitor.
   Per.   Even in his throat, unless it be the king,
That calls me traitor, I return the lie.
   Sim.   [*Aside*] Now, by the gods, I do applaud his courage.
   Per.   My actions are as noble as my thoughts,
That never relished of a base descent.
I came unto your court for honour's cause,
And not to be a rebel to her state;
And he that otherwise accounts of me,
This sword shall prove, he 's honour's enemy.
   Sim.   No?
Here comes my daughter, she can witness it.

                    Enter THAISA

   Per.   Then, as you are as virtuous as fair,
Resolve your angry father, if my tongue
Did e'er solicit, or my hand subscribe
To any syllable that made love to you?
   Thai.   Why, sir, say if you had,
Who takes offence at that would make me glad?
   Sim.   Yea, mistress, are you so peremptory?—
[*Aside*] I am glad on 't with all my heart.—
I 'll tame you; I 'll bring you in subjection.

Will you, although not having my consent,
Bestow your love and your affections
Upon a stranger? [aside] who, for aught I know,
May be—nor can I think the contrary—
As great in royal blood as I myself.—
Therefore, hear you, my mistress; either frame
Your will to mine; and you, sir, hear you.
Either be ruled by me, or I will make you—
Man and wife.
Nay, come, your hands and lips must seal it too;
And being joined, I 'll thus your hopes destroy;
And for a further grief,—God give you joy!—
What, are you both pleased?

    Thai.   Yes, if you love me, sir.
    Per.   Even as my life, or blood that fosters it.
    Sim.   What! are you both agreed?
    Both.   Yes, if 't please your majesty.
    Sim.   It pleaseth me so well, I 'll see you wed;
Then, with what haste you can, get you to bed.   [*Exeunt*

ACT THREE

Enter GOWER

    Gow. Now sleep-yslakéd hath the rout;
No din but snores the house about,
Made louder by the o'er-fed breast
Of this most pompous marriage-feast.
The cat, with eyne of burning coal,
Now couches fore the mouse's hole;
And crickets sing at the oven's mouth,
All the blither for their drouth.
Hymen hath brought the bride to bed,
Where, by the loss of maidenhead,
A babe is moulded.—Be attent,
And time that is so briefly spent
With your fine fancies quaintly eche:
What 's dumb in show, I'll plain with speech.

DUMB-SHOW

Enter from one side, PERICLES *and* SIMONIDES, *with Attendants;
a Messenger meets them, kneels, and gives* PERICLES *a
letter:* PERICLES *shows it to* SIMONIDES; *the Lords
kneel to* PERICLES. *Then enter* THAISA *with child, and*
LYCHORIDA: SIMONIDES *shows his daughter the letter;
she rejoices: she and* PERICLES *take leave of her father,
and all depart.*

    Gow. By many a dern and painful perch
Of Pericles the careful search

By the four opposing coigns
Which the world together joins,
Is made, with all due diligence
That horse, and sail, and high expense,
Can stead the quest. At last from Tyre—
Fame answering the most strange inquire—
To the court of King Simonides
Are letters brought, the tenor these:—
Antiochus and his daughter dead;
The men of Tyrus on the head
Of Helicanus would set on
The crown of Tyre, but he will none:
The mutiny there he hastes t' oppress;
Says to 'em, if King Pericles
Come not home in twice six moons,
He, obedient to their dooms,
Will take the crown. The sum of this,
Brought hither to Pentapolis,
Yravishéd the regions round,
And every one with claps can sound,
"Our heir-apparent is a king!
Who dreamed, who thought of such a thing?"
Brief, he must hence depart to Tyre:
His queen, with child, makes her desire
(Which who shall cross?) along to go;
Omit we all their dole and woe:
Lychorida, her nurse, she takes,
And so to sea. Their vessel shakes
On Neptune's billow; half the flood
Hath their keel cut: but fortune's mood
Varies again; the grizzly north
Disgorges such a tempest forth,
That, as a duck for life that dives,
So up and down the poor ship drives.
The lady shrieks, and well-a-near
Does fall in travail with her fear:
And what ensues in this fell storm
Shall for itself itself perform.
I nill relate, for action may
Conveniently the rest convey,
Which might not what by me is told.
In your imagination hold
This stage the ship, upon whose deck
The sea-tost Pericles appears to speak.   *[Exit*

Scene I

Enter Pericles, *on shipboard*

   Per. Thou God of this great vast, rebuke these surges,
Which wash both heaven and hell; and thou, that hast

Upon the winds command, bind them in brass,
Having recalled them from the deep. O, still
Thy deafening, dreadful thunders; gently quench
Thy nimble, sulphurous flashes!—O, how, Lychorida,
How does my queen?—Thou stormest venomously;
Wilt thou spit all thyself?—The seaman's whistle
Is as a whisper in the ears of death,
Unheard. Lychorida!—Lucina, O!
Divinest patroness, and midwife gentle
To those that cry by night, convey thy deity
Aboard our dancing boat; make swift the pangs
Of my queen's travails!—Now, Lychorida!

Enter LYCHORIDA, *with an Infant*

   Lyc. Here is a thing too young for such a place,
Who, if it had conceit, would die, as I
Am like to do. Take in your arms this piece
Of your dead queen.
   Per.   How, how, Lychorida!
   Lyc. Patience, good sir; do not assist the storm.
Here 's all that is left living of your queen,
A little daughter: for the sake of it,
Be manly, and take comfort.
   Per.   O you gods!
Why do you make us love your goodly gifts,
And snatch them straight away? We here below
Recall not what we give, and therein may
Vie honour with you.
   Lyc.   Patience, good sir,
Even for this charge.
   Per.   Now, mild may be thy life!
For a more blusterous birth had never babe:
Quiet and gentle thy conditions!
For thou 'rt the rudeliest welcome to this world,
That e'er was prince's child. Happy what follows!
Thou hast as chiding a nativity,
As fire, air, water, earth, and heaven can make,
To herald thee from the womb: even at the first,
Thy loss is more than can thy portage quit
With all thou canst find here.—Now the good gods
Throw their best eyes upon 't!

Enter two Sailors

   First Sail. What courage, sir? God save you!
   Per. Courage enough. I do not fear the flaw;
It has done to me the worst. Yet for the love
Of this poor infant, this fresh new sea-farer,
I would it would be quiet.
   First Sail. Slack the bowlines there! Thou wilt not, wilt
thou? Blow, and split thyself.

Sec. Sail. But sea-room, an the brine and cloudy billow kiss the moon, I care not.

First Sail. Sir, your queen must overboard: the sea works high, the wind is loud, and will not lie till the ship be cleared of the dead.

Per. That's your superstition.

First Sail. Pardon us, sir; with us at sea it hath been still observed, and we are strong in custom. Therefore briefly yield her, for she must overboard straight.

Per. As you think meet.—Most wretched queen!

Lyc. Here she lies, sir.

Per. A terrible childbed hast thou had, my dear;
No light, no fire: the unfriendly elements
Forgot thee utterly; nor have I time
To give thee hallowed to thy grave, but straight
Must cast thee, scarcely coffined, in the ooze;
Where, for a monument upon thy bones,
And aye remaining lamps, the belching whale
And humming water must o'erhelm thy corse,
Lying with simple shells.—O Lychorida!
Bid Nestor bring me spices, ink and paper,
My casket and my jewels; and bid Nicander
Bring me the satin coffer: lay the babe
Upon the pillow. Hie thee, whiles I say
A priestly farewell to her: suddenly, woman.

[Exit Lychorida

Sec. Sail. Sir, we have a chest beneath the hatches, caulked and bituméd ready.

Per. I thank thee. Mariner, say what coast is this?

Sec. Sail. We are near Tarsus.

Per. Thither, gentle mariner,
Alter thy course from Tyre. When canst thou reach it?

Sec. Sail. By break of day, if the wind cease.

Per. O, make for Tarsus.—
There will I visit Cleon, for the babe
Cannot hold out to Tyrus: there I'll leave it
At careful nursing.—Go thy ways, good mariner:
I'll bring the body presently.   *[Exeunt*

SCENE II.—Ephesus. A Room in CERIMON's House

Enter CERIMON, *a Servant, and some Persons who have been shipwrecked*

Cer. Philemon, ho!

Enter PHILEMON

Phil. Doth my lord call?

Cer. Get fire and meat for these poor men:
It has been a turbulent and stormy night.

Serv. I have been in many; but such a night as this,
Till now I ne'er endured.
    Cer. Your master will be dead ere you return:
There's nothing can be ministered to nature,
That can recover him.—[*To Philemon*] Give this to the
        pothecary,
And tell me how it works.   [*Exeunt all but Cerimon*

Enter two Gentlemen

First Gent.   Good morrow.
    Sec. Gent. Good morrow to your lordship.
    Cer.   Gentlemen,
Why do you stir so early?
    First Gent. Sir,
Our lodgings, standing bleak upon the sea,
Shook as the earth did quake;
The very principals did seem to rend,
And all to topple. Pure surprise and fear
Made me to quit the house.
    Sec. Gent. That is the cause we trouble you so early;
'T is not our husbandry.
    Cer.   O, you say well.
    First Gent. But I much marvel that your lordship
        having
Rich tire about you, should at these early hours
Shake off the golden slumber of repose.
'T is most strange,
Nature should be so conversant with pain,
Being thereto not compelled.
    Cer.   I held it ever,
Virtue and cunning were endowments greater
Than nobleness and riches: careless heirs
May the two latter darken and expand;
But immortality attends the former,
Making a man a god. 'T is known, I ever
Have studied physic, through which secret art,
By turning o'er authorities, I have—
Together with my practice—made familiar
To me and to my aid the blest infusions
That dwell in vegetives, in metals, stones;
And I can speak of the disturbances
That nature works, and of her cures; which give me
A more content in course of true delight
Than to be thirsty after tottering honour,
Or tie my treasure up in silken bags
To please the fool and death.
    Sec. Gent. Your honour has through Ephesus poured
        forth
Your charity, and hundreds call themselves
Your creatures, who by you have been restored:

And not your knowledge, personal pain, but even
Your purse, still open, hath built Lord Cerimon
Such strong renown as never shall decay.

Enter two or three Servants with a chest

    Serv. So; lift there.
    Cer.   What is that?
    Serv.   Sir, even now
Did the sea toss upon our shore this chest:
'T is of some wreck.
    Cer.   Set it down; let's look upon 't.
    Sec. Gent. 'T is like a coffin, sir.
    Cer.   Whate'er it be,
'T is wondrous heavy. Wrench it open straight:
If the sea's stomach be o'ercharged with gold,
'T is a good strain of fortune belched upon us.
    Sec. Gent. 'T is so, my lord.
    Cer. How close 't is caulked and bitumed!
Did the sea cast it up?
    Serv. I never saw so huge a billow, sir,
As tossed it upon shore.
    Cer.   Come, wrench it open.
Soft!—it smells most sweetly in my sense.
    Sec. Gent. A delicate odour.
    Cer. As ever hit my nostril. So, up with it.
O you most potent gods! what's here? a corse!
    First Gent. Most strange!
    Cer. Shrouded in cloth of state; balmed and entreasured
With spices and full bags! A passport too:
Apollo, perfect me i' the characters! [*Reads from a scroll*

> Here I give to understand,
> (If e'er this coffin drive a-land),
> I, King Pericles, have lost
> This queen, worth all our mundane cost.
> Who finds her, give her burying;
> She was the daughter of a king:
> Besides this treasure for a fee,
> The gods requite his charity!

If thou liv'st, Pericles, thou hast a heart
That even cracks for woe!—This chanced to-night.
    Sec. Gent. Most likely, sir.
    Cer.   Nay, certainly, to-night;
For look, how fresh she looks. They were too rough,
That threw her in the sea. Make fire within:
Fetch hither all the boxes in my closet. [*Exit a Servant*
Death may usurp on nature many hours,
And yet the fire of life kindle again
The o'erpressed spirits. I heard of an Egyptian,

That had nine hours lien dead,
Who was by good appliances recovered.

Re-enter Servant, with boxes, napkins, and fire

Well said, well said; the fire and the cloths.—
The rough and woful music that we have,
Cause it to sound, beseech you.
The vial once more;—how thou stirr'st, thou block!—
The music there! I pray you, give her air.
Gentlemen,
This queen will live: nature awakes; a warmth
Breathes out of her: she hath not been entranced
Above five hours. See, how she gins to blow
Into life's flower again!
   First Gent.   The heavens,
Through you, increase our wonder, and set up
Your fame for ever.
   Cer.   She is alive! behold,
Her eyelids, cases to those heavenly jewels
Which Pericles hath lost, begin to part
Their fringes of bright gold: the diamonds
Of a most praiséd water do appear
To make the world twice rich. O live, and make
Us weep to hear your fate, fair creature,
Rare as you seem to be!   [*She moves*
   Thai.   O dear Diana!
Where am I? Where's my lord? What world is this?
   Sec. Gent.   Is not this strange?
   First Gent.   Most rare.
   Cer.   Hush, gentle neighbours!
Lend me your hands; to the next chamber bear her.
Get linen: now this matter must be looked to,
For her relapse is mortal. Come, come, come;
And Æsculapius guide us!
               [*Exeunt, carrying Thaisa away*

Scene III.—Tarsus. A Room in Cleon's House

Enter Pericles, Cleon, Dionyza, Lychorida, *with*
Marina *in her arms*

   Per. Most honoured Cleon, I must needs be gone:
My twelve months are expired, and Tyrus stands
In a litigious peace. You and your lady
Take, from my heart, all thankfulness; the gods
Make up the rest upon you!
   Cle. Your shafts of fortune, though they hurt you
        mortally,
Yet glance full wanderingly on us.

Dion.   O your sweet queen!
That the strict fates had pleased you had brought her
       hither,
To have blessed mine eyes with her!
Per.   We cannot but obey
The powers above us. Could I rage and roar
As doth the sea she lies in, yet the end
Must be as 't is. My gentle babe Marina—whom,
For she was born at sea, I have named so—here
I charge your charity withal, and leave her
The infant of your care, beseeching you
To give her princely training, that she may
Be mannered as she is born.
Cle.   Fear not, my lord, but think
Your grace, that fed my country with your corn—
For which the people's prayers still fall upon you—
Must in your child be thought on. If neglection
Should therein make me vile, the common body,
By you relieved, would force me to my duty;
But if to that my nature need a spur,
The gods revenge it upon me and mine,
To the end of generation!
Per.   I believe you;
Your honour and your goodness teach me to 't,
Without your vows. Till she be married, madam,
By bright Diana, whom we honour, all
Unscissared shall this hair of mine remain,
Though I show ill in 't. So I take my leave.
Good madam, make me blessèd in your care
In bringing up my child.
Dion.   I've one myself,
Who shall not be more dear to my respect,
Than yours, my lord.
Per.   Madam, my thanks and prayers.
Cle. We'll bring your grace even to the edge o' the
       shore;
Then give you up to the masked Neptune, and
The gentlest winds of heaven.
Per.   I will embrace
Your offer. Come, dear'st madam.—O, no tears,
Lychorida, no tears:
Look to your little mistress, on whose grace
You may depend hereafter.—Come, my lord.   [*Exeunt*

SCENE IV.—Ephesus. A Room in CERIMON'S House

Enter CERIMON *and* THAISA

Cer. Madam, this letter, and some certain jewels,
Lay with you in your coffer: which are now

At your command. Know you the character?
    Thai.   It is my lord's.
That I was shipped at sea, I well remember,
Even on my eaning time; but whether there
Delivered, by the holy gods,
I cannot rightly say. But since King Pericles,
My wedded lord, I ne'er shall see again,
A vestal livery I will take me to,
And never more have joy.
    Cer.   Madam, if this you purpose as ye speak,
Diana's temple is not distant far,
Where you may dwell until your date expire.
Moreover, if you please, a niece of mine
Shall there attend you.
    Thai.   My recompense is thanks, that's all;
Yet my good will is great, though the gift small.   [*Exeunt*

ACT FOUR

Enter GOWER

    Gow.   Imagine Pericles arrived at Tyre,
Welcomed and settled to his own desire.
His woful queen we leave at Ephesus,
Unto Diana there a votaress.
Now to Marina bend your mind,
Whom our fast-growing scene must find
At Tarsus, and by Cleon trained
In music, letters; who hath gained
Of education all the grace,
Which makes her both the heart and place
Of general wonder. But, alack!
That monster envy, oft the wrack
Of earnèd praise, Marina's life
Seeks to take off by treason's knife.
And in this kind hath our Cleon
One daughter, and a wench full grown,
Even ripe for marriage-rite: this maid
Hight Philoten; and it is said
For certain in our story, she
Would ever with Marina be:
Be't when she weaved the sleided silk
With fingers long, small, white as milk;
Or when she would with sharp neeld wound
The cambric, which she made more sound
By hurting it; or when to the lute
She sung, and made the night-bird mute,
That still records with moan; or when
She would with rich and constant pen
Vail to her mistress Dian; still
126

This Philoten contends in skill
With absolute Marina: so
With the dove of Paphos might the crow
Vie feathers white.   Marina gets
All praises, which are paid as debts,
And not as given.   This so darks
In Philoten all graceful marks,
That Cleon's wife, with envy rare,
A present murderer does prepare
For good Marina, that her daughter
Might stand peerless by this slaughter.
The sooner her vile thoughts to stead,
Lychorida, our nurse, is dead:
And cursèd Dionyza hath
The pregnant instrument of wrath
Prest for this blow.   The unborn event
I do commend to your content:
Only I carry wingèd time
Post on the lame feet of my rhyme;
Which never could I so convey,
Unless your thoughts went on my way.—
Dionyza doth appear,
With Leonine, a murderer.   [*Exit*

SCENE I.—Tarsus. An Open Place near the Seashore:

Enter DIONYZA *and* LEONINE

Dion.   Thy oath remember; thou hast sworn to do't
'T is but a blow, which never shall be known.
Thou canst not do a thing i' the world so soon,
To yield thee so much profit.   Let not conscience,
Which is but cold, inflaming love i' thy bosom,
Inflame too nicely; nor let pity, which
Even women have cast off, melt thee, but be
A soldier to thy purpose.
Leon.   I'll do't; but yet she is a goodly creature.
Dion.   The fitter, then, the gods should have her.
Here she comes weeping her old nurse's death.
Thou art resolved?
Leon.   I am resolved.

Enter MARINA, *with a basket of flowers*

Mar.   No, I will rob fair Tellus of her weed,
To strew thy grave with flowers: the yellows, blues,
The purple violets, and marigolds,
Shall as a carpet hang upon thy grave,
While summer-days do last.   Ah me, poor maid!
Born in a tempest when my mother died,
This world to me is like a lasting storm,

Whirring me from my friends.
   Dion. How now, Marina! why do you keep alone?
How chance my daughter is not with you? Do not
Consume your blood with sorrowing: you have
A nurse of me. Lord, how your favour's changed
With this unprofitable woe! Come, come,
Give me your flowers, ere the sea shall mar it.
Walk with Leonine; there the air is quick,
It pierces, and makes sharp the stomach. Come,
Leonine, take her by the arm, walk with her.
   Mar. No, I pray you;
I'll not bereave you of your servant.
   Dion.   Come,
I love the king your father, and yourself,
With more than foreign heart. We every day
Expect him here: when he shall come, and find
Our paragon to all reports thus blasted,
He will repent the breadth of his great voyage,
Blame both my lord and me, that we have ta'en
No care to your best courses. Go, I pray you;
Walk, and be cheerful once again: preserve
That excellent complexion, which did steal
The eyes of young and old. Care not for me;
I can go home alone.
   Mar.   Well, I will go;
But yet I've no desire to it.
   Dion.   Come, come,
I know 't is good for you.—
Walk half an hour, Leonine, at the least.—
Remember what I have said.
   Leon.   I warrant you, madam.
   Dion. I'll leave you, my sweet lady, for a while.
Pray you, walk softly, do not heat your blood:
What! I must have care of you.
   Mar.   My thanks, sweet madam.—
                          [*Exit Dionyza*
Is the wind westerly that blows?
   Leon.   South-west.
   Mar. When I was born, the wind was north.
   Leon.   Was't so?
   Mar. My father, as nurse said, did never fear,
But cried "Good seamen!" to the sailors, galling
His kingly hands with haling of the ropes;
And, clasping to the mast, endured a sea
That almost burst the deck.
   Leon. When was this?
   Mar. When I was born:
Never were waves nor wind more violent;
And from the ladder-tackle washes off
A canvas-climber. "Ha!" says one, "wilt out?"

And with a dropping industry they skip
From stem to stern: the boatswain whistles, and
The master calls, and trebles their confusion.
   Leon.   Come; say your prayers.
   Mar.   What mean you?
   Leon.   If you require a little space for prayer,
I grant it.   Pray; but be not tedious,
For the gods are quick of ear, and I am sworn
To do my work with haste.
   Mar.   Why will you kill me?
   Leon.   To satisfy my lady.
   Mar.   Why would she have me killed?
Now, as I can remember, by my troth,
I never did her hurt in all my life.
I never spake bad word, nor did ill turn
To any living creature: believe me, la,
I never killed a mouse, nor hurt a fly:
I trod upon a worm against my will,
But I wept for it.   How have I offended,
Wherein my death might yield her any profit,
Or life imply her danger?
   Leon.   My commission
Is not to reason of the deed, but do 't.
   Mar.   You will not do 't for all the world, I hope.
You are well-favoured, and your looks foreshow
You have a gentle heart.   I saw you lately
When you caught hurt in parting two that fought:
Good sooth, it showed well in you: do so now.
Your lady seeks my life; come you between,
And save poor me, the weaker.
   Leon.   I am sworn,
And will despatch.   [*Seizes her*

Enter Pirates

   First Pir.   Hold, villain!   [*Leonine runs away*
   Sec. Pir.   A prize! a prize!
   Third Pir.   Half-part, mates, half-part.   Come, let's have
her aboard suddenly.   [*Exeunt Pirates with Marina*

SCENE II.—Near the Same

Enter LEONINE

   Leon.   These roguing thieves serve the great pirate
        Valdes;
And they have seized Marina.   Let her go:
There's no hope she 'll return.   I'll swear she's dead,
And thrown into the sea.—But I'll see further;
Perhaps they will but please themselves upon her,
Not carry her aboard.   If she remain,
Whom they have ravished must by me be slain.   [*Exit*

129

SCENE III.—Mitylene. A Room in a Brothel

Enter Pander, Bawd, and BOULT

Pand. Boult!

Boult. Sir?

Pand. Search the market narrowly; Mitylene is full of gallants: we lost too much money this mart, by being too wenchless.

Bawd. We were never so much out of creatures. We have but poor three, and they can do no more than they can do; and they with continual action are even as good as rotten.

Pand. Therefore, let's have fresh ones, whate'er we pay for them. If there be not a conscience to be used in every trade, we shall never prosper.

Bawd. Thou say'st true: 't is not the bringing up of poor bastards,—as I think, I have brought up some eleven—

Boult. Ay, to eleven; and brought them down again. But shall I search the market?

Bawd. What else, man? The stuff we have, a strong wind will blow it to pieces, they are so pitifully sodden.

Pand. Thou say'st true; they're too unwholesome, o' conscience. The poor Transylvanian is dead, that lay with the little baggage.

Boult. Ay, she quickly pooped him; she made him roast-meat for worms. But I'll go search the market.

[*Exit*

Pand. Three or four thousand chequins were as pretty a proportion to live quietly, and so give over.

Bawd. Why to give over, I pray you? is it a shame to get when we are old?

Pand. O, our credit comes not in like the commodity; nor the commodity wages not with the danger: therefore, if in our youths we could pick up some pretty estate, 't were not amiss to keep our door hatched. Besides, the sore terms we stand upon with the gods, will be strong with us for giving over.

Bawd. Come, other sorts offend as well as we.

Pand. As well as we? ay, and better too; we offend worse. Neither is our profession any trade, it 's no calling. But here comes Boult.

Re-enter BOULT, *with the Pirates and* MARINA

Boult. [*To Marina*] Come your ways.—
My masters, you say she's a virgin?

First Pir. O, sir, we doubt it not.

Boult. Master, I have gone through for this piece, you see: if you like her, so; if not, I have lost my earnest.

Bawd. Boult, has she any qualities?

Boult. She has a good face, speaks well, and has excellent good clothes: there's no further necessity of qualities can make her be refused.

Bawd. What's her price, Boult?

Boult. I cannot be bated one doit of a thousand pieces.

Pand. Well, follow me, my masters, you shall have your money presently. Wife, take her in: instruct her what she has to do, that she may not be raw in her entertainment.   [*Exeunt Pander and Pirates*

Bawd. Boult, take you the marks of her, the colour of her hair, complexion, height, her age, with warrant of her virginity, and cry, "He that will give most, shall have her first." Such a maidenhead were no cheap thing, if men were as they have been. Get this done as I command you.

Boult. Performance shall follow.   [*Exit*

Mar. Alack, that Leonine was so slack, so slow!
He should have struck, not spoke; or that these pirates—
Not enough barbarous—had not o'erboard thrown me
To seek my mother!

Bawd. Why lament you, pretty one?

Mar. That I am pretty.

Bawd. Come, the gods have done their part in you.

Mar. I accuse them not.

Bawd. You are light into my hands, where you are like to live.

Mar. The more my fault
To scape his hands where I was like to die.

Bawd. Ay, and you shall live in pleasure.

Mar. No.

Bawd. Yes, indeed, shall you, and taste gentlemen of all fashions. You shall fare well: you shall have the difference of all complexions. What, do you stop your ears?

Mar. Are you a woman?

Bawd. What would you have me be, an I be not a woman?

Mar. An honest woman, or not a woman.

Bawd. Marry, whip thee, gosling: I think I shall have something to do with you. Come, you're a young foolish sapling, and must be bowed as I would have you.

Mar. The gods defend me!

Bawd. If it please the gods to defend you by men, then men must comfort you, men must feed you, men must stir you up.—Boult 's returned.

Re-enter BOULT

Now, sir, hast thou cried her through the market?

Boult. I have cried her almost to the number of her hairs: I have drawn her picture with my voice.

Bawd. And, I pr'ythee, tell me, how dost thou find the inclination of the people, especially of the younger sort?

Boult. Faith, they listened to me, as they would have hearkened to their father's testament. There was a Spaniard's mouth so watered, that he went to bed to her very description.

Bawd. We shall have him here to-morrow with his best ruff on.

Boult. To-night, to-night. But, mistress, do you know the French knight that cowers i' the hams?

Bawd. Who? Monsieur Veroles?

Boult. Ay: he offered to cut a caper at the proclamation; but he made a groan at it, and swore he would see her to-morrow.

Bawd. Well, well; as for him, he brought his disease hither; here he does but repair it. I know, he will come in our shadow, to scatter his crowns in the sun.

Boult. Well, if we had of every nation a traveller, we should lodge them with this sign.

Bawd. [*To Marina*] Pray you, come hither awhile. You have fortunes coming upon you. Mark me: you must seem to do that fearfully, which you commit willingly; to despise profit, where you have most gain. To weep that you live as ye do, makes pity in your lovers: seldom, but that pity begets you a good opinion, and that opinion a mere profit.

Mar. I understand you not.

Boult. O, take her home, mistress, take her home: these blushes of hers must be quenched with some present practice.

Bawd. Thou say'st true, i' faith, so they must: for your bride goes to that with shame, which is her way to go with warrant.

Boult. Faith, some do, and some do not. But, mistress, if I have bargained for the joint,—

Bawd. Thou may'st cut a morsel off the spit.

Boult. I may so?

Bawd. Who should deny it? Come, young one, I like the manner of your garments well.

Boult. Ay, by my faith, they shall not be changed yet.

Bawd. Boult, spend thou that in the town: report what a sojourner we have; you'll lose nothing by custom. When nature framed this piece, she meant thee a good turn; therefore, say what a paragon she is, and thou hast the harvest out of thine own report.

Boult. I warrant you, mistress, thunder shall not so awake the beds of eels, as my giving out her beauty stir up the lewdly-inclined. I'll bring home some to-night.

Bawd. Come your ways; follow me.

Mar. If fires be hot, knives sharp, or waters deep,

Untied I still my virgin knot will keep.
Diana, aid my purpose!
    Bawd. What have we to do with Diana?
Pray you, will you go with us?   *[Exeunt*

SCENE IV.—Tarsus. A Room in CLEON'S House

Enter CLEON *and* DIONYZA

    Dion. Why, are you foolish? Can it be undone?
    Cle. O Dionyza! such a piece of slaughter
The sun and moon ne'er looked upon.
    Dion.   I think
You'll turn a child again.
    Cle. Were I chief lord of all this spacious world,
I'd give it to undo the deed. O lady,
Much less in blood than virtue, yet a princess
To equal any single crown o' the earth,
I' the justice of compare! O villain Leonine!
Whom thou hast poisoned too.
If thou hadst drunk to him, 't had been a kindness
Becoming well thy fact: what canst thou say,
When noble Pericles shall demand his child?
    Dion. That she is dead. Nurses are not the fates,
To foster it, nor ever to preserve.
She died at night; I'll say so. Who can cross it?
Unless you play the pious innocent,
And, for an honest attribute, cry out,
"She died by foul play."
    Cle.   O, go to. Well, well,
Of all the faults beneath the heavens, the gods
Do like this worst.
    Dian.   Be one of those that think
The petty wrens of Tarsus will fly hence
And open this to Pericles. I do shame
To think of what a noble strain you are,
And of how coward a spirit.
    Cle.   To such proceeding
Who ever but his approbation added
Though not his prime consent, he did not flow
From honourable sources.
    Dion.   Be it so, then;
Yet none does know, but you, how she came dead,
Nor none can know, Leonine being gone.
She did distain my child, and stood between
Her and her fortunes: none would look on her,
But cast their gazes on Marina's face;
Whilst ours was blurted at, and held a malkin
Not worth the time of day. It pierced me through;
And though you call my course unnatural,
You not your child well loving, yet I find,

It greets me as an enterprise of kindness,
Performed to your sole daughter.
    Cle.   Heavens forgive it!
    Dion.   And as for Pericles,
What should he say?   We wept after her hearse,
And yet we mourn for her: her monument
Is almost finished, and her epitaphs
In glittering golden characters express
A general praise to her, and care in us
At whose expense 't is done.
    Cle.   Thou 'rt like the harpy,
Which, to betray, dost, with thine angel's face,
Seize with thine eagle's talons.
    Dion.   You are like one that superstitiously
Doth swear to the gods that winter kills the flies:
But yet, I know, you 'll do as I advise.   [*Exeunt*

    Enter GOWER, *before the monument of* MARINA *at Tarsus*

    Gow.   Thus time we waste, and longest leagues make
        short;
Sail seas in cockles, have a wish but for 't;
Making—to take thus your imagination—
From bourn to bourn, region to region.
By you being pardoned, we commit no crime
To use one language in each several clime
Where our scenes seem to live. I do beseech you
To learn of me, who stand i' the gaps to teach you,
The stages of our story.—Pericles
Is now again thwarting the wayward seas,
Attended on by many a lord and knight,
To see his daughter, all his life's delight.
Old Escanes, whom Helicanus late
Advanced in time to great and high estate,
Is left to govern. Bear you it in mind,
Old Helicanus goes along behind.
Well-sailing ships and bounteous winds have brought
This king to Tarsus—think his pilot thought,
So with his steerage shall your thoughts grow on—
To fetch his daughter home, who first is gone.
Like motes and shadows see them move awhile;
Your ears unto your eyes I'll reconcile.

DUMB-SHOW

Enter from one side PERICLES, *with his Train; from the
other* CLEON *and* DIONYZA. CLEON *shows* PERICLES *the
tomb of* MARINA; *whereat* PERICLES *makes lamenta-
tion, puts on sackcloth, and in a mighty passion departs.
Then exeunt* CLEON *and* DIONYZA.

    Gow.   See, how belief may suffer by foul show!
This borrowed passion stands for true old woe;

And Pericles, in sorrow all devoured,
With sighs shot through, and biggest tears o'er-showered,
Leaves Tarsus, and again embarks.   He swears
Never to wash his face, nor cut his hairs;
He puts on sackcloth, and to sea.   He bears
A tempest, which his mortal vessel tears,
And yet he rides it out.   Now please you wit
The epitaph is for Marina writ
By wicked Dionyza.

> [*Reads the inscription on Marina's monument*

> *The fairest, sweet'st, and best, lies here,*
> *Who withered in her spring of year:*
> *She was of Tyrus the king's daughter,*
> *On whom foul death hath made this slaughter.*
> *Marina was she called; and at her birth,*
> *Thetis, being proud, swallowed some part o' the earth:*
> *Therefore the earth, fearing to be o'erflowed,*
> *Hath Thetis' birth-child on the heavens bestowed:*
> *Wherefore she does (and swears she'll never stint)*
> *Make raging battery upon shores of flint.*

No visor does become black villainy
So well as soft and tender flattery.
Let Pericles believe his daughter 's dead,
And bear his courses to be orderéd
By Lady Fortune; while our scene must play
His daughter's woe and heavy well-a-day,
In her unholy service.   Patience then,
And think you now are all in Mitylen.   [*Exit*

Scene V.—Mitylene.   A Street before the Brothel

Enter, from the brothel, two Gentlemen

First Gent.   Did you ever hear the like?
Sec. Gent.   No, nor never shall do in such a place as this,
she being once gone.
First Gent.   But to have divinity preached there! did
you ever dream of such a thing?
Sec. Gent.   No, no.   Come, I am for no more bawdy-
houses.   Shall 's go hear the vestals sing?
First Gent.   I'll do anything now that is virtuous; but I
am out of the road of rutting for ever.   [*Exeunt*

Scene VI.—The Same.   A Room in the Brothel

Enter Pander, Bawd, and BOULT

Pand.   Well, I had rather than twice the worth of her,
she had ne'er come here.

Bawd. Fie, fie upon her! she is able to freeze the god Priapus, and undo a whole generation: we must either get her ravished, or be rid of her. When she should do for clients her fitment, and do me the kindness of our profession, she has me her quirks, her reasons, her master-reasons, her prayers, her knees, that she would make a puritan of the devil, if he should cheapen a kiss of her.

Boult. Faith, I must ravish her, or she 'll disfurnish us of all our cavaliers, and make all our swearers priests.

Pand. Now, the pox upon her green-sickness for me!

Bawd. Faith, there 's no way to be rid on't, but by the way to the pox. Here comes the Lord Lysimachus, disguised.

Boult. We should have both lord and lown, if the peevish baggage would but give way to customers.

Enter LYSIMACHUS

Lys. How now! How a dozen of virginities?

Bawd. Now, the gods to-bless your honour!

Boult. I am glad to see your honour in good health.

Lys. You may so; 't is the better for you that your resorters stand upon sound legs. How now, wholesome iniquity! have you that a man may deal withal, and defy the surgeon?

Bawd. We have here one, sir, if she would—but there never came her like in Mitylene.

Lys. If she 'd do the deed of darkness, thou wouldst say.

Bawd. Your honour knows what 't is to say, well enough.

Lys. Well; call forth, call forth.

Boult. For flesh and blood, sir, white and red, you shall see a rose; and she were a rose indeed, if she had but—

Lys. What, pr'ythee?

Boult. O, sir! I can be modest.

Lys. That dignifies the renown of a bawd, no less than it gives a good report to a number to be chaste.

Enter MARINA

Bawd. Here comes that which grows to the stalk;— never plucked yet, I can assure you.—Is she not a fair creature?

Lys. Faith, she would serve after a long voyage at sea. Well, there's for you: leave us.

Bawd. I beseech your honour, give me leave, a word, and I'll have done presently.

Lys. I beseech you, do.

Bawd. [*To Marina*] First, I would have you note, this is an honourable man.

Mar. I do desire to find him so, that I may worthily note him.

Bawd. Next, he 's the governor of this country, and a man whom I am bound to.

Mar. If he govern the country, you are bound to him indeed; but how honourable he is in that, I know not.

Bawd. Pray you, without any more virginal fencing, will you use him kindly? He will line your apron with gold.

Mar. What he will do graciously, I will thankfully receive.

Lys. Have you done?

Bawd. My lord, she's not paced yet; you must take some pains to work her to your manage. Come, we will leave his honour and her together.

Lys. Go thy ways. [*Exeunt Bawd, Pander, and Boult* —Now, pretty one, how long have you been at this trade?

Mar. What trade, sir?

Lys. Why, I cannot name 't but I shall offend.

Mar. I cannot be offended with my trade. Please you to name it.

Lys. How long have you been of this profession?

Mar. E'er since I can remember.

Lys. Did you go to it so young? Were you a gamester at five, or at seven?

Mar. Earlier too, sir, if now I be one.

Lys. Why, the house you dwell in proclaims you to be a creature of sale.

Mar. Do you know this house to be a place of such resort, and will come into 't? I hear say, you are of honourable parts, and are the governor of this place.

Lys. Why, hath your principal made known unto you who I am?

Mar. Who is my principal?

Lys. Why, your herb-woman; she that sets seed and roots of shame and iniquity. O, you have heard something of my power, and so stand aloof for more serious wooing. But I protest to thee, pretty one, my authority shall not see thee, or else, look friendly upon thee. Come, bring me to some private place: come, come.

Mar. If you were born to honour, show it now;
If put upon you, make the judgment good
That thought you worthy of it.

Lys. How 's this? how 's this?—Some more:—be sage.

Mar.   For me,
That am a maid, though most ungentle fortune
Hath placed me in this sty, where, since I came,
Diseases have been sold dearer than physic,—
O, that the gods
Would set me free from this unhallowed place,

Though they did change me to the meanest bird
That flies i' the purer air!
    Lys.   I did not think
Thou couldst have spoke so well; ne'er dreamed thou couldst.
Had I brought hither a corrupted mind,
Thy speech had altered it. Hold, here's gold for thee:
Perséver in the clear way that thou goest,
And the gods strengthen thee!
    Mar.   The gods preserve you!
    Lys. For me, be your thought only
That with no ill intent I came; to me
The very doors and windows savour vilely.
Farewell. Thou art a piece of virtue, and
I doubt not but thy training hath been noble.
Hold, here's more gold for thee.
A curse upon him, die he like a thief,
That robs thee of thy goodness! If thou dost
Hear more from me, it shall be for thy good.

Re-enter BOULT

    Boult. I beseech your honour, one piece for me.
    Lys. Avaunt, thou damnéd door-keeper!
Your house, but for this virgin that doth prop it,
Would sink, and overwhelm you. Away!   *[Exit*
    Boult. How's this? We must take another course with
you. If your peevish chastity, which is not worth a break-
fast in the cheapest country under the cope, shall undo
a whole household, let me be gelded like a spaniel. Come
your ways.
    Mar. Whither would you have me?
    Boult. I must have your maidenhead taken off, or the
common hangman shall execute it. Come your ways.
We'll have no more gentlemen driven away. Come your
ways, I say.

Re-enter Bawd

    Bawd. How now! what's the matter?
    Boult. Worse and worse, mistress: she has here spoken
holy words to the Lord Lysimachus.
    Bawd. O, abominable!
    Boult. She makes our profession as it were to stink
afore the face of the gods.
    Bawd. Marry, hang her up for ever!
    Boult. The nobleman would have dealt with her like
a nobleman, and she sent him away as cold as a snow-ball;
saying his prayers, too.
    Bawd. Boult, take her away; use her at thy pleasure:
crack the glass of her virginity, and make the rest malleable.
    Boult. An if she were a thornier piece of ground than
she is, she shall be ploughed.

Mar. Hark, hark, you gods!

Bawd. She conjures: away with her! Would she had never come within my doors!—Marry, hang you!—She's born to undo us.—Will you not go the way of womankind? Marry, come up, my dish of chastity with rosemary and bays!   [*Exit*

Boult. Come, mistress; come your way with me.

Mar. Whither wilt thou have me?

Boult. To take from you the jewel you hold so dear.

Mar. Pr'ythee, tell me one thing first.

Boult. Come now, your one thing.

Mar. What canst thou wish thine enemy to be?

Boult. Why, I could wish him to be my master, or rather, my mistress.

Mar. Neither of these are so bad as thou art,
Since they do better thee in their command.
Thou hold'st a place, for which the pained'st fiend
Of hell would not in reputation change:
Thou art damnéd door-keeper to every
Coystril that comes inquiring for his Tib;
Unto the choleric fist of every rogue
Thy ear is liable; thy food is such
As hath been belched on by infected lungs.

Boult. What would you have me do? go to the wars, would you? where a man may serve seven years for the loss of a leg, and have not enough money in the end to buy him a wooden one?

Mar. Do anything but this thou doest. Empty
Old réceptacles, or common sewers, of filth;
Serve by indenture to the common hangman:
Any of these ways are yet better than this;
For what thou art, a baboon, could he speak,
Would own a name too dear. O that the gods
Would from this place safely deliver me!
Here, here is gold for thee.
If that thy master would gain gold by me,
Proclaim that I can sing, weave, sew, and dance,
With other virtues, which I'll keep from boast;
And I will undertake all these to teach.
I doubt not but this populous city will
Yield many scholars.

Boult. But can you teach all this you speak of?

Mar. Prove that I cannot, take me home again
And prostitute me to the basest groom
That doth frequent your house.

Boult. Well, I will see what I can do for thee; if I can place thee, I will.

Mar. But amongst honest women.

Boult. Faith, my acquaintance lies little amongst them But since my master and mistress hath bought you, there's

no going but by their consent; therefore, I will make
them acquainted with your purpose, and I doubt not
but I shall find them tractable enough. Come; I'll do
for thee what I can: come your ways.   [*Exeunt*

ACT FIVE

Enter GOWER

Gow.   Marina thus the brothel scapes, and chances
   Into an honest house, our story says.
She sings like one immortal, and she dances
   As goddess-like to her admiréd lays.
Deep clerks she dumbs; and with her neeld composes
   Nature's own shape, of bud, bird, branch, or berry,
That even her art sisters the natural roses;
   Her inkle, silk, twin with the rubied cherry;
That pupils lacks she none of noble race,
   Who pour their bounty on her; and her gain
She gives the curséd bawd.   Here we her place,
   And to her father turn our thoughts again,
Where we left him, on the sea.   We there him lost,
   Whence, driven before the winds, he is arrived
Here where his daughter dwells: and on this coast
   Suppose him anchored now.   The city strived
God Neptune's annual feast to keep: from whence
   Lysimachus our Tyrian ship espies,
His banners sable, trimmed with rich expense;
   And to him in his barge with fervour hies.
In your supposing once more put your sight;
   Of heavy Pericles think this the bark:
Where, what is done in action, more, if might,
   Shall be discovered; please you, sit and hark.   [*Exit*

SCENE I.—On board PERICLES' ship, off Mitylene. A
   Pavilion on deck, with a curtain before it; PERICLES
   within it, reclining on a couch. A barge lying beside
   the Tyrian vessel.

*Enter two Sailors, one belonging to the Tyrian vessel, the
   other to the barge; to them* HELICANUS

   Tyr. Sail.   [*To the Sailor of Mitylene*]   Where is Lord
      Helicane? he can resolve you.
O, here he is.—
Sir, there's a barge put off from Mitylene,
And in it is Lysimachus, the governor,
Who craves to come aboard.   What is your will?

Hel. That he have his. Call up some gentlemen.
Tyr. Sail. Ho, gentlemen! my lord calls.

Enter two or three Gentlemen

First Gent. Doth your lordship call?
Hel. Gentlemen, there is some of worth would come
aboard: I pray you greet them fairly.
[*Gentlemen and Sailors descend, and go on board the barge*

Enter, from thence, LYSIMACHUS *and Lords; the Tyrian
Gentlemen and the two Sailors.*

Tyr. Sail. Sir,
This is the man that can in aught you would
Resolve you.
    Lys. Hail, reverend sir! the gods preserve you!
Hel. And you, sir, to outlive the age I am,
And die as I would do.
                    You wish me well.
Being on shore, honouring Neptune's triumphs,
Seeing this goodly vessel ride before us,
I made to it, to know of whence you are.
    Hel. First, what is your place?
    Lys. I'm governor of this place you lie before.
    Hel. Sir,
Our vessel is of Tyre, in it the king;
A man, who for this three months hath not spoken
To any one, nor taken sustenance,
But to prorogue his grief.
    Lys. Upon what ground is his distemperature?
    Hel. 'T would be too tedious to repeat;
But the main grief springs from the loss
Of a belovéd daughter and a wife.
    Lys. May we not see him?
    Hel. You may;
But bootless is your sight: he will not speak
To any.
    Lys. Yet, let me obtain my wish.
    Hel. Behold him. [*Pericles discovered*] This was a
        goodly person,
Till the disaster that, one mortal night,
Drove him to this.
    Lys. Sir king, all hail! the gods preserve you!
Hail, royal sir!
    Hel. It is in vain; he will not speak to you!
    First Lord. Sir, we have a maid in Mitylene, I durst
        wager,
Would win some words of him.
    Lys.   'T is well bethought.
She, questionless, with her sweet harmony,
141

And other choice attractions, would allure,
And make a battery through his deafened parts,
Which now are midway stopped:
She is all happy as the fair'st of all,
And with her fellow-maids is now upon
The leafy shelter that abuts against
The island's side.
             [*Whispers one of the attendant Lords. Exit Lord*
    Hel.   Effectless, sure; yet nothing we'll omit,
That bears recovery's name. But, since your kindness
We have stretched thus far, let us to this beseech you,
That for our gold we may provision have,
Wherein we are not destitute for want,
But weary for the staleness.
    Lys.   O, sir, a courtesy,
Which if we should deny, the most just gods
For every graff would send a caterpillar,
And so inflict our province.—Yet once more
Let me entreat to know at large the cause
Of your king's sorrow.
    Hel.   Sit, sir, I will recount it to you;—
But see, I am prevented.

        Re-enter Lord, with MARINA *and a young Lady*

    Lys.   O, here is
The lady that I sent for.—Welcome, fair one!—
Is't not a goodly presence?
    Hel.   She's a gallant lady.
    Lys.   She 's such a one, that were I well assured
She came of gentle kind, and noble stock,
I'd wish no better choice, and think me rarely wed.—
Fair one, all goodness that consists in bounty
Expect even here, where is a kingly patient:
If that thy prosperous and artificial feat
Can draw him but to answer thee in aught,
Thy sacred physic shall receive such pay
As thy desires can wish.
    Mar.   Sir, I will use
My utmost skill in his recovery,
Provided
That none but I and my companion maid
Be suffered to come near him.
    Lys.   Come, let us leave her,
And the gods make her prosperous!—[MARINA *sings*
Marked he your music?
    Mar.   No, nor looked on us.
    Lys.   See, she will speak to him.
    Mar.   Hail, sir! my lord, lend ear.
    Per.   Hum! ha!

Mar. I am a maid,
My lord, that ne'er before invited eyes,
But hath been gazed on like a comet: she speaks,
My lord, that, may be, hath endured a grief
Might equal yours, if both were justly weighed.
Though wayward fortune did malign my state,
My derivation was from ancestors
Who stood equivalent with mighty kings;
But time hath rooted out my parentage,
And to the world and awkward casualties
Bound me in servitude.—[*Aside*]   I will desist;
But there is something glows upon my cheek,
And whispers in mine ear, "Go not till he speak."
    Per. My fortunes—parentage—good parentage—
To equal mine!—was it not thus? what say you?
    Mar. I said, my lord, if you did know my parentage,
You would not do me violence.
    Per. I do think so.—Pray you, turn your eyes upon me.
You are like something that—What country-woman?
Here of these shores?
    Mar.   No, nor of any shores;
Yet I was mortally brought forth, and am
No other than I appear.
    Per. I am great with woe, and shall deliver weeping.
My dearest wife was like this maid, and such a one
My daughter might have been: my queen's square brows;
Her stature to an inch; as wand-like straight;
As silver-voiced; her eyes as jewel like,
And cased as richly; in pace another Juno;
Who starves the ears she feeds, and makes them hungry,
The more she gives them speech.—Where do you live?
    Mar. Where I am but a stranger: from the deck
You may discern the place.
    Per.   Where were you bred?
And how achieved you these endowments, which
You make more rich to owe?
    Mar. If I should tell my history, it would seem
Like lies, disdained in the reporting.
    Per.   Prithee, speak:
Falseness cannot come from thee, for thou look'st
Modest as justice, and thou seem'st a palace
For the crowned truth to dwell in.   I'll believe thee,
And make my senses credit thy relation
To points that seem impossible; for thou look'st
Like one I loved indeed.   What were thy friends?
Didst thou not say, when I did push thee back—
Which was when I perceived thee—that thou cam'st
From good descending?
    Mar.   So indeed I did.
    Per. Report thy parentage.   I think thou saidst
143

Thou hadst been tossed from wrong to injury,
And that thou thought'st thy griefs might equal mine,
If both were opened.
    Mar.   Some such thing
I said, and said no more but what my thoughts
Did warrant me was likely.
    Per.   Tell thy story;
If thine considered prove the thousandth part
Of my endurance, thou art a man, and I
Have suffered like a girl: yet thou dost look
Like Patience gazing on kings' graves and smiling
Extremity out of act. What were thy friends?
How lost thou them? Thy name, my most kind virgin?
Recount, I do beseech thee. Come, sit by me.
    Mar. My name is Marina.
    Per.   O, I am mocked,
And thou by some incensèd god sent hither
To make the world to laugh at me.
    Mar.   Patience, good sir,
Or here I'll cease.
    Per.   Nay, I'll be patient.
Thou little know'st how thou dost startle me,
To call thyself Marina.
    Mar.   The name
Was given me by one that had some power;
My father, and a king.
    Per.   How! a king's daughter?
And called Marina?
    Mar.   You said you would believe me;
But, not to be a troubler of your peace,
I will end here.
    Per.   But are you flesh and blood?
Have you a working pulse? and are no fairy?—
Motion!—Well; speak on. Where were you born?
And wherefore called Marina?
    Mar.   Called Marina,
For I was born at sea.
    Per.   At sea! what mother?
    Mar. My mother was the daughter of a king,
Who died the minute I was born,
As my good nurse Lychorida hath oft
Delivered weeping.
    Per.   O! stop there a little.—
[*Aside*] This is the rarest dream that e'er dull sleep
Did mock sad fools withal; this cannot be.
My daughter's buried.—Well: where were you bred?
I'll hear you more, to the bottom of your story,
And never interrupt you.
    Mar. You scorn to believe me; 't were best I did give
      o'er.

Per.   I will believe you by the syllable
Of what you shall deliver.   Yet, give me leave:—
How came you in these parts? where were you bred?
   Mar.   The king, my father, did in Tarsus leave me,
Till cruel Cleon, with his wicked wife,
Did seek to murder me: and having wooed
A villain to attempt it, who having drawn to do 't,
A crew of pirates came and rescued me;
Brought me to Mitylene.   But, good sir,
Whither will you have me?   Why do you weep?   It
      may be,
You think me an imposter: no, good faith;
I am the daughter to King Pericles,
If good King Pericles be.
   Per.   Ho, Helicanus!
   Hel.   Calls my lord?
   Per.   Thou art a grave and noble counsellor,
Most wise in general: tell me, if thou canst,
What this maid is, or what is like to be,
That thus hath made me weep?
   Hel.   I know not; but
Here is the regent, sir, of Mitylene,
Speaks nobly of her.
   Lys.   Never she would tell
Her parentage; being demanded that,
She would sit still and weep.
   Per.   O Helicanus! strike me, honoured sir;
Give me a gash, put me to present pain;
Lest this great sea of joys rushing upon me,
O'erbear the shores of my mortality,
And drown me with their sweetness.   O, come hither,
Thou that begett'st him that did thee beget;
Thou that wast born at sea, buried at Tarsus,
And found at sea again.—O Helicanus!
Down on thy knees, thank the holy gods as loud
As thunder threatens us: this is Marina.—
What was thy mother's name? tell me but that,
For truth can never be confirmed enough,
Though doubts did ever sleep.
   Mar.   First, sir, I pray,
What is your title?
   Per.   I am Pericles of Tyre: but tell me now
My drowned queen's name—as in the rest you said
Thou hast been godlike perfect,—thou'rt heir of kingdoms,
And another life to Pericles thy father.
   Mar.   Is it no more to be your daughter, than
To say, my mother's name was Thaisa?
Thaisa was my mother, who did end
The minute I began.
   Per.   Now, blessing on thee! rise; thou art my child.

Give me fresh garments! Mine own, Helicanus;
She is not dead at Tarsus, as she should have been,
By savage Cleon: she shall tell thee all;
When thou shalt kneel, and justify in knowledge,
She is thy very princess.—Who is this?
   Hel.   Sir, 't is the governor of Mitylene,
Who, hearing of your melancholy state,
Did come to see you.
   Per.   I embrace you.—
Give me my robes: I am wild in my beholding.
O heavens, bless my girl! But hark! what music?—
Tell Helicanus, my Marina, tell him
O'er, point by point, for yet he seems to doubt,
How sure you are my daughter.—But what music?
   Hel.   My lord, I hear none.
   Per.   None?
The music of the spheres! List, my Marina.
   Lys.   It is not good to cross him: give him way.
   Per.   Rarest sounds! Do ye not hear?—
   Lys.   My lord, I hear.   *[Music*
   Per.   Most heavenly music:
It nips me unto listening, and thick slumber
Hangs upon mine eyes: let me rest.   *[Sleeps*
   Lys.   A pillow for his head.
      [The curtain before the pavilion of PERICLES *is closed*
So, leave him all.—Well, my companion-friends,
If this but answer to my just belief,
I'll well remember you.   *[Exeunt all but Pericles*

SCENE II.—The Same

PERICLES *on the deck asleep;* DIANA *appearing to him in a vision*

   Dia.   My temple stands in Ephesus: hie thee thither,
And do upon mine altar sacrifice.
There, when my maiden priests are met together,
Before the people all,
Reveal how thou at sea didst lose thy wife:
To mourn thy crosses, with thy daughter's call,
And give them repetition to the life.
Perform my bidding, or thou liv'st in woe:
Do it, and happy, by my silver bow!
Awake, and tell thy dream.   *[Disappears*
   Per.   Celestial Dian, goddess argentine,
I will obey thee!—Helicanus!

    Enter LYSIMACHUS, HELICANUS, *and* MARINA
   Hel.   Sir?
   Per.   My purpose was for Tarsus, there to strike

146

The inhospitable Cleon; but I am
For other service first: toward Ephesus
Turn our blown sails; eftsoons I'll tell thee why.—
Shall we refresh us, sir, upon your shore,
And give you gold for such provision
As our intents will need?
   Lys. Sir,
With all my heart; and when you come ashore,
I have another suit.
   Per.   You shall prevail,
Were it to woo my daughter; for it seems
You have been noble towards her.
   Lys.   Sir, lend your arm.
   Per. Come, my Marina.   *[Exeunt*

Enter GOWER, *before the Temple of* DIANA *at* Ephesus

   Gow. Now our sands are almost run;
More a little, and then dumb.
This, my last boon, pray you give me,
For such kindness must relieve me,
That you aptly will suppose
What pageantry, what feats, what shows,
What minstrelsy, and pretty din,
The regent made in Mitylen,
To greet the king. So well he thrived,
That he is promised to be wived
To fair Marina; but in no wise
Till he had done his sacrifice,
As Dian bade: whereto being bound,
The interim, pray you, all confound.
In feathered briefness sails are filled,
And wishes fall out as they're willed.
At Ephesus, the temple see,
Our king, and all his company.
That he can hither come so soon,
Is by your fancy's thankful doom.   *[Exit*

SCENE III.—The Temple of DIANA at Ephesus; THAISA
      standing near the altar, as high priestess; a number
      of Virgins on each side; CERIMON and other In-
      habitants of Ephesus attending

Enter PERICLES, *with his Train;* LYSIMACHUS,
    HELICANUS, MARINA, *and a Lady*

   Per. Hail, Dian! to perform thy just command,
I here confess myself the King of Tyre;
Who, frighted from my country, did wed,

At Pentapólis, the fair Thaisa.
At sea in childbed died she, but brought forth
A maid-child called Marina; who, O goddess!
Wears yet thy silver livery. She at Tarsus
Was nursed with Cleon, whom at fourteen years
He sought to murder: but her better stars
Brought her to Mitylene; against whose shore
Riding, her fortunes brought the maid aboard us,
Where, by her own most clear remembrance, she
Made known herself my daughter.
  Thai.   Voice and favour:—
You are, you are—O royal Pericles!—   [*Faints*
  Per. What means the woman? she dies: help, gentle-
   men!
  Cer. Noble sir,
If you have told Diana's altar true,
This is your wife.
  Per.   Reverend appearer, no:
I threw her o'erboard with these very arms.
  Cer. Upon this coast, I warrant you.
  Per.   'T is most certain.
  Cer. Look to the lady.—O! she's but o'erjoyed.
Early in blustering morn this lady was
Thrown on this shore. I oped the coffin, found
Rich jewels there; recovered her, and placed her
Here in Diana's temple.
  Per.   May we see them?
  Cer. Great sir, they shall be brought you to my house,
Whither I invite you. Look! Thaisa is
Recovered.
  Thai. O, let me look!
If he be none of mine, my sanctity
Will to my sense bend no licentious ear,
But curb it, spite of seeing. Like him you speak,
Like him you are. Did you not name a tempest,
A birth, and death?
  Per.   The voice of dead Thaisa!
  Thai. That Thaisa am I, supposéd dead
And drowned.
  Per. Immortal Dian!
  Thai.   Now I know you better.
When we with tears parted Pentapolis,
The king, my father, gave you such a ring.
           [*Shows a ring*
  Per. This, this: no more, you gods! your present
   kindness
Makes my past miseries sports: you shall do well,
That on touching of her lips I may
Melt, and no more be seen. O, come, be buried
A second time within these arms.

Mar.   My heart
Leaps to be gone into my mother's bosom.
                                    [Kneels to Thaisa
   Per. Look, who kneels here.   Flesh of thy flesh, Thaisa;
Thy burden at the sea, and called Marina,
For she was yielded there.
    Thai.   Blessed, and mine own!
    Hel. Hail, madam, and my queen!
    Thai.   I know you not.
    Per. You have heard me say, when I did fly from
         Tyre,
I left behind an ancient substitute:
Can you remember what I called the man?
I have named him off.
    Thai.   'T was Helicanus then.
    Per. Still confirmation!
Embrace him, dear Thaisa; this is he.
Now do I long to hear how you were found,
How possibly preserved, and whom to thank,
Besides the gods, for this great miracle.
    Thai. Lord Cerimon, my lord; this is the man,
Through whom the gods have shown their power, that
         can
From first to last resolve you.
    Per.   Reverend sir,
The gods can have no mortal officer
More like a god than you.   Will you deliver
How this dead queen re-lives?
    Cer.   I will, my lord:
Beseech you, first go with me to my house,
Where shall be shown you all was found with her;
How she came to be placed here in the temple;
No needful thing omitted.
    Per. Pure Dian! bless thee for thy vision; I
Will offer night-oblations to thee.   Thaisa,
This prince, the fair-betrothéd of your daughter,
Shall marry her at Pentapolis.   And now,
This ornament,
Makes me look dismal, will I clip to form;
And what this fourteen years no razor touched,
To grace thy marriage-day, I'll beautify.
    Thai. Lord Cerimon hath letters of good credit, sir,
My father's dead.
    Per. Heavens, make a star of him!   Yet there, my
         queen,
We'll celebrate their nuptials, and ourselves
Will in that kingdom spend our following days:
Our son and daughter shall in Tyrus reign.
Lord Cerimon, we do our longing stay
To hear the rest untold.—Sir, lead 's the way.   *[Exeunt*

Enter GOWER

Gow.   In Antiochus and his daughter you have heard
Of monstrous lust the due and just reward:
In Pericles, his queen, and daughter, seen,
Although assailed with fortune fierce and keen,
Virtue preserved from fell destruction's blast,
Led on by heaven and crowned with joy at last.
In Helicanus may you well descry
A figure of truth, of faith, of loyalty.
In reverend Cerimon there well appears
The worth that learnéd charity aye wears.
For wicked Cleon and his wife, when fame
Had spread their curséd deed, and honoured name
Of Pericles, to rage the city turn,
That him and his they in his palace burn;
The gods for murder seeméd so content
To punish them,—although not done, but meant.
So on your patience evermore attending,
New joy wait on you!   Here our play has ending.   [*Exit*

The Rape of Lucrece

THE RAPE OF LUCRECE

FROM the besieged Ardea all in post,
Borne by the trustless wings of false desire,
Lust-breathed Tarquin leaves the Roman host,
And to Collatium bears the lightless fire   4
Which, in pale embers hid, lurks to aspire,
    And girdle with embracing flames the waist
    Of Collatine's fair love, Lucrece the chaste.

Haply that name of chaste unhappily set   8
This bateless edge on his keen appetite;
When Collatine unwisely did not let
To praise the clear unmatched red and white
Which triumph'd in that sky of his delight,   12
    Where mortal stars, as bright as heaven's beauties,
    With pure aspects did him peculiar duties.

For he the night before, in Tarquin's tent,
Unlock'd the treasure of his happy state;   16
What priceless wealth the heavens had him lent
In the possession of his beauteous mate;
Reckoning his fortune at such high-proud rate,
    That kings might be espoused to more fame,   20
    But king nor peer to such a peerless dame.

O happiness enjoy'd but of a few!
And, if possess'd, as soon decay'd and done
As is the morning's silver-melting dew   24
Against the golden splendour of the sun;
An expir'd date, cancell'd ere well begun:
    Honour and beauty, in the owner's arms,
    Are weakly fortress'd from a world of harms.   28

Beauty itself doth of itself persuade
The eyes of men without an orator;
What needeth then apology be made
To set forth that which is so singular ?   32
Or why is Collatine the publisher
   Of that rich jewel he should keep unknown
   From thievish ears, because it is his own ?

Perchance his boast of Lucrece' sovereignty   36
Suggested this proud issue of a king;
For by our ears our hearts oft tainted be:
Perchance that envy of so rich a thing,
Braving compare, disdainfully did sting   40
   His high-pitch'd thoughts, that meaner men should
      vaunt
   That golden hap which their superiors want.

But some untimely thought did instigate
His all-too-timeless speed, if none of those: 44
His honour, his affairs, his friends, his state,
Neglected all, with swift intent he goes
To quench the coal which in his liver glows.
   O ! rash false heat, wrapp'd in repentant cold,   48
   Thy hasty spring still blasts, and ne'er grows old.

When at Collatium this false lord arriv'd,
Well was he welcom'd by the Roman dame,
Within whose face beauty and virtue striv'd   52
Which of them both should underprop her fame:
When virtue bragg'd, beauty would blush for shame;
   When beauty boasted blushes, in despite
   Virtue would stain that o'er with silver white.   56

But beauty, in that white intituled,
From Venus' doves doth challenge that fair field;
Then virtue claims from beauty beauty's red,
Which virtue gave the golden age to gild   60
Their silver cheeks, and call'd it then their shield;
   Teaching them thus to use it in the fight,
   When shame assail'd, the red should fence the white.

This heraldry in Lucrece' face was seen,   64
Argu'd by beauty's red and virtue's white:
Of either's colour was the other queen,
Proving from world's minority their right:
Yet their ambition makes them still to fight;   68
  The sovereignty of either being so great,
  That oft they interchange each other's seat.

This silent war of lilies and of roses,
Which Tarquin view'd in her fair face's field,   72
In their pure ranks his traitor eye encloses;
Where, lest between them both it should be kill'd,
The coward captive vanquished doth yield
  To those two armies that would let him go,   76
  Rather than triumph in so false a foe.

Now thinks he that her husband's shallow tongue—
The niggard prodigal that prais'd her so—
In that high task hath done her beauty wrong,   80
Which far exceeds his barren skill to show:
Therefore that praise which Collatine doth owe
  Enchanted Tarquin answers with surmise,
  In silent wonder of still-gazing eyes.   84

This earthly saint, adored by this devil,
Little suspecteth the false worshipper;
For unstain'd thoughts do seldom dream on evil,
Birds never lim'd no secret bushes fear: 88
So guiltless she securely gives good cheer
  And reverend welcome to her princely guest,
  Whose inward ill no outward harm express'd:

For that he colour'd with his high estate,   92
Hiding base sin in plaits of majesty;
That nothing in him seem'd inordinate,
Save sometime too much wonder of his eye,
Which, having all, all could not satisfy;   96
  But, poorly rich, so wanteth in his store,
  That, cloy'd with much, he pineth still for more.

But she, that never cop'd with stranger eyes,
Could pick no meaning from their parling looks,   100
Nor read the subtle-shining secrecies
Writ in the glassy margents of such books:
She touch'd no unknown baits, nor fear'd no hooks;
  Nor could she moralize his wanton sight,   104
  More than his eyes were open'd to the light.

He stories to her ears her husband's fame,
Won in the fields of fruitful Italy;
And decks with praises Collatine's high name,   108
Made glorious by his manly chivalry
With bruised arms and wreaths of victory:
  Her joy with heav'd-up hand she doth express,
  And wordless so greets heaven for his success.   112

Far from the purpose of his coming thither,
He makes excuses for his being there:
No cloudy show of stormy blustering weather
Doth yet in his fair welkin once appear;   116
Till sable Night, mother of Dread and Fear,
  Upon the world dim darkness doth display,
  And in her vaulty prison stows the Day.

For then is Tarquin brought unto his bed,   120
Intending weariness with heavy spright;
For after supper long he questioned
With modest Lucrece, and wore out the night:
Now leaden slumber with life's strength doth fight,
  And every one to rest themselves betake,   125
  Save thieves, and cares, and troubled minds, that wake.

As one of which doth Tarquin lie revolving
The sundry dangers of his will's obtaining;   128
Yet ever to obtain his will resolving,
Though weak-built hopes persuade him to abstaining:
Despair to gain doth traffic oft for gaining;
  And when great treasure is the meed propos'd,   132
  Though death be adjunct, there 's no death suppos'd.

Those that much covet are with gain so fond,
For what they have not, that which they possess
They scatter and unloose it from their bond,   136
And so, by hoping more, they have but less ;
Or, gaining more, the profit of excess
    Is but to surfeit, and such griefs sustain,
    That they prove bankrupt in this poor-rich gain.

The aim of all is but to nurse the life   141
With honour, wealth, and ease, in waning age ;
And in this aim there is such thwarting strife,
That one for all, or all for one we gage ;   144
As life for honour in fell battles' rage ;
    Honour for wealth ; and oft that wealth doth cost
    The death of all, and all together lost.

So that in venturing ill we leave to be   148
The things we are for that which we expect ;
And this ambitious foul infirmity,
In having much, torments us with defect
Of that we have : so then we do neglect   152
    The thing we have, and, all for want of wit,
    Make something nothing by augmenting it.

Such hazard now must doting Tarquin make,
Pawning his honour to obtain his lust,   156
And for himself himself he must forsake :
Then where is truth, if there be no self-trust ?
When shall he think to find a stranger just,
    When he himself himself confounds, betrays   160
    To slanderous tongues and wretched hateful days ?

Now stole upon the time the dead of night,
When heavy sleep had closed up mortal eyes ;
No comfortable star did lend his light,   164
No noise but owls' and wolves' death-boding cries ;
Now serves the season that they may surprise
    The silly lambs ; pure thoughts are dead and still,
    While lust and murder wake to stain and kill.   168

And now this lustful lord leap'd from his bed,
Throwing his mantle rudely o'er his arm;
Is madly toss'd between desire and dread;
Th' one sweetly flatters, th' other feareth harm;   172
But honest fear, bewitch'd with lust's foul charm,
   Doth too too oft betake him to retire,
   Beaten away by brain-sick rude desire.

His falchion on a flint he softly smiteth,   176
That from the cold stone sparks of fire do fly;
Whereat a waxen torch forthwith he lighteth,
Which must be lode-star to his lustful eye;
And to the flame thus speaks advisedly: 180
   ' As from this cold flint I enforc'd this fire,
   So Lucrece must I force to my desire.'

Here pale with fear he doth premeditate
The dangers of his loathsome enterprise,   184
And in his inward mind he doth debate
What following sorrow may on this arise:
Then looking scornfully, he doth despise
   His naked armour of still-slaughter'd lust,   188
   And justly thus controls his thoughts unjust:

' Fair torch, burn out thy light, and lend it not
To darken her whose light excelleth thine;
And die, unhallow'd thoughts, before you blot   192
With your uncleanness that which is divine;
Offer pure incense to so pure a shrine:
   Let fair humanity abhor the deed
   That spots and stains love's modest snow-white weed.

' O shame to knighthood and to shining arms.   197
O foul dishonour to my household's grave!
O impious act, including all foul harms!
A martial man to be soft fancy's slave!   200
True valour still a true respect should have;
   Then my digression is so vile, so base,
   That it will live engraven in my face.

'Yea, though I die, the scandal will survive,   204
And be an eye-sore in my golden coat;
Some loathsome dash the herald will contrive,
To cipher me how fondly I did dote;
That my posterity sham'd with the note,   208
   Shall curse my bones, and hold it for no sin
   To wish that I their father had not been.

'What win I if I gain the thing I seek?
A dream, a breath, a froth of fleeting joy.   212
Who buys a minute's mirth to wail a week?
Or sells eternity to get a toy?
For one sweet grape who will the vine destroy?
   Or what fond beggar, but to touch the crown,   216
   Would with the sceptre straight be strucken down?

'If Collatinus dream of my intent,
Will he not wake, and in a desperate rage
Post hither, this vile purpose to prevent?   220
This siege that hath engirt his marriage,
This blur to youth, this sorrow to the sage,
   This dying virtue, this surviving shame,
   Whose crime will bear an ever-during blame?   224

'O! what excuse can my invention make,
When thou shalt charge me with so black a deed?
Will not my tongue be mute, my frail joints shake,
Mine eyes forego their light, my false heart bleed?
The guilt being great, the fear doth still exceed;   229
   And extreme fear can neither fight nor fly,
   But coward-like with trembling terror die.

'Had Collatinus kill'd my son or sire,   232
Or lain in ambush to betray my life,
Or were he not my dear friend, this desire
Might have excuse to work upon his wife,
As in revenge or quittal of such strife: 236
   But as he is my kinsman, my dear friend,
   The shame and fault finds no excuse nor end.

THE RAPE OF LUCRECE

'Shameful it is; ay, if the fact be known:
Hateful it is; there is no hate in loving:
I'll beg her love; but she is not her own:
The worst is but denial and reproving:
My will is strong, past reason's weak removing.
　Who fears a sentence or an old man's saw,
　Shall by a painted cloth be kept in awe.'

240

244

Thus, graceless, holds he disputation
'Tween frozen conscience and hot burning will,
And with good thoughts makes dispensation,
Urging the worser sense for vantage still;
Which in a moment doth confound and kill
　All pure effects, and doth so far proceed,
　That what is vile shows like a virtuous deed.

248

252

Quoth he, 'She took me kindly by the hand,
And gaz'd for tidings in my eager eyes,
Fearing some hard news from the warlike band
Where her beloved Collatinus lies.
O! how her fear did make her colour rise:
　First red as roses that on lawn we lay,
　Then white as lawn, the roses took away.

256

'And how her hand, in my hand being lock'd,
Forc'd it to tremble with her loyal fear!
Which struck her sad, and then it faster rock'd,
Until her husband's welfare she did hear;
Whereat she smiled with so sweet a cheer,
　That had Narcissus seen her as she stood,
　Self-love had never drown'd him in the flood.

260

264

'Why hunt I then for colour or excuses?
All orators are dumb when beauty pleadeth;
Poor wretches have remorse in poor abuses;
Love thrives not in the heart that shadows dreadeth:
Affection is my captain, and he leadeth;
　And when his gaudy banner is display'd,
　The coward fights, and will not be dismay'd.

268

272

160

'Then, childish fear, avaunt! debating, die!
Respect and reason, wait on wrinkled age!
My heart shall never countermand mine eye: 276
Sad pause and deep regard beseems the sage;
My part is youth, and beats these from the stage.
　　Desire my pilot is, beauty my prize;
　　Then who fears sinking where such treasure lies?'

As corn o'ergrown by weeds, so heedful fear   281
Is almost chok'd by unresisted lust.
Away he steals with open listening ear,
Full of foul hope, and full of fond mistrust;   284
Both which, as servitors to the unjust,
　　So cross him with their opposite persuasion,
　　That now he vows a league, and now invasion.

Within his thought her heavenly image sits,   288
And in the self-same seat sits Collatine:
That eye which looks on her confounds his wits;
That eye which him beholds, as more divine,
Unto a view so false will not incline;   292
　　But with a pure appeal seeks to the heart,
　　Which once corrupted, takes the worser part;

And therein heartens up his servile powers,
Who, flatter'd by their leader's jocund show,   296
Stuff up his lust, as minutes fill up hours;
And as their captain, so their pride doth grow,
Paying more slavish tribute than they owe.
　　By reprobate desire thus madly led,   300
　　The Roman lord marcheth to Lucrece' bed.

The locks between her chamber and his will,
Each one by him enforc'd, retires his ward;
But as they open they all rate his ill,   304
Which drives the creeping thief to some regard:
The threshold grates the door to have him heard;
　　Night-wandering weasels shriek to see him there;
　　They fright him, yet he still pursues his fear.   308

As each unwilling portal yields him way,
Through little vents and crannies of the place
The wind wars with his torch to make him stay,
And blows the smoke of it into his face,   312
Extinguishing his conduct in this case;
  But his hot heart, which fond desire doth scorch,
  Puffs forth another wind that fires the torch:

And being lighted, by the light he spies   316
Lucretia's glove, wherein her needle sticks:
He takes it from the rushes where it lies,
And griping it, the neeld his finger pricks;
As who should say, 'This glove to wanton tricks   320
  Is not inur'd; return again in haste;
  Thou seest our mistress' ornaments are chaste.'

But all these poor forbiddings could not stay him;
He in the worst sense construes their denial: 324
The door, the wind, the glove, that did delay him,
He takes for accidental things of trial;
Or as those bars which stop the hourly dial,
  Who with a lingering stay his course doth let,   328
  Till every minute pays the hour his debt.

'So, so,' quoth he, 'these lets attend the time,
Like little frosts that sometime threat the spring,
To add a more rejoicing to the prime,   332
And give the sneaped birds more cause to sing.
Pain pays the income of each precious thing;
  Huge rocks, high winds, strong pirates, shelves and
    sands,
  The merchant fears, ere rich at home he lands.'

Now is he come unto the chamber door,   337
That shuts him from the heaven of his thought,
Which with a yielding latch, and with no more,
Hath barr'd him from the blessed thing he sought.
So from himself impiety hath wrought,   341
  That for his prey to pray he doth begin,
  As if the heavens should countenance his sin.

But in the midst of his unfruitful prayer,   344
Having solicited the eternal power
That his foul thoughts might compass his fair fair,
And they would stand auspicious to the hour,
Even there he starts: quoth he, 'I must deflower;
   The powers to whom I pray abhor this fact,   349
   How can they then assist me in the act?

'Then Love and Fortune be my gods, my guide!
My will is back'd with resolution: 352
Thoughts are but dreams till their effects be tried;
The blackest sin is clear'd with absolution;
Against love's fire fear's frost hath dissolution.
   The eye of heaven is out, and misty night   356
   Covers the shame that follows sweet delight.'

This said, his guilty hand pluck'd up the latch,
And with his knee the door he opens wide.
The dove sleeps fast that this night-owl will catch:
Thus treason works ere traitors be espied.   361
Who sees the lurking serpent steps aside;
   But she, sound sleeping, fearing no such thing,
   Lies at the mercy of his mortal sting.   364

Into the chamber wickedly he stalks,
And gazeth on her yet unstained bed.
The curtains being close, about he walks,
Rolling his greedy eyeballs in his head: 368
By their high treason is his heart misled;
   Which gives the watchword to his hand full soon,
   To draw the cloud that hides the silver moon.

Look, as the fair and fiery-pointed sun,   372
Rushing from forth a cloud, bereaves our sight;
Even so, the curtain drawn, his eyes begun
To wink, being blinded with a greater light:
Whether it is that she reflects so bright,   376
   That dazzleth them, or else some shame supposed,
   But blind they are, and keep themselves enclosed.

O! had they in that darksome prison died,
Then had they seen the period of their ill;   380
Then Collatine again, by Lucrece' side,
In his clear bed might have reposed still:
But they must ope, this blessed league to kill,
   And holy-thoughted Lucrece to their sight   384
   Must sell her joy, her life, her world's delight.

Her lily hand her rosy cheek lies under,
Cozening the pillow of a lawful kiss;
Who, therefore angry, seems to part in sunder,   388
Swelling on either side to want his bliss;
Between whose hills her head entombed is:
   Where, like a virtuous monument she lies,
   To be admir'd of lewd unhallow'd eyes.   392

Without the bed her other fair hand was,
On the green coverlet; whose perfect white
Show'd like an April daisy on the grass,
With pearly sweat, resembling dew of night.   396
Her eyes, like marigolds, had sheath'd their light,
   And canopied in darkness sweetly lay,
   Till they might open to adorn the day.

Her hair, like golden threads, play'd with her breath;
O modest wantons! wanton modesty!   401
Showing life's triumph in the map of death,
And death's dim look in life's mortality:
Each in her sleep themselves so beautify,   404
   As if between them twain there were no strife,
   But that life liv'd in death, and death in life.

Her breasts, like ivory globes circled with blue,
A pair of maiden worlds unconquered,   408
Save of their lord no bearing yoke they knew,
And him by oath they truly honoured.
These worlds in Tarquin new ambition bred;
   Who, like a foul usurper, went about   412
   From this fair throne to heave the owner out.

THE RAPE OF LUCRECE

What could he see but mightily he noted?
What did he note but strongly he desir'd?
What he beheld, on that he firmly doted,   416
And in his will his wilful eye he tir'd.
With more than admiration he admir'd
   Her azure veins, her alabaster skin,
   Her coral lips, her snow-white dimpled chin.   420

As the grim lion fawneth o'er his prey,
Sharp hunger by the conquest satisfied,
So o'er this sleeping soul doth Tarquin stay,
His rage of lust by gazing qualified;   424
Slack'd, not suppress'd; for standing by her side,
   His eye, which late this mutiny restrains,
   Unto a greater uproar tempts his veins:

And they, like straggling slaves for pillage fighting,
Obdurate vassals fell exploits effecting,   429
In bloody death and ravishment delighting,
Nor children's tears nor mother's groans respecting,
Swell in their pride, the onset still expecting: 432
   Anon his beating heart, alarum striking,
   Gives the hot charge and bids them do their liking.

His drumming heart cheers up his burning eye,
His eye commends the leading to his hand;   436
His hand, as proud of such a dignity,
Smoking with pride, march'd on to make his stand
On her bare breast, the heart of all her land;
   Whose ranks of blue veins, as his hand did scale,
   Left their round turrets destitute and pale.   441

They, mustering to the quiet cabinet
Where their dear governess and lady lies,
Do tell her she is dreadfully beset,   444
And fright her with confusion of their cries:
She, much amaz'd, breaks ope her lock'd-up eyes,
   Who, peeping forth this tumult to behold,
   Are by his flaming torch dimm'd and controll'd.

165

Imagine her as one in dead of night   449
From forth dull sleep by dreadful fancy waking,
That thinks she hath beheld some ghastly sprite,
Whose grim aspect sets every joint a-shaking ;   452
What terror 'tis ! but she, in worser taking,
  From sleep disturbed, heedfully doth view
  The sight which makes supposed terror true.

Wrapp'd and confounded in a thousand fears,   456
Like to a new-kill'd bird she trembling lies ;
She dares not look ; yet, winking, there appears
Quick-shifting antics, ugly in her eyes :
Such shadows are the weak brain's forgeries ;   460
  Who, angry that the eyes fly from their lights,
  In darkness daunts them with more dreadful sights.

His hand, that yet remains upon her breast,—
Rude ram to batter such an ivory wall !—   464
May feel her heart,—poor citizen,—distress'd,
Wounding itself to death, rise up and fall,
Beating her bulk, that his hand shakes withal.
  This moves in him more rage and lesser pity,   468
  To make the breach and enter this sweet city.

First, like a trumpet, doth his tongue begin
To sound a parley to his heartless foe ;
Who o'er the white sheet peers her whiter chin,   472
The reason of this rash alarm to know,
Which he by dumb demeanour seeks to show ;
  But she with vehement prayers urgeth still
  Under what colour he commits this ill.   476

Thus he replies : ' The colour in thy face,
That even for anger makes the lily pale,
And the red rose blush at her own disgrace,
Shall plead for me and tell my loving tale ;   480
Under that colour am I come to scale
  Thy never-conquer'd fort : the fault is thine,
  For those thine eyes betray thee unto mine.

' Thus I forestall thee, if thou mean to chide :   484
Thy beauty hath ensnar'd thee to this night,
Where thou with patience must my will abide,
My will that marks thee for my earth's delight,
Which I to conquer sought with all my might ;   488
   But as reproof and reason beat it dead,
   By thy bright beauty was it newly bred.

' I see what crosses my attempt will bring ;
I know what thorns the growing rose defends ;   492
I think the honey guarded with a sting ;
All this, beforehand, counsel comprehends :
But will is deaf and hears no heedful friends ;
   Only he hath an eye to gaze on beauty,   496
   And dotes on what he looks, 'gainst law or duty.

' I have debated, even in my soul,
What wrong, what shame, what sorrow I shall breed ;
But nothing can affection's course control,   500
Or stop the headlong fury of his speed.
I know repentant tears ensue the deed,
   Reproach, disdain, and deadly enmity ;
   Yet strive I to embrace mine infamy.'   504

This said, he shakes aloft his Roman blade,
Which like a falcon towering in the skies,
Coucheth the fowl below with his wings' shade,
Whose crooked beak threats if he mount he dies :   508
So under his insulting falchion lies
   Harmless Lucretia, marking what he tells
   With trembling fear, as fowl hear falcon's bells.

' Lucrece,' quoth he, ' this night I must enjoy thee :
If thou deny, then force must work my way,   513
For in thy bed I purpose to destroy thee :
That done, some worthless slave of thine I'll slay,
To kill thine honour with thy life's decay ;   516
   And in thy dead arms do I mean to place him,
   Swearing I slew him, seeing thee embrace him.

'So thy surviving husband shall remain
The scornful mark of every open eye ;   520
Thy kinsmen hang their heads at this disdain,
Thy issue blurr'd with nameless bastardy :
And thou, the author of their obloquy,
    Shalt have thy trespass cited up in rimes,   524
    And sung by children in succeeding times.

'But if thou yield, I rest thy secret friend :
The fault unknown is as a thought unacted ;
A little harm done to a great good end,   528
For lawful policy remains enacted.
The poisonous simple sometime is compacted
    In a pure compound ; being so applied,
    His venom in effect is purified.   532

'Then for thy husband and thy children's sake,
Tender my suit : bequeath not to their lot
The shame that from them no device can take,
The blemish that will never be forgot ;   536
Worse than a slavish wipe or birth-hour's blot :
    For marks descried in men's nativity
    Are nature's faults, not their own infamy.'

Here with a cockatrice' dead-killing eye   540
He rouseth up himself, and makes a pause ;
While she, the picture of pure piety,
Like a white hind under the gripe's sharp claws,
Pleads in a wilderness where are no laws,   544
    To the rough beast that knows no gentle right,
    Nor aught obeys but his foul appetite.

But when a black-fac'd cloud the world doth threat,
In his dim mist the aspiring mountains hiding,   548
From earth's dark womb some gentle gust doth get,
Which blows these pitchy vapours from their biding,
Hindering their present fall by this dividing ;
    So his unhallow'd haste her words delays,   552
    And moody Pluto winks while Orpheus plays.

Yet, foul night-waking cat, he doth but dally,
While in his hold-fast foot the weak mouse panteth:
Her sad behaviour feeds his vulture folly,   556
A swallowing gulf that even in plenty wanteth:
His ear her prayers admits, but his heart granteth
    No penetrable entrance to her plaining:
    Tears harden lust though marble wear with raining.

Her pity-pleading eyes are sadly fix'd   561
In the remorseless wrinkles of his face;
Her modest eloquence with sighs is mix'd,
Which to her oratory adds more grace.   564
She puts the period often from his place,
    And midst the sentence so her accent breaks,
    That twice she doth begin ere once she speaks.

She conjures him by high almighty Jove,   568
By knighthood, gentry, and sweet friendship's oath,
By her untimely tears, her husband's love,
By holy human law, and common troth,
By heaven and earth, and all the power of both,   572
    That to his borrow'd bed he make retire,
    And stoop to honour, not to foul desire.

Quoth she, ' Reward not hospitality
With such black payment as thou hast pretended;
Mud not the fountain that gave drink to thee;   577
Mar not the thing that cannot be amended;
End thy ill aim before thy shoot be ended;
    He is no woodman that doth bend his bow   580
    To strike a poor unseasonable doe.

' My husband is thy friend, for his sake spare me;
Thyself art mighty, for thine own sake leave me;
Myself a weakling, do not, then, ensnare me;   584
Thou look'dst not like deceit, do not deceive me.
My sighs, like whirlwinds, labour hence to heave thee;
    If ever man were mov'd with woman's moans,
    Be moved with my tears, my sighs, my groans.

' All which together, like a troubled ocean, 589
Beat at thy rocky and wrack-threatening heart,
To soften it with their continual motion;
For stones dissolv'd to water do convert. 592
O! if no harder than a stone thou art,
 Melt at my tears, and be compassionate;
 Soft pity enters at an iron gate.

' In Tarquin's likeness I did entertain thee; 596
Hast thou put on his shape to do him shame?
To all the host of heaven I complain me,
Thou wrong'st his honour, wound'st his princely name.
Thou art not what thou seem'st; and if the same,
 Thou seem'st not what thou art, a god, a king;
 For kings like gods should govern every thing.

' How will thy shame be seeded in thine age,
When thus thy vices bud before thy spring! 604
If in thy hope thou dar'st do such outrage,
What dar'st thou not when once thou art a king?
O! be remembered, no outrageous thing
 From vassal actors can be wip'd away; 608
 Then kings' misdeeds cannot be hid in clay.

' This deed will make thee only lov'd for fear;
But happy monarchs still are fear'd for love:
With foul offenders thou perforce must bear, 612
When they in thee the like offences prove:
If but for fear of this, thy will remove;
 For princes are the glass, the school, the book,
 Where subjects' eyes do learn, do read, do look.

' And wilt thou be the school where Lust shall learn?
Must he in thee read lectures of such shame?
Wilt thou be glass wherein it shall discern
Authority for sin, warrant for blame, 620
To privilege dishonour in thy name?
 Thou back'st reproach against long-living laud,
 And mak'st fair reputation but a bawd.

' Hast thou command ? by him that gave it thee,
From a pure heart command thy rebel will: 625
Draw not thy sword to guard iniquity,
For it was lent thee all that brood to kill.
Thy princely office how canst thou fulfil,   628
  When, pattern'd by thy fault, foul sin may say,
  He learn'd to sin, and thou didst teach the way ?

' Think but how vile a spectacle it were,
To view thy present trespass in another.   632
Men's faults do seldom to themselves appear;
Their own transgressions partially they smother:
This guilt would seem death-worthy in thy brother.   636
  O ! how are they wrapp'd in with infamies
  That from their own misdeeds askance their eyes.

' To thee, to thee, my heav'd-up hands appeal,
Not to seducing lust, thy rash relier :
I sue for exil'd majesty's repeal ;   640
Let him return, and flattering thoughts retire :
His true respect will prison false desire,
  And wipe the dim mist from thy doting eyne,
  That thou shalt see thy state and pity mine.'   644

' Have done,' quoth he ; ' my uncontrolled tide
Turns not, but swells the higher by this let.
Small lights are soon blown out, huge fires abide,
And with the wind in greater fury fret :   648
The petty streams that pay a daily debt
  To their salt sovereign, with their fresh falls' haste
  Add to his flow, but alter not his taste.'

' Thou art,' quoth she, ' a sea, a sovereign king ;   652
And lo ! there falls into thy boundless flood
Black lust, dishonour, shame, misgoverning,
Who seek to stain the ocean of thy blood.
If all these petty ills shall change thy good,   656
  Thy sea within a puddle's womb is hears'd,
  And not the puddle in thy sea dispers'd.

' So shall these slaves be king, and thou their slave ;
Thou nobly base, they basely dignified ;   660
Thou their fair life, and they thy fouler grave ;
Thou loathed in their shame, they in thy pride :
The lesser thing should not the greater hide ;
   The cedar stoops not to the base shrub's foot,   664
   But low shrubs wither at the cedar's root.

' So let thy thoughts, low vassals to thy state '—
' No more,' quoth he ; ' by heaven, I will not hear thee :
Yield to my love ; if not, enforced hate,   668
Instead of love's coy touch, shall rudely tear thee ;
That done, despitefully I mean to bear thee
   Unto the base bed of some rascal groom,
   To be thy partner in this shameful doom.'   672

This said, he sets his foot upon the light,
For light and lust are deadly enemies :
Shame folded up in blind concealing night,
When most unseen, then most doth tyrannize.   676
The wolf hath seiz'd his prey, the poor lamb cries ;
   Till with her own white fleece her voice controll'd
   Entombs her outcry in her lips' sweet fold :

For with the nightly linen that she wears   680
He pens her piteous clamours in her head,
Cooling his hot face in the chastest tears
That ever modest eyes with sorrow shed.
O ! that prone lust should stain so pure a bed,   684
   The spots whereof could weeping purify,
   Her tears should drop on them perpetually.

But she hath lost a dearer thing than life,
And he hath won what he would lose again ;   688
This forced league doth force a further strife ;
This momentary joy breeds months of pain ;
This hot desire converts to cold disdain :
   Pure Chastity is rifled of her store,   692
   And Lust, the thief, far poorer than before.

Look! as the full-fed hound or gorged hawk,
Unapt for tender smell or speedy flight,
Make slow pursuit, or altogether balk   696
The prey wherein by nature they delight;
So surfeit-taking Tarquin fares this night:
  His taste delicious, in digestion souring,
    Devours his will, that liv'd by foul devouring.   700

O! deeper sin than bottomless conceit
Can comprehend in still imagination;
Drunken Desire must vomit his receipt,
Ere he can see his own abomination.   704
While Lust is in his pride, no exclamation
  Can curb his heat, or rein his rash desire,
    ill, like a jade, Self-will himself doth tire.

And then with lank and lean discolour'd cheek,   708
With heavy eye, knit brow, and strengthless pace,
Feeble Desire, all recreant, poor, and meek,
Like to a bankrupt beggar wails his case:
The flesh being proud, Desire doth fight with Grace,
  For there it revels; and when that decays,   713
    The guilty rebel for remission prays.

So fares it with this faultful lord of Rome,
Who this accomplishment so hotly chas'd;   716
For now against himself he sounds this doom,
That through the length of times he stands disgrac'd;
Besides, his soul's fair temple is defac'd;
  To whose weak ruins muster troops of cares,   720
    To ask the spotted princess how she fares.

She says, her subjects with foul insurrection
Have batter'd down her consecrated wall,
And by their mortal fault brought in subjection   724
Her immortality, and made her thrall
To living death and pain perpetual:
  Which in her prescience she controlled still,
    But her foresight could not forestall their will.   728

Even in this thought through the dark night he stealeth,
A captive victor that hath lost in gain;
Bearing away the wound that nothing healeth,
The scar that will despite of cure remain; 732
Leaving his spoil perplex'd in greater pain.
　She bears the load of lust he left behind,
　And he the burden of a guilty mind.

He like a thievish dog creeps sadly thence, 736
She like a wearied lamb lies panting there;
He scowls and hates himself for his offence,
She desperate with her nails her flesh doth tear;
He faintly flies, sweating with guilty fear, 740
　She stays, exclaiming on the direful night;
　He runs, and chides his vanish'd, loath'd delight.

He thence departs a heavy convertite,
She there remains a hopeless castaway; 744
He in his speed looks for the morning light;
She prays she never may behold the day;
'For day,' quoth she, 'night's 'scapes doth open lay,
　And my true eyes have never practis'd how 748
　To cloak offences with a cunning brow.

'They think not but that every eye can see
The same disgrace which they themselves behold;
And therefore would they still in darkness be, 752
To have their unseen sin remain untold;
For they their guilt with weeping will unfold,
　And grave, like water that doth eat in steel,
　Upon my cheeks what helpless shame I feel.' 756

Here she exclaims against repose and rest,
And bids her eyes hereafter still be blind.
She wakes her heart by beating on her breast,
And bids it leap from thence, where it may find 760
Some purer chest to close so pure a mind.
　Frantic with grief thus breathes she forth her spite
　Against the unseen secrecy of night:

'O comfort-killing Night, image of hell!   764
Dim register and notary of shame!
Black stage for tragedies and murders fell!
Vast sin-concealing chaos! nurse of blame!
Blind muffled bawd! dark harbour for defame!   768
    Grim cave of death! whispering conspirator
    With close-tongu'd treason and the ravisher!

'O hateful, vaporous, and foggy Night!
Since thou art guilty of my cureless crime,   772
Muster thy mists to meet the eastern light,
Make war against proportion'd course of time;
Or if thou wilt permit the sun to climb
    His wonted height, yet ere he go to bed,   776
    Knit poisonous clouds about his golden head.

'With rotten damps ravish the morning air;
Let their exhal'd unwholesome breaths make sick
The life of purity, the supreme fair,   780
Ere he arrive his weary noontide prick;
And let thy misty vapours march so thick,
    That in their smoky ranks his smother'd light
    May set at noon and make perpetual night.   784

'Were Tarquin Night, as he is but Night's child,
The silver-shining queen he would distain;
Her twinkling handmaids too, by him defil'd,
Through Night's black bosom should not peep again:
So should I have co-partners in my pain;   789
    And fellowship in woe doth woe assuage,
    As palmers' chat makes short their pilgrimage.

'Where now I have no one to blush with me,   792
To cross their arms and hang their heads with mine,
To mask their brows and hide their infamy;
But I alone alone must sit and pine,
Seasoning the earth with showers of silver brine,   796
    Mingling my talk with tears, my grief with groans,
    Poor wasting monuments of lasting moans.

'O Night! thou furnace of foul-reeking smoke,
Let not the jealous Day behold that face 800
Which underneath thy black all-hiding cloak
Immodestly lies martyr'd with disgrace:
Keep still possession of thy gloomy place,
    That all the faults which in thy reign are made
    May likewise be sepulchred in thy shade. 805

'Make me not object to the tell-tale Day!
The light will show, character'd in my brow,
The story of sweet chastity's decay, 808
The impious breach of holy wedlock vow:
Yea, the illiterate, that know not how
    To 'cipher what is writ in learned books,
    Will quote my loathsome trespass in my looks. 812

The nurse, to still her child, will tell my story,
And fright her crying babe with Tarquin's name;
The orator, to deck his oratory,
Will couple my reproach to Tarquin's shame; 816
Feast-finding minstrels, tuning my defame,
    Will tie the hearers to attend each line,
    How Tarquin wronged me, I Collatine.

'Let my good name, that senseless reputation, 820
For Collatine's dear love be kept unspotted:
If that be made a theme for disputation,
The branches of another root are rotted,
And undeserv'd reproach to him allotted 824
    That is as clear from this attaint of mine,
    As I ere this was pure to Collatine.

'O unseen shame! invisible disgrace!
O unfelt sore! crest-wounding, private scar! 828
Reproach is stamp'd in Collatinus' face,
And Tarquin's eye may read the mot afar,
How he in peace is wounded, not in war.
    Alas! how many bear such shameful blows, 832
    Which not themselves, but he that gives them knows.

' If, Collatine, thine honour lay in me,
From me by strong assault it is bereft.
My honey lost, and I, a drone-like bee, 836
Have no perfection of my summer left,
But robb'd and ransack'd by injurious theft :
  In thy weak hive a wandering wasp hath crept,
  And suck'd the honey which thy chaste bee kept.

' Yet am I guilty of thy honour's wrack ; 841
Yet for thy honour did I entertain him ;
Coming from thee, I could not put him back,
For it had been dishonour to disdain him : 844
Besides, of weariness he did complain him,
  And talk'd of virtue : O ! unlook'd-for evil,
  When virtue is profan'd in such a devil.

' Why should the worm intrude the maiden bud ?
Or hateful cuckoos hatch in sparrows' nests ? 849
Or toads infect fair founts with venom mud ?
Or tyrant folly lurk in gentle breasts ?
Or kings be breakers of their own behests ? 852
  But no perfection is so absolute,
  That some impurity doth not pollute.

' The aged man that coffers up his gold
Is plagu'd with cramps and gouts and painful fits ;
And scarce hath eyes his treasure to behold, 857
But like still-pining Tantalus he sits,
And useless barns the harvest of his wits ;
  Having no other pleasure of his gain 860
  But torment that it cannot cure his pain.

' So then he hath it when he cannot use it,
And leaves it to be master'd by his young ;
Who in their pride do presently abuse it : 864
Their father was too weak, and they too strong,
To hold their cursed-blessed fortune long.
  The sweets we wish for turn to loathed sours
  Even in the moment that we call them ours. 868

'Unruly blasts wait on the tender spring;
Unwholesome weeds take root with precious flowers;
The adder hisses where the sweet birds sing;
What virtue breeds iniquity devours: 872
We have no good that we can say is ours,
   But ill-annexed Opportunity
   Or kills his life, or else his quality.

'O Opportunity! thy guilt is great,   876
'Tis thou that execut'st the traitor's treason;
Thou sett'st the wolf where he the lamb may get;
Whoever plots the sin, thou point'st the season;
'Tis thou that spurn'st at right, at law, at reason;
   And in thy shady cell, where none may spy him,
   Sits Sin to seize the souls that wander by him.

'Thou makest the vestal violate her oath;   883
Thou blow'st the fire when temperance is thaw'd;
Thou smother'st honesty, thou murder'st troth;
Thou foul abettor! thou notorious bawd!
Thou plantest scandal and displacest laud:
   Thou ravisher, thou traitor, thou false thief,   888
   Thy honey turns to gall, thy joy to grief!

'Thy secret pleasure turns to open shame,
Thy private feasting to a public fast,
Thy smoothing titles to a ragged name,   892
Thy sugar'd tongue to bitter wormwood taste:
Thy violent vanities can never last.
   How comes it then, vile Opportunity,
   Being so bad, such numbers seek for thee?   896

'When wilt thou be the humble suppliant's friend,
And bring him where his suit may be obtain'd?
When wilt thou sort an hour great strifes to end?
Or free that soul which wretchedness hath chain'd?
Give physic to the sick, ease to the pain'd?   901
   The poor, lame, blind, halt, creep, cry out for thee;
   But they ne'er meet with Opportunity.

' The patient dies while the physician sleeps ;   904
The orphan pines while the oppressor feeds ;
Justice is feasting while the widow weeps ;
Advice is sporting while infection breeds :
Thou grant'st no time for charitable deeds :   908
    Wrath, envy, treason, rape, and murder's rages,
    Thy heinous hours wait on them as their pages.

' When Truth and Virtue have to do with thee,
A thousand crosses keep them from thy aid :   912
They buy thy help ; but Sin ne'er gives a fee,
He gratis comes ; and thou art well appaid
As well to hear as grant what he hath said.
    My Collatine would else have come to me   916
    When Tarquin did, but he was stay'd by thee.

' Guilty thou art of murder and of theft,
Guilty of perjury and subornation,
Guilty of treason, forgery, and shift,   920
Guilty of incest, that abomination ;
An accessary by thine inclination
    To all sins past and all that are to come,
    From the creation to the general doom.   924

' Mis-shapen Time, copesmate of ugly Night,
Swift subtle post, carrier of grisly care,
Eater of youth, false slave to false delight,
Base watch of woes, sin's pack-horse, virtue's snare ;
Thou nursest all, and murderest all that are :   929
    O ! hear me then, injurious, shifting Time,
    Be guilty of my death, since of my crime.

' Why hath thy servant Opportunity   932
Betray'd the hours thou gav'st me to repose ?
Cancell'd my fortunes, and enchained me
To endless date of never-ending woes ?
Time's office is to fine the hate of foes,   936
    To eat up errors by opinion bred,
    Not spend the dowry of a lawful bed.

'Time's glory is to calm contending kings,
To unmask falsehood and bring truth to light,   940
To stamp the seal of time in aged things,
To wake the morn and sentinel the night,
To wrong the wronger till he render right,
  To ruinate proud buildings with thy hours,   944
  And smear with dust their glittering golden towers ;

'To fill with worm-holes stately monuments,
To feed oblivion with decay of things,
To blot old books and alter their contents,   948
To pluck the quills from ancient ravens' wings,
To dry the old oak's sap and cherish springs,
  To spoil antiquities of hammer'd steel,
  And turn the giddy round of Fortune's wheel ;   952

'To show the beldam daughters of her daughter,
To make the child a man, the man a child,
To slay the tiger that doth live by slaughter,
To tame the unicorn and lion wild,   956
To mock the subtle, in themselves beguil'd,
  To cheer the ploughman with increaseful crops,
  And waste huge stones with little water-drops.

'Why work'st thou mischief in thy pilgrimage,   960
Unless thou couldst return to make amends ?
One poor retiring minute in an age
Would purchase thee a thousand thousand friends,
Lending him wit that to bad debtors lends :   964
  O ! this dread night, wouldst thou one hour come back,
  I could prevent this storm and shun thy wrack.

'Thou ceaseless lackey to eternity,
With some mischance cross Tarquin in his flight :   968
Devise extremes beyond extremity,
To make him curse this cursed crimeful night :
Let ghastly shadows his lewd eyes affright,
  And the dire thought of his committed evil   972
  Shape every bush a hideous shapeless devil.

' Disturb his hours of rest with restless trances,
Afflict him in his bed with bedrid groans ;
Let there bechance him pitiful mischances,   976
To make him moan, but pity not his moans :
Stone him with harden'd hearts, harder than stones ;
　　And let mild women to him lose their mildness,
　　Wilder to him than tigers in their wildness.   980

' Let him have time to tear his curled hair,
Let him have time against himself to rave,
Let him have time of Time's help to despair,
Let him have time to live a loathed slave,   984
Let him have time a beggar's orts to crave,
　　And time to see one that by alms doth live
　　Disdain to him disdained scraps to give.

' Let him have time to see his friends his foes,   988
And merry fools to mock at him resort ;
Let him have time to mark how slow time goes
In time of sorrow, and how swift and short
His time of folly and his time of sport ;   992
　　And ever let his unrecalling crime
　　Have time to wail the abusing of his time.

' O Time ! thou tutor both to good and bad,
Teach me to curse him that thou taught'st this ill ;
At his own shadow let the thief run mad,   997
Himself himself seek every hour to kill :
Such wretched hands such wretched blood should spill ;
　　For who so base would such an office have   1000
　　As slanderous deathsman to so base a slave ?

' The baser is he, coming from a king,
To shame his hope with deeds degenerate :
The mightier man, the mightier is the thing   1004
That makes him honour'd, or begets him hate ;
For greatest scandal waits on greatest state,
　　The moon being clouded presently is miss'd,
　　But little stars may hide them when they list.   1008

' The crow may bathe his coal-black wings in mire,
And unperceiv'd fly with the filth away;
But if the like the snow-white swan desire,
The stain upon his silver down will stay.   1012
Poor grooms are sightless night, kings glorious day :
  Gnats are unnoted wheresoe'er they fly,
  But eagles gaz'd upon with every eye.

' Out, idle words ! servants to shallow fools,   1016
Unprofitable sounds, weak arbitrators !
Busy yourselves in skill-contending schools ;
Debate where leisure serves with dull debaters ;
To trembling clients be you mediators ;   1020
  For me, I force not argument a straw,
  Since that my case is past the help of law.

' In vain I rail at Opportunity,
At Time, at Tarquin, and uncheerful Night ;   1024
In vain I cavil with mine infamy,
In vain I spurn at my confirm'd despite ;
This helpless smoke of words doth me no right.
  The remedy indeed to do me good,   1028
  Is to let forth my foul-defiled blood.

' Poor hand, why quiver'st thou at this decree ?
Honour thyself to rid me of this shame ;
For if I die, my honour lives in thee,   1032
But if I live, thou liv'st in my defame ;
Since thou couldst not defend thy loyal dame,
  And wast afeard to scratch her wicked foe,
  Kill both thyself and her for yielding so.'   1036.

This said, from her be-tumbled couch she starteth,
To find some desperate instrument of death ;
But this no slaughter-house no tool imparteth
To make more vent for passage of her breath ;   1040
Which, thronging through her lips, so vanisheth
  As smoke from Ætna, that in air consumes,
  Or that which from discharged cannon fumes.

'In vain,' quoth she, 'I live, and seek in vain   1044
Some happy mean to end a hapless life.
I fear'd by Tarquin's falchion to be slain,
Yet for the self-same purpose seek a knife :
But when I fear'd I was a loyal wife :   1048
  So am I now : O no ! that cannot be ;
  Of that true type hath Tarquin rifled me.

' O ! that is gone for which I sought to live,
And therefore now I need not fear to die.   1052
To clear this spot by death, at least I give
A badge of fame to slander's livery,
A dying life to living infamy :
  Poor helpless help, the treasure stol'n away,   1056
  To burn the guiltless casket where it lay !

' Well, well, dear Collatine, thou shalt not know
The stained taste of violated troth ;
I will not wrong thy true affection so,   1060
To flatter thee with an infringed oath ;
This bastard graff shall never come to growth ;
  He shall not boast who did thy stock pollute
  That thou art doting father of his fruit.   1064

' Nor shall he smile at thee in secret thought,
Nor laugh with his companions at thy state ;
But thou shalt know thy interest was not bought
Basely with gold, but stol'n from forth thy gate.
For me, I am the mistress of my fate,   1069
  And with my trespass never will dispense,
  Till life to death acquit my forc'd offence.

' I will not poison thee with my attaint,   1072
Nor fold my fault in cleanly-coin'd excuses ;
My sable ground of sin I will not paint,
To hide the truth of this false night's abuses :
My tongue shall utter all ; mine eyes, like sluices,
  As from a mountain-spring that feeds a dale,   1077
  Shall gush pure streams to purge my impure tale.

SH. II   * L l

THE RAPE OF LUCRECE

By this, lamenting Philomel had ended
The well-tun'd warble of her nightly sorrow,   1080
And solemn night with slow sad gait descended
To ugly hell; when, lo! the blushing morrow
Lends light to all fair eyes that light will borrow:
  But cloudy Lucrece shames herself to see,   1084
  And therefore still in night would cloister'd be.

Revealing day through every cranny spies,
And seems to point her out where she sits weeping;
To whom she sobbing speaks: ' O eye of eyes,   1088
Why pry'st thou through my window? leave thy peeping;
Mock with thy tickling beams eyes that are sleeping:
  Brand not my forehead with thy piercing light,
  For day hath nought to do what 's done by night.'

Thus cavils she with everything she sees   1093
True grief is fond and testy as a child,
Who wayward once, his mood with nought agrees:
Old woes, not infant sorrows, bear them mild;
Continuance tames the one; the other wild,   1097
  Like an unpractis'd swimmer plunging still,
  With too much labour drowns for want of skill.

So she, deep-drenched in a sea of care,   1100
Holds disputation with each thing she views,
And to herself all sorrow doth compare;
No object but her passion's strength renews,
And as one shifts, another straight ensues: 1104
  Sometime her grief is dumb and hath no words;
  Sometime 'tis mad and too much talk affords.

The little birds that tune their morning's joy
Make her moans mad with their sweet melody: 1108
For mirth doth search the bottom of annoy;
Sad souls are slain in merry company;
Grief best is pleas'd with grief's society:
  True sorrow then is feelingly suffic'd   1112
  When with like semblance it is sympathiz'd.

184

'Tis double death to drown in ken of shore;
He ten times pines that pines beholding food;   1115
To see the salve doth make the wound ache more;
Great grief grieves most at that would do it good;
Deep woes roll forward like a gentle flood,
  Who, being stopp'd, the bounding banks o'erflows;
  Grief dallied with nor law nor limit knows.   1120

' You mocking birds,' quoth she, ' your tunes entomb
Within your hollow-swelling feather'd breasts,
And in my hearing be you mute and dumb:
My restless discord loves no stops nor rests;   1124
A woeful hostess brooks not merry guests:
  Relish your nimble notes to pleasing ears;
  Distress likes dumps when time is kept with tears.

' Come, Philomel, that sing'st of ravishment,   1128
Make thy sad grove in my dishevell'd hair:
As the dank earth weeps at thy languishment,
So I at each sad strain will strain a tear,
And with deep groans the diapason bear;   1132
  For burthen-wise I'll hum on Tarquin still,
  While thou on Tereus descant'st better skill.

' And whiles against a thorn thou bear'st thy part,
To keep thy sharp woes waking, wretched I,   1136
To imitate thee well, against my heart
Will fix a sharp knife to affright mine eye,
Who, if it wink, shall thereon fall and die.
  These means, as frets upon an instrument,   1140
  Shall tune our heart-strings to true languishment.

' And for, poor bird, thou sing'st not in the day,
As shaming any eye should thee behold,
Some dark deep desert, seated from the way,   1144
That knows not parching heat nor freezing cold,
Will we find out; and there we will unfold
  To creatures stern sad tunes, to change their kinds:
  Since men prove beasts, let beasts bear gentle minds.'

As the poor frighted deer, that stands at gaze, 1149
Wildly determining which way to fly,
Or one encompass'd with a winding maze,
That cannot tread the way out readily ;
So with herself is she in mutiny, 1153
    To live or die which of the twain were better,
    When life is sham'd, and death reproach's debtor.

' To kill myself,' quoth she, ' alack ! what were it
But with my body my poor soul's pollution ? 1157
They that lose half with greater patience bear it
Than they whose whole is swallow'd in confusion.
That mother tries a merciless conclusion, 1160
    Who, having two sweet babes, when death takes one,
    Will slay the other and be nurse to none.

' My body or my soul, which was the dearer,
When the one pure, the other made divine ? 1164
Whose love of either to myself was nearer,
When both were kept for heaven and Collatine ?
Ay me ! the bark peel'd from the lofty pine,
    His leaves will wither and his sap decay ; 1168
    So must my soul, her bark being peel'd away.

' Her house is sack'd, her quiet interrupted,
Her mansion batter'd by the enemy ;
Her sacred temple spotted, spoil'd, corrupted, 1172
Grossly engirt with daring infamy :
Then let it not be call'd impiety,
    If in this blemish'd fort I make some hole
    Through which I may convey this troubled soul.

' Yet die I will not till my Collatine 1177
Have heard the cause of my untimely death ;
That he may vow, in that sad hour of mine,
Revenge on him that made me stop my breath.
My stained blood to Tarquin I'll bequeath, 1181
    Which by him tainted, shall for him be spent,
    And as his due writ in my testament.

' My honour I'll bequeath unto the knife 1184
That wounds my body so dishonoured.
'Tis honour to deprive dishonour'd life ;
The one will live, the other being dead :
So of shame's ashes shall my fame be bred ; 1188
   For in my death I murder shameful scorn :
   My shame so dead, mine honour is new-born.

' Dear lord of that dear jewel I have lost,
What legacy shall I bequeath to thee ? 1192
My resolution, love, shall be thy boast,
By whose example thou reveng'd mayst be.
How Tarquin must be us'd, read it in me :
   Myself, thy friend, will kill myself, thy foe, 1196
   And for my sake serve thou false Tarquin so.

' This brief abridgment of my will I make :
My soul and body to the skies and ground ; 1199
My resolution, husband, do thou take ;
Mine honour be the knife's that makes my wound ;
My shame be his that did my fame confound ;
   And all my fame that lives disbursed be 1203
   To those that live, and think no shame of me.

' Thou, Collatine, shalt oversee this will ;
How was I overseen that thou shalt see it !
My blood shall wash the slander of mine ill ;
My life's foul deed, my life's fair end shall free it. 1208
Faint not, faint heart, but stoutly say ' So be it : '
   Yield to my hand ; my hand shall conquer thee :
   Thou dead, both die, and both shall victors be.'

This plot of death when sadly she had laid, 1212
And wip'd the brinish pearl from her bright eyes,
With untun'd tongue she hoarsely calls her maid,
Whose swift obedience to her mistress hies ;
For fleet-wing'd duty with thought's feathers flies.
   Poor Lucrece' cheeks unto her maid seem so 1217
   As winter meads when sun doth melt their snow.

Her mistress she doth give demure good-morrow,
With soft slow tongue, true mark of modesty,   1220
And sorts a sad look to her lady's sorrow,
For why her face wore sorrow's livery;
But durst not ask of her audaciously
   Why her two suns were cloud-eclipsed so,   1224
   Nor why her fair cheeks over-wash'd with woe.

But as the earth doth weep, the sun being set,
Each flower moisten'd like a melting eye;
Even so the maid with swelling drops 'gan wet   1228
Her circled eyne, enforc'd by sympathy
Of those fair suns set in her mistress' sky,
   Who in a salt-wav'd ocean quench their light,
   Which makes the maid weep like the dewy night.

A pretty while these pretty creatures stand,   1233
Like ivory conduits coral cisterns filling:
One justly weeps, the other takes in hand
No cause, but company, of her drops spilling:
Their gentle sex to weep are often willing,   1237
   Grieving themselves to guess at others' smarts,
   And then they drown their eyes or break their hearts.

For men have marble, women waxen, minds,   1240
And therefore are they form'd as marble will;
The weak oppress'd, the impression of strange kinds
Is form'd in them by force, by fraud, or skill:
Then call them not the authors of their ill,   1244
   No more than wax shall be accounted evil
   Wherein is stamp'd the semblance of a devil.

Their smoothness, like a goodly champaign plain,
Lays open all the little worms that creep;   1248
In men, as in a rough-grown grove, remain
Cave-keeping evils that obscurely sleep:
Through crystal walls each little mote will peep:
   Though men can cover crimes with bold stern looks,
   Poor women's faces are their own faults' books.

No man inveigh against the wither'd flower,
But chide rough winter that the flower hath kill'd :
Not that devour'd, but that which doth devour,   1256
Is worthy blame. O ! let it not be hild
Poor women's faults, that they are so fulfill'd
    With men's abuses : those proud lords, to blame,
    Make weak-made women tenants to their shame.

The precedent whereof in Lucrece view,   1261
Assail'd by night with circumstances strong
Of present death, and shame that might ensue
By that her death, to do her husband wrong :
Such danger to resistance did belong,   1265
    That dying fear through all her body spread ;
    And who cannot abuse a body dead ?

By this, mild patience bid fair Lucrece speak   1268
To the poor counterfeit of her complaining :
' My girl,' quoth she, ' on what occasion break
Those tears from thee, that down thy cheeks are raining ?
If thou dost weep for grief of my sustaining,   1272
    Know, gentle wench, it small avails my mood :
    If tears could help, mine own would do me good.

' But tell me, girl, when went '—and there she stay'd
Till after a deep groan—' Tarquin from hence ? '—
' Madam, ere I was up,' replied the maid,   1277
' The more to blame my sluggard negligence :
Yet with the fault I thus far can dispense ;
    Myself was stirring ere the break of day,   1280
    And, ere I rose, was Tarquin gone away.

' But, lady, if your maid may be so bold,
She would request to know your heaviness.'
' O ! peace,' quoth Lucrece ; ' if it should be told,
The repetition cannot make it less ;   1285
For more it is than I can well express :
    And that deep torture may be call'd a hell,
    When more is felt than one hath power to tell.   1288

' Go, get me hither paper, ink, and pen :
Yet save that labour, for I have them here.
What should I say ?   One of my husband's men
Bid thou be ready, by and by, to bear   1292
A letter to my lord, my love, my dear :
   Bid him with speed prepare to carry it ;
   The cause craves haste, and it will soon be writ.'

Her maid is gone, and she prepares to write,   1296
First hovering o'er the paper with her quill :
Conceit and grief an eager combat fight ;
What wit sets down is blotted straight with will ;
This is too curious-good, this blunt and ill :   1300
   Much like a press of people at a door,
   Throng her inventions, which shall go before.

At last she thus begins : ' Thou worthy lord
Of that unworthy wife that greeteth thee,   1304
Health to thy person ! next vouchsafe t' afford—
If ever, love, thy Lucrece thou wilt see—
Some present speed to come and visit me.
   So I commend me from our house in grief :   1308
   My woes are tedious, though my words are brief.'

Here folds she up the tenour of her woe,
Her certain sorrow writ uncertainly.
By this short schedule Collatine may know   1312
Her grief, but not her grief's true quality :
She dares not thereof make discovery,
   Lest he should hold it her own gross abuse,
   Ere she with blood had stain'd her stain'd excuse.

Besides, the life and feeling of her passion   1317
She hoards, to spend when he is by to hear her ;
When sighs, and groans, and tears may grace the fashion
Of her disgrace, the better so to clear her   1320
From that suspicion which the world might bear her.
   To shun this blot, she would not blot the letter
   With words, till action might become them better.

To see sad sights moves more than hear them told ;
For then the eye interprets to the ear   1325
The heavy motion that it doth behold,
When every part a part of woe doth bear.
'Tis but a part of sorrow that we hear ;   1328
   Deep sounds make lesser noise than shallow fords,
   And sorrow ebbs, being blown with wind of words.

Her letter now is seal'd, and on it writ
' At Ardea to my lord with more than haste '.   1332
The post attends, and she delivers it,
Charging the sour-fac'd groom to hie as fast
As lagging fowls before the northern blast :
   Speed more than speed but dull and slow she deems :
   Extremity still urgeth such extremes.   1337

The homely villein curtsies to her low ;
And, blushing on her, with a steadfast eye
Receives the scroll without or yea or no,   1340
And forth with bashful innocence doth hie.
But they whose guilt within their bosoms lie
   Imagine every eye beholds their blame ;
   For Lucrece thought he blush'd to see her shame :

When, silly groom ! God wot, it was defect   1345
Of spirit, life, and bold audacity.
Such harmless creatures have a true respect
To talk in deeds, while others saucily
Promise more speed, but do it leisurely :   1349
   Even so this pattern of the worn-out age
   Pawn'd honest looks, but laid no words to gage.

His kindled duty kindled her mistrust,   1352
That two red fires in both their faces blaz'd ;
She thought he blush'd, as knowing Tarquin's lust,
And, blushing with him, wistly on him gaz'd ;
Her earnest eye did make him more amaz'd :   1356
   The more she saw the blood his cheeks replenish,
   The more she thought he spied in her some blemish.

But long she thinks till he return again,
And yet the duteous vassal scarce is gone.   1360
The weary time she cannot entertain,
For now 'tis stale to sigh, to weep, and groan:
So woe hath wearied woe, moan tired moan,
  That she her plaints a little while doth stay,   1364
  Pausing for means to mourn some newer way.

At last she calls to mind where hangs a piece
Of skilful painting, made for Priam's Troy;
Before the which is drawn the power of Greece,   1368
For Helen's rape the city to destroy,
Threat'ning cloud-kissing Ilion with annoy;
  Which the conceited painter drew so proud,
  As heaven, it seem'd, to kiss the turrets bow'd.

A thousand lamentable objects there,   1373
In scorn of nature, art gave lifeless life;
Many a dry drop seem'd a weeping tear,
Shed for the slaughter'd husband by the wife: 1376
The red blood reek'd, to show the painter's strife;
  And dying eyes gleam'd forth their ashy lights,
  Like dying coals burnt out in tedious nights.

There might you see the labouring pioner   1380
Begrim'd with sweat, and smeared all with dust;
And from the towers of Troy there would appear
The very eyes of men through loop-holes thrust,
Gazing upon the Greeks with little lust: 1384
  Such sweet observance in this work was had,
  That one might see those far-off eyes look sad.

In great commanders grace and majesty
You might behold, triumphing in their faces;   1388
In youth quick bearing and dexterity;
And here and there the painter interlaces
Pale cowards, marching on with trembling paces;
  Which heartless peasants did so well resemble,
  That one would swear he saw them quake and tremble.

In Ajax and Ulysses, O ! what art
Of physiognomy might one behold ;
The face of either cipher'd either's heart ;   1396
Their face their manners most expressly told :
In Ajax' eyes blunt rage and rigour roll'd ;
   But the mild glance that sly Ulysses lent
   Show'd deep regard and smiling government.   1400

There pleading might you see grave Nestor stand,
As 'twere encouraging the Greeks to fight ;
Making such sober action with his hand,
That it beguil'd attention, charm'd the sight :   1404
In speech, it seem'd, his beard, all silver white,
   Wagg'd up and down, and from his lips did fly
   Thin winding breath, which purl'd up to the sky.

About him were a press of gaping faces,   1408
Which seem'd to swallow up his sound advice ;
All jointly listening, but with several graces,
As if some mermaid did their ears entice,
Some high, some low, the painter was so nice ;   1412
   The scalps of many, almost hid behind,
   To jump up higher seem'd, to mock the mind.

Here one man's hand lean'd on another's head,   1415
His nose being shadow'd by his neighbour's ear ;
Here one being throng'd bears back, all boll'n and red ;
Another smother'd, seems to pelt and swear ;
And in their rage such signs of rage they bear,
   As, but for loss of Nestor's golden words,   1420
   It seem'd they would debate with angry swords.

For much imaginary work was there ;
Conceit deceitful, so compact, so kind,
That for Achilles' image stood his spear,   1424
Grip'd in an armed hand ; himself behind
Was left unseen, save to the eye of mind :
   A hand, a foot, a face, a leg, a head,
   Stood for the whole to be imagined.   1428

And from the walls of strong-besieged Troy,
When their brave hope, bold Hector, march'd to field,
Stood many Trojan mothers, sharing joy
To see their youthful sons bright weapons wield ;   1432
And to their hope they such odd action yield,
  That through their light joy seemed to appear,—
  Like bright things stain'd—a kind of heavy fear.

And from the strand of Dardan, where they fought,
To Simois' reedy banks the red blood ran,   1437
Whose waves to imitate the battle sought
With swelling ridges ; and their ranks began
To break upon the galled shore, and than   1440
  Retire again, till meeting greater ranks
  They join, and shoot their foam at Simois' banks.

To this well-painted piece is Lucrece come,
To find a face where all distress is stell'd.   1444
Many she sees where cares have carved some,
But none where all distress and dolour dwell'd,
Till she despairing Hecuba beheld,   1447
  Staring on Priam's wounds with her old eyes,
  Which bleeding under Pyrrhus' proud foot lies.

In her the painter had anatomiz'd
Time's ruin, beauty's wrack, and grim care's reign :
Her cheeks with chaps and wrinkles were disguis'd ;
Of what she was no semblance did remain :   1453
Her blue blood chang'd to black in every vein,
  Wanting the spring that those shrunk pipes had fed,
  Show'd life imprison'd in a body dead.   1456

On this sad shadow Lucrece spends her eyes,
And shapes her sorrow to the beldam's woes,
Who nothing wants to answer her but cries,
And bitter words to ban her cruel foes :   1460
The painter was no god to lend her those ;
  And therefore Lucrece swears he did her wrong,
  To give her so much grief and not a tongue.

'Poor instrument,' quoth she, 'without a sound,   1464
I'll tune thy woes with my lamenting tongue;
And drop sweet balm in Priam's painted wound,
And rail on Pyrrhus that hath done him wrong;
And with my tears quench Troy that burns so long;
   And with my knife scratch out the angry eyes
   Of all the Greeks that are thine enemies.

'Show me the strumpet that began this stir,
That with my nails her beauty I may tear.   1472
Thy heat of lust, fond Paris, did incur
This load of wrath that burning Troy doth bear:
Thy eye kindled the fire that burneth here;
   And here in Troy, for trespass of thine eye,   1476
   The sire, the son, the dame, and daughter die.

'Why should the private pleasure of some one
Become the public plague of many moe?
Let sin, alone committed, light alone
Upon his head that hath transgressed so;   1581
Let guiltless souls be freed from guilty woe;
   For one's offence why should so many fall,
   To plague a private sin in general?   1484

'Lo! here weeps Hecuba, here Priam dies,
Here manly Hector faints, here Troilus swounds,
Here friend by friend in bloody channel lies,
And friend to friend gives unadvised wounds,   1488
And one man's lust these many lives confounds:
   Had doting Priam check'd his son's desire,
   Troy had been bright with fame and not with fire.'

Here feelingly she weeps Troy's painted woes;   1492
For sorrow, like a heavy-hanging bell,
Once set on ringing, with his own weight goes;
Then little strength rings out the doleful knell:
So Lucrece, set a-work, sad tales doth tell   1496
   To pencil'd pensiveness and colour'd sorrow;
   She lends them words, and she their looks doth borrow.

She throws her eyes about the painting round,
And whom she finds forlorn she doth lament :   1500
At last she sees a wretched image bound,
That piteous looks to Phrygian shepherds lent ;
His face, though full of cares, yet show'd content ;
  Onward to Troy with the blunt swains he goes,   1504
  So mild, that Patience seem'd to scorn his woes.

In him the painter labour'd with his skill
To hide deceit, and give the harmless show
An humble gait, calm looks, eyes wailing still,   1508
A brow unbent that seem'd to welcome woe ;
Cheeks neither red nor pale, but mingled so
  That blushing red no guilty instance gave,
  Nor ashy pale the fear that false hearts have.   1512

But, like a constant and confirmed devil,
He entertain'd a show so seeming-just,
And therein so ensconc'd his secret evil,
That jealousy itself could not mistrust   1516
False-creeping craft and perjury should thrust
  Into so bright a day such black-fac'd storms,
  Or blot with hell-born sin such saint-like forms.

The well-skill'd workman this mild image drew   1520
For perjur'd Sinon, whose enchanting story
The credulous old Priam after slew ;
Whose words like wildfire burnt the shining glory
Of rich-built Ilion, that the skies were sorry,   1524
  And little stars shot from their fixed places,
  When their glass fell wherein they view'd their faces.

This picture she advisedly perus'd,
And chid the painter for his wondrous skill,   1528
Saying, some shape in Sinon's was abus'd ;
So fair a form lodg'd not a mind so ill :
And still on him she gaz'd, and gazing still,
  Such signs of truth in his plain face she spied,   1532
  That she concludes the picture was belied.

'It cannot be,' quoth she, 'that so much guile '—
She would have said—'can lurk in such a look ; '
But Tarquin's shape came in her mind the while,
And from her tongue 'can lurk ' from 'cannot ' took :
'It cannot be,' she in that sense forsook,
   And turn'd it thus, 'It cannot be, I find,
   But such a face should bear a wicked mind :   1540

'For even as subtle Sinon here is painted,
So sober-sad, so weary, and so mild,
As if with grief or travail he had fainted,
To me came Tarquin armed ; so beguil'd   1544
With outward honesty, but yet defil'd
   With inward vice ; as Priam him did cherish,
   So did I Tarquin ; so my Troy did perish.

'Look, look, how listening Priam wets his eyes,   1548
To see those borrow'd tears that Sinon sheds !
Priam, why art thou old and yet not wise ?
For every tear he falls a Trojan bleeds :
His eye drops fire, no water thence proceeds ;   1552
   Those round clear pearls of his, that move thy pity,
   Are balls of quenchless fire to burn thy city.

'Such devils steal effects from lightless hell ;   1555
For Sinon in his fire doth quake with cold,
And in that cold hot-burning fire doth dwell ;
These contraries such unity do hold,
Only to flatter fools and make them bold :   1559
   So Priam's trust false Sinon's tears doth flatter,
   That he finds means to burn his Troy with water.'

Here, all enrag'd, such passion her assails,
That patience is quite beaten from her breast.
She tears the senseless Sinon with her nails,   1564
Comparing him to that unhappy guest
Whose deed hath made herself herself detest :
   At last she smilingly with this gives o'er ;
   'Fool, fool !' quoth she, 'his wounds will not be sore.'

Thus ebbs and flows the current of her sorrow,   1569
And time doth weary time with her complaining.
She looks for night, and then she longs for morrow,
And both she thinks too long with her remaining :
Short time seems long in sorrow's sharp sustaining :
    Though woe be heavy, yet it seldom sleeps ;
    And they that watch see time how slow it creeps.

While all this time hath overslipp'd her thought,
That she with painted images hath spent ;   1577
Being from the feeling of her own grief brought
By deep surmise of others' detriment ;
Losing her woes in shows of discontent.
    It easeth some, though none it ever cur'd,   1581
    To think their dolour others have endur'd.

But now the mindful messenger, come back,
Brings home his lord and other company ;   1584
Who finds his Lucrece clad in mourning black ;
And round about her tear-distained eye
Blue circles stream'd, like rainbows in the sky :
    These water-galls in her dim element   1588
    Foretell new storms to those already spent.

Which when her sad-beholding husband saw,
Amazedly in her sad face he stares :
Her eyes, though sod in tears, look'd red and raw,
Her lively colour kill'd with deadly cares.   1593
He hath no power to ask her how she fares :
    Both stood like old acquaintance in a trance,
    Met far from home, wondering each other's chance.

At last he takes her by the bloodless hand,   1597
And thus begins : ' What uncouth ill event
Hath thee befall'n, that thou dost trembling stand ?
Sweet love, what spite hath thy fair colour spent ?
Why art thou thus attir'd in discontent ?   1601
    Unmask, dear dear, this moody heaviness,
    And tell thy grief, that we may give redress.'

Three times with sighs she gives her sorrow fire,   1604
Ere once she can discharge one word of woe :
At length address'd to answer his desire,
She modestly prepares to let them know
Her honour is ta'en prisoner by the foe ;   1608
   While Collatine and his consorted lords
   With sad attention long to hear her words.

And now this pale swan in her watery nest
Begins the sad dirge of her certain ending.   1612
' Few words,' quoth she, ' shall fit the trespass best,
Where no excuse can give the fault amending ;
In me moe woe than words are now depending ;
   And my laments would be drawn out too long,   1616
   To tell them all with one poor tired tongue.

' Then be this all the task it hath to say :
Dear husband, in the interest of thy bed
A stranger came, and on that pillow lay   1620
Where thou wast wont to rest thy weary head ;
And what wrong else may be imagined
   By foul enforcement might be done to me,
   From that, alas ! thy Lucrece is not free.   1624

' For in the dreadful dead of dark midnight,
With shining falchion in my chamber came
A creeping creature with a flaming light,
And softly cried, "Awake, thou Roman dame,   1628
And entertain my love ; else lasting shame
   On thee and thine this night I will inflict,
   If thou my love's desire do contradict.

' " For some hard-favour'd groom of thine," quoth he,
" Unless thou yoke thy liking to my will,   1633
I'll murder straight, and then I'll slaughter thee,
And swear I found you where you did fulfil
The loathsome act of lust, and so did kill   1636
   The lechers in their deed ; this act will be
   My fame, and thy perpetual infamy."

' With this I did begin to start and cry,
And then against my heart he set his sword,   1640
Swearing, unless I took all patiently,
I should not live to speak another word ;
So should my shame still rest upon record,
    And never be forgot in mighty Rome   1644
    Th' adulterate death of Lucrece and her groom.

' Mine enemy was strong, my poor self weak,
And far the weaker with so strong a fear :
My bloody judge forbade my tongue to speak ;   1648
No rightful plea might plead for justice there :
His scarlet lust came evidence to swear
    That my poor beauty had purloin'd his eyes ;
    And when the judge is robb'd the prisoner dies.

' O ! teach me how to make mine own excuse,   1653
Or, at the least, this refuge let me find ;
Though my gross blood be stain'd with this abuse,
Immaculate and spotless is my mind ;
That was not forc'd ; that never was inclin'd   1657
    To accessary yieldings, but still pure
    Doth in her poison'd closet yet endure.'

Lo ! here the helpless merchant of this loss,   1660
With head declin'd, and voice damm'd up with woe
With sad set eyes, and wretched arms across,
From lips new-waxen pale begins to blow
The grief away that stops his answer so :   1664
    But, wretched as he is, he strives in vain ;
    What he breathes out his breath drinks up again.

As through an arch the violent roaring tide
Outruns the eye that doth behold his haste,   1668
Yet in the eddy boundeth in his pride
Back to the strait that forc'd him on so fast ;
In rage sent out, recall'd in rage, being past :
    Even so his sighs, his sorrows, make a saw,   1672
    To push grief on, and back the same grief draw.

Which speechless woe of his poor she attendeth,
And his untimely frenzy thus awaketh :
' Dear lord, thy sorrow to my sorrow lendeth   1676
Another power ; no flood by raining slaketh.
My woe too sensible thy passion maketh
    More feeling-painful : let it then suffice
      To drown one woe, one pair of weeping eyes.   1680

' And for my sake, when I might charm thee so,
For she that was thy Lucrece, now attend me :
Be suddenly revenged on my foe,   1683
Thine, mine, his own : suppose thou dost defend me
From what is past : the help that thou shalt lend me
    Comes all too late, yet let the traitor die ;
      For sparing justice feeds iniquity.   1687

' But ere I name him, you fair lords,' quoth she,—
Speaking to those that came with Collatine,—
' Shall plight your honourable faiths to me,
With swift pursuit to venge this wrong of mine ;
For 'tis a meritorious fair design   1692
    To chase injustice with revengeful arms :
      Knights, by their oaths, should right poor ladies' harms.

At this request, with noble disposition
Each present lord began to promise aid,   1696
As bound in knighthood to her imposition,
Longing to hear the hateful foe bewray'd.
But she, that yet her sad task hath not said,   1699
    The protestation stops. ' O ! speak,' quoth she,
      ' How may this forced stain be wip'd from me ?

' What is the quality of mine offence,
Being constrain'd with dreadful circumstance ?
May my pure mind with the foul act dispense,   1704
My low-declined honour to advance ?
May any terms acquit me from this chance ?
    The poison'd fountain clears itself again ;
      And why not I from this compelled stain ? '   1708

With this, they all at once began to say,
Her body's stain her mind untainted clears ;
While with a joyless smile she turns away
The face, that map which deep impression bears   1712
Of hard misfortune, carv'd in it with tears.
   ' No, no,' quoth she, ' no dame, hereafter living,
   By my excuse shall claim excuse's giving.'

Here with a sigh, as if her heart would break,   1716
She throws forth Tarquin's name, ' He, he,' she says,
But more than ' he ' her poor tongue could not speak ;
Till after many accents and delays,
Untimely breathings, sick and short assays,   1720
   She utters this, ' He, he, fair lords, 'tis he,
   That guides this hand to give this wound to me.'

Even here she sheathed in her harmless breast
A harmful knife, that thence her soul unsheath'd :
That blow did bail it from the deep unrest   1725
Of that polluted prison where it breath'd ;
Her contrite sighs unto the clouds bequeath'd
   Her winged sprite, and through her wounds doth fly
   Life's lasting date from cancell'd destiny.   1729

Stone-still, astonish'd with this deadly deed,
Stood Collatine and all his lordly crew ;
Till Lucrece' father, that beholds her bleed,   1732
Himself on her self-slaughter'd body threw ;
And from the purple fountain Brutus drew
   The murderous knife, and as it left the place,
   Her blood, in poor revenge, held it in chase ;   1736

And bubbling from her breast, it doth divide
In two slow rivers, that the crimson blood
Circles her body in on every side,
Who, like a late-sack'd island, vastly stood,   1740
Bare and unpeopled in this fearful flood.
   Some of her blood still pure and red remain'd,
   And some look'd black, and that false Tarquin stain'd.

About the mourning and congealed face 1744
Of that black blood a watery rigol goes,
Which seems to weep upon the tainted place :
And ever since, as pitying Lucrece' woes,
Corrupted blood some watery token shows ; 1748
    And blood untainted still doth red abide,
    Blushing at that which is so putrified.

' Daughter, dear daughter ! ' old Lucretius cries,
' That life was mine which thou hast here depriv'd.
If in the child the father's image lies, 1753
Where shall I live now Lucrece is unliv'd ?
Thou wast not to this end from me deriv'd.
    If children pre-decease progenitors, 1756
    We are their offspring, and they none of ours.

' Poor broken glass, I often did behold
In thy sweet semblance my old age new born ;
But now that fair fresh mirror, dim and old, 1760
Shows me a bare-bon'd death by time outworn :
O ! from thy cheeks my image thou hast torn,
    And shiver'd all the beauty of my glass,
    That I no more can see what once I was. 1764

' O Time ! cease thou thy course and last no longer,
If they surcease to be that should survive.
Shall rotten death make conquest of the stronger,
And leave the faltering feeble souls alive ? 1768
The old bees die, the young possess their hive :
    Then live, sweet Lucrece, live again and see
    Thy father die, and not thy father thee ! '

By this, starts Collatine as from a dream, 1772
And bids Lucretius give his sorrow place ;
And then in key-cold Lucrece' bleeding stream
He falls, and bathes the pale fear in his face,
And counterfeits to die with her a space ; 1776
    Till manly shame bids him possess his breath
    And live to be revenged on her death.

The deep vexation of his inward soul
Hath serv'd a dumb arrest upon his tongue ;   1780
Who, mad that sorrow should his use control,
Or keep him from heart-easing words so long,
Begins to talk ; but through his lips do throng
  Weak words, so thick come in his poor heart's aid,
  That no man could distinguish what he said.   1785

Yet sometime ' Tarquin ' was pronounced plain,
But through his teeth, as if the name he tore.
This windy tempest, till it blow up rain,   1788
Held back his sorrow's tide, to make it more ;
At last it rains, and busy winds give o'er :
  Then son and father weep with equal strife
  Who should weep most, for daughter or for wife.

The one doth call her his, the other his,   1793
Yet neither may possess the claim they lay.
The father says, ' She 's mine.' ' O ! mine she is,'
Replies her husband ; ' do not take away
My sorrow's interest ; let no mourner say   1797
  He weeps for her, for she was only mine,
  And only must be wail'd by Collatine.'

' O ! ' quoth Lucretius, ' I did give that life   1800
Which she too early and too late hath spill'd.'
' Woe, woe,' quoth Collatine, ' she was my wife,
I ow'd her, and 'tis mine that she hath kill'd.'
' My daughter ' and ' my wife ' with clamours fill'd
  The dispers'd air, who, holding Lucrece' life,   1805
  Answer'd their cries, ' my daughter ' and ' my wife '.

Brutus, who pluck'd the knife from Lucrece' side,
Seeing such emulation in their woe,   1808
Began to clothe his wit in state and pride,
Burying in Lucrece' wound his folly's show.
He with the Romans was esteemed so
  As silly-jeering idiots are with kings,   1812
  For sportive words and uttering foolish things :

But now he throws that shallow habit by,
Wherein deep policy did him disguise ;
And arm'd his long-hid wits advisedly,   1816
To check the tears in Collatinus' eyes.
' Thou wronged lord of Rome,' quoth he, ' arise :
    Let my unsounded self, suppos'd a fool,
    Now set thy long-experienc'd wit to school.   1820

' Why, Collatine, is woe the cure for woe ?
Do wounds help wounds, or grief help grievous deeds ?
Is it revenge to give thyself a blow
For his foul act by whom thy fair wife bleeds ?   1824
Such childish humour from weak minds proceeds :
    Thy wretched wife mistook the matter so,
    To slay herself, that should have slain her foe.

' Courageous Roman, do not steep thy heart   1828
In such relenting dew of lamentations ;
But kneel with me and help to bear thy part,
To rouse our Roman gods with invocations,
That they will suffer these abominations,   1832
    Since Rome herself in them doth stand disgrac'd,
    By our strong arms from forth her fair streets chas'd.

' Now, by the Capitol that we adore,
And by this chaste blood so unjustly stain'd,   1836
By heaven's fair sun that breeds the fat earth's store,
By all our country rights in Rome maintain'd,
And by chaste Lucrece' soul that late complain'd
    Her wrongs to us, and by this bloody knife,   1840
    We will revenge the death of this true wife.'

This said, he struck his hand upon his breast,
And kiss'd the fatal knife to end his vow ;
And to his protestation urg'd the rest,   1844
Who, wondering at him, did his words allow :
Then jointly to the ground their knees they bow ;
    And that deep vow, which Brutus made before,
    He doth again repeat, and that they swore.   1848

When they had sworn to this advised doom,
They did conclude to bear dead Lucrece thence ;
To show her bleeding body thorough Rome,
And so to publish Tarquin's foul offence :   1852
Which being done with speedy diligence,
   The Romans plausibly did give consent
   To Tarquin's everlasting banishment.

Sonnets

SONNETS

I

From fairest creatures we desire increase,
That thereby beauty's rose might never die,
But as the riper should by time decease,
His tender heir might bear his memory :
But thou, contracted to thine own bright eyes,
Feed'st thy light's flame with self-substantial fuel,   6
Making a famine where abundance lies,
Thyself thy foe, to thy sweet self too cruel.
Thou that art now the world's fresh ornament
And only herald to the gaudy spring,
Within thine own bud buriest thy content
And, tender churl, mak'st waste in niggarding.   12
   Pity the world, or else this glutton be,
    To eat the world's due, by the grave and thee.

209

II

When forty winters shall besiege thy brow,
And dig deep trenches in thy beauty's field,
Thy youth's proud livery, so gaz'd on now,
Will be a tatter'd weed, of small worth held:
Then being ask'd where all thy beauty lies,
Where all the treasure of thy lusty days, 6
To say, within thine own deep-sunken eyes,
Were an all-eating shame and thriftless praise.
How much more praise deserv'd thy beauty's use,
If thou couldst answer ' This fair child of mine
Shall sum my count, and make my old excuse,'
Proving his beauty by succession thine ! 12
    This were to be new made when thou art old,
    And see thy blood warm when thou feel'st it cold.

III

Look in thy glass, and tell the face thou viewest
Now is the time that face should form another;
Whose fresh repair if now thou not renewest,
Thou dost beguile the world, unbless some mother.
For where is she so fair whose unear'd womb
Disdains the tillage of thy husbandry ? 6
Or who is he so fond will be the tomb
Of his self-love, to stop posterity ?
Thou art thy mother's glass, and she in thee
Calls back the lovely April of her prime ;
So thou through windows of thine age shalt see,
Despite of wrinkles, this thy golden time. 12
    But if thou live, remember'd not to be,
    Die single, and thine image dies with thee.

IV

Unthrifty loveliness, why dost thou spend
Upon thyself thy beauty's legacy ?
Nature's bequest gives nothing, but doth lend,
And being frank, she lends to those are free:
Then, beauteous niggard, why dost thou abuse
The bounteous largess given thee to give ? 6

Profitless usurer, why dost thou use
So great a sum of sums, yet canst not live ?
For having traffic with thyself alone,
Thou of thyself thy sweet self dost deceive :
Then how, when Nature calls thee to be gone,
What acceptable audit canst thou leave ?   12
   Thy unus'd beauty must be tomb'd with thee,
   Which, used, lives th' executor to be.

V

Those hours, that with gentle work did frame
The lovely gaze where every eye doth dwell,
Will play the tyrants to the very same
And that unfair which fairly doth excel ;
For never-resting time leads summer on
To hideous winter, and confounds him there ;   6
Sap check'd with frost, and lusty leaves quite gone,
Beauty o'ersnow'd and bareness every where :
Then, were not summer's distillation left,
A liquid prisoner pent in walls of glass,
Beauty's effect with beauty were bereft,
Nor it, nor no remembrance what it was :   12
   But flowers distill'd, though they with winter meet,
   Leese but their show ; their substance still lives sweet.

VI

Then let not winter's ragged hand deface
In thee thy summer, ere thou be distill'd :
Make sweet some vial ; treasure thou some place
With beauty's treasure, ere it be self-kill'd.
That use is not forbidden usury,
Which happies those that pay the willing loan ;   6
That 's for thyself to breed another thee,
Or ten times happier, be it ten for one ;
Ten times thyself were happier than thou art,
If ten of thine ten times refigur'd thee ;
Then what could death do, if thou shouldst depart,
Leaving thee living in posterity ?   12
   Be not self-will'd, for thou art much too fair
   To be death's conquest and make worms thine heir.

SONNETS

VII

Lo ! in the orient when the gracious light
Lifts up his burning head, each under eye
Doth homage to his new-appearing sight,
Serving with looks his sacred majesty ;
And having climb'd the steep-up heavenly hill,
Resembling strong youth in his middle age,   6
Yet mortal looks adore his beauty still,
Attending on his golden pilgrimage ;
But when from highmost pitch, with weary car,
Like feeble age, he reeleth from the day,
The eyes, 'fore duteous, now converted are
From his low tract, and look another way :   12
  So thou, thyself outgoing in thy noon,
  Unlook'd on diest, unless thou get a son.

VIII

Music to hear, why hear'st thou music sadly ?
Sweets with sweets war not, joy delights in joy :
Why lov'st thou that which thou receiv'st not gladly,
Or else receiv'st with pleasure thine annoy ?
If the true concord of well-tuned sounds,
By unions married, do offend thine ear,   6
They do but sweetly chide thee, who confounds
In singleness the parts that thou shouldst bear.
Mark how one string, sweet husband to another,
Strikes each in each by mutual ordering ;
Resembling sire and child and happy mother,
Who, all in one, one pleasing note do sing :   12
  Whose speechless song, being many, seeming one,
  Sings this to thee : ' Thou single wilt prove none.'

IX

Is it for fear to wet a widow's eye
That thou consum'st thyself in single life ?
Ah ! if thou issueless shalt hap to die,
The world will wail thee, like a makeless wife ;
The world will be thy widow, and still weep
That thou no form of thee hast left behind,   6

When every private widow well may keep
By children's eyes her husband's shape in mind.
Look ! what an unthrift in the world doth spend
Shifts but his place, for still the world enjoys it ;
But beauty's waste hath in the world an end,
And kept unus'd, the user so destroys it.　　　　12
　　No love toward others in that bosom sits
　　That on himself such murderous shame commits.

X

For shame ! deny that thou bear'st love to any,
Who for thyself art so unprovident.
Grant, if thou wilt, thou art belov'd of many,
But that thou none lov'st is most evident ;
For thou art so possess'd with murderous hate
That 'gainst thyself thou stick'st not to conspire,　　6
Seeking that beauteous roof to ruinate
Which to repair should be thy chief desire.
O ! change thy thought, that I may change my mind :
Shall hate be fairer lodg'd than gentle love ?
Be, as thy presence is, gracious and kind,
Or to thyself at least kind-hearted prove :　　　　12
　　Make thee another self, for love of me,
　　That beauty still may live in thine or thee.

XI

As fast as thou shalt wane, so fast thou grow'st
In one of thine, from that which thou departest ;
And that fresh blood which youngly thou bestow'st
Thou mayst call thine when thou from youth convertest
Herein lives wisdom, beauty and increase ;
Without this, folly, age and cold decay :　　　　6
If all were minded so, the times should cease
And threescore year would make the world away.
Let those whom Nature hath not made for store,
Harsh, featureless, and rude, barrenly perish :
Look, whom she best endow'd she gave the more ;
Which bounteous gift thou shouldst in bounty cherish :
　　She carv'd thee for her seal, and meant thereby　13
　　Thou shouldst print more, not let that copy die.

XII

When I do count the clock that tells the time,
And see the brave day sunk in hideous night;
When I behold the violet past prime,
And sable curls, all silver'd o'er with white;
When lofty trees I see barren of leaves,
Which erst from heat did canopy the herd,   6
And summer's green all girded up in sheaves,
Borne on the bier with white and bristly beard,
Then of thy beauty do I question make,
That thou among the wastes of time must go,
Since sweets and beauties do themselves forsake
And die as fast as they see others grow;   12
   And nothing 'gainst Time's scythe can make defence
   Save breed, to brave him when he takes thee hence.

XIII

O! that you were yourself; but, love, you are
No longer yours than you yourself here live:
Against this coming end you should prepare,
And your sweet semblance to some other give:
So should that beauty which you hold in lease
Find no determination; then you were   6
Yourself again, after yourself's decease,
When your sweet issue your sweet form should bear.
Who lets so fair a house fall to decay,
Which husbandry in honour might uphold
Against the stormy gusts of winter's day
And barren rage of death's eternal cold?   12
   O! none but unthrifts. Dear my love, you know
   You had a father: let your son say so.

XIV

Not from the stars do I my judgment pluck;
And yet methinks I have astronomy,
But not to tell of good or evil luck,
Of plagues, of dearths, or seasons' quality;
Nor can I fortune to brief minutes tell,
Pointing to each his thunder, rain, and wind,   6

Or say with princes if it shall go well,
By oft predict that I in heaven find :
But from thine eyes my knowledge I derive,
And, constant stars, in them I read such art
As ' Truth and beauty shall together thrive,
If from thyself to store thou wouldst convert'; 12
 Or else of thee this I prognosticate :
 ' Thy end is truth's and beauty's doom and date.'

XV

When I consider every thing that grows
Holds in perfection but a little moment,
That this huge stage presenteth nought but shows
Whereon the stars in secret influence comment ;
When I perceive that men as plants increase,
Cheered and check'd even by the self-same sky, 6
Vaunt in their youthful sap, at height decrease,
And wear their brave state out of memory ;
Then the conceit of this inconstant stay
Sets you most rich in youth before my sight,
Where wasteful Time debateth with Decay,
To change your day of youth to sullied night ; 12
 And, all in war with Time for love of you,
 As he takes from you, I engraft you new.

XVI

But wherefore do not you a mightier way
Make war upon this bloody tyrant, Time ?
And fortify yourself in your decay
With means more blessed than my barren rime ?
Now stand you on the top of happy hours,
And many maiden gardens, yet unset, 6
With virtuous wish would bear you living flowers,
Much liker than your painted counterfeit :
So should the lines of life that life repair,
Which this, Time's pencil, or my pupil pen,
Neither in inward worth nor outward fair,
Can make you live yourself in eyes of men. 12
 To give away yourself keeps yourself still ;
 And you must live, drawn by your own sweet skill.

XVII

Who will believe my verse in time to come,
If it were fill'd with your most high deserts?
Though yet, heaven knows, it is but as a tomb
Which hides your life and shows not half your parts.
If I could write the beauty of your eyes
And in fresh numbers number all your graces,   6
The age to come would say 'This poet lies;
Such heavenly touches ne'er touch'd earthly faces.'
So should my papers, yellow'd with their age,
Be scorn'd, like old men of less truth than tongue,
And your true rights be term'd a poet's rage
And stretched metre of an antique song: 12
   But were some child of yours alive that time,
   You should live twice,—in it and in my rime.

XVIII

Shall I compare thee to a summer's day?
Thou art more lovely and more temperate:
Rough winds do shake the darling buds of May,
And summer's lease hath all too short a date:
Sometime too hot the eye of heaven shines,
And often is his gold complexion dimm'd;   6
And every fair from fair sometime declines,
By chance, or nature's changing course untrimm'd;
But thy eternal summer shall not fade,
Nor lose possession of that fair thou ow'st,
Nor shall death brag thou wander'st in his shade,
When in eternal lines to time thou grow'st: 12
   So long as men can breathe, or eyes can see,
   So long lives this, and this gives life to thee.

XIX

Devouring Time, blunt thou the lion's paws,
And make the earth devour her own sweet brood;
Pluck the keen teeth from the fierce tiger's jaws,
And burn the long-liv'd phœnix in her blood;
Make glad and sorry seasons as thou fleets,
And do whate'er thou wilt, swift-footed Time,   6

SONNETS

To the wide world and all her fading sweets;
But I forbid thee one most heinous crime:
O! carve not with thy hours my love's fair brow,
Nor draw no lines there with thine antique pen;
Him in thy course untainted do allow
For beauty's pattern to succeeding men.   12
   Yet, do thy worst, old Time: despite thy wrong,
   My love shall in my verse ever live young.

XX

A woman's face with Nature's own hand painted
Hast thou, the master-mistress of my passion;
A woman's gentle heart, but not acquainted
With shifting change, as is false women's fashion;
An eye more bright than theirs, less false in rolling,
Gilding the object whereupon it gazeth;   6
A man in hue all ' hues ' in his controlling,
Which steals men's eyes and women's souls amazeth.
And for a woman wert thou first created;
Till Nature, as she wrought thee, fell a-doting,
And by addition me of thee defeated,
By adding one thing to my purpose nothing.   12
   But since she prick'd thee out for women's pleasure,
   Mine be thy love, and thy love's use their treasure.

XXI

So is it not with me as with that Muse
Stirr'd by a painted beauty to his verse,
Who heaven itself for ornament doth use
And every fair with his fair doth rehearse,
Making a couplement of proud compare,   5
With sun and moon, with earth and sea's rich gems,
With April's first-born flowers, and all things rare
That heaven's air in this huge rondure hems.
O! let me, true in love, but truly write,
And then believe me, my love is as fair
As any mother's child, though not so bright
As those gold candles fix'd in heaven's air: 12
   Let them say more that like of hear-say well;
   I will not praise that purpose not to sell.

XXII

My glass shall not persuade me I am old,
So long as youth and thou are of one date ;
But when in thee time's furrows I behold,
Then look I death my days should expiate.
For all that beauty that doth cover thee
Is but the seemly raiment of my heart,   6
Which in thy breast doth live, as thine in me :
How can I then be elder than thou art ?
O ! therefore, love, be of thyself so wary
As I, not for myself, but for thee will ;
Bearing thy heart, which I will keep so chary
As tender nurse her babe from faring ill.   12
   Presume not on thy heart when mine is slain ;
   Thou gav'st me thine, not to give back again.

XXIII

As an unperfect actor on the stage,
Who with his fear is put besides his part,
Or some fierce thing replete with too much rage,
Whose strength's abundance weakens his own heart ;
So I, for fear of trust, forget to say
The perfect ceremony of love's rite,   6
And in mine own love's strength seem to decay,
O'ercharg'd with burthen of mine own love's might.
O ! let my books be then the eloquence
And dumb presagers of my speaking breast,
Who plead for love, and look for recompense,
More than that tongue that more hath more express'd.
   O ! learn to read what silent love hath writ :   13
   To hear with eyes belongs to love's fine wit.

XXIV

Mine eye hath play'd the painter and hath stell'd
Thy beauty's form in table of my heart ;
My body is the frame wherein 'tis held,
And perspective it is best painter's art.
For through the painter must you see his skill,
To find where your true image pictur'd lies,   6

Which in my bosom's shop is hanging still,
That hath his windows glazed with thine eyes.
Now see what good turns eyes for eyes have done:
Mine eyes have drawn thy shape, and thine for me
Are windows to my breast, where-through the sun
Delights to peep, to gaze therein on thee ;   12
   Yet eyes this cunning want to grace their art,
   They draw but what they see, know not the heart.

XXV

Let those who are in favour with their stars
Of public honour and proud titles boast,
Whilst I, whom fortune of such triumph bars
Unlook'd for joy in that I honour most.
Great princes' favourites their fair leaves spread
But as the marigold at the sun's eye,   6
And in themselves their pride lies buried,
For at a frown they in their glory die.
The painful warrior famoused for fight,
After a thousand victories once foil'd,
Is from the book of honour razed quite,
And all the rest forgot for which he toil'd: 12
   Then happy I, that love and am belov'd,
   Where I may not remove nor be remov'd.

XXVI

Lord of my love, to whom in vassalage
Thy merit hath my duty strongly knit,
To thee I send this written ambassage,
To witness duty, not to show my wit:
Duty so great, which wit so poor as mine   5
May make seem bare, in wanting words to show it,
But that I hope some good conceit of thine
In thy soul's thought, all naked, will bestow it ;
Till whatsoever star that guides my moving,
Points on me graciously with fair aspect,
And puts apparel on my tatter'd loving,
To show me worthy of thy sweet respect :   12
   Then may I dare to boast how I do love thee ;
   Till then not show my head where thou mayst prove
     me.

XXVII

Weary with toil, I haste me to my bed,
The dear repose for limbs with travel tir'd;
But then begins a journey in my head
To work my mind, when body's work 's expir'd:
For then my thoughts—from far where I abide—
Intend a zealous pilgrimage to thee,   6
And keep my drooping eyelids open wide,
Looking on darkness which the blind do see:
Save that my soul's imaginary sight
Presents thy shadow to my sightless view,
Which, like a jewel hung in ghastly night,   11
Makes black night beauteous and her old face new.
  Lo ! thus, by day my limbs, by night my mind,
  For thee, and for myself no quiet find.

XXVIII

How can I then return in happy plight,
That am debarr'd the benefit of rest ?
When day's oppression is not eas'd by night,
But day by night and night by day oppress'd,
And each, though enemies to either's reign,
Do in consent shake hands to torture me,   6
The one by toil, the other to complain
How far I toil, still farther off from thee.
I tell the day, to please him thou art bright,
And dost him grace when clouds do blot the heaven:
So flatter I the swart-complexion'd night;   11
When sparkling stars twire not thou gild'st the even.
  But day doth daily draw my sorrows longer,
  And night doth nightly make grief's strength seem
    stronger.

XXIX

When in disgrace with fortune and men's eyes
I all alone beweep my outcast state,
And trouble deaf heaven with my bootless cries,
And look upon myself, and curse my fate,
Wishing me like to one more rich in hope,
Featur'd like him, like him with friends possess'd, 6

Desiring this man's art, and that man's scope,
With what I most enjoy contented least ;
Yet in these thoughts myself almost despising,
Haply I think on thee,—and then my state,
Like to the lark at break of day arising
From sullen earth, sings hymns at heaven's gate ;   12
  For thy sweet love remember'd such wealth brings
  That then I scorn to change my state with kings.

XXX

When to the sessions of sweet silent thought
I summon up remembrance of things past,
I sigh the lack of many a thing I sought,
And with old woes new wail my dear times' waste :
Then can I drown an eye, unus'd to flow,
For precious friends hid in death's dateless night,   6
And weep afresh love's long since cancell'd woe,
And moan the expense of many a vanish'd sight :
Then can I grieve at grievances foregone,
And heavily from woe to woe tell o'er
The sad account of fore-bemoaned moan,
Which I new pay as if not paid before.   12
  But if the while I think on thee, dear friend,
  All losses are restor'd and sorrows end.

XXXI

Thy bosom is endeared with all hearts,
Which I by lacking have supposed dead ;
And there reigns Love, and all Love's loving parts,
And all those friends which I thought buried.
How many a holy and obsequious tear
Hath dear religious love stol'n from mine eye,   6
As interest of the dead, which now appear
But things remov'd that hidden in thee lie !
Thou art the grave where buried love doth live,
Hung with the trophies of my lovers gone,
Who all their parts of me to thee did give,
That due of many now is thine alone :   12
  Their images I lov'd I view in thee,
  And thou—all they—hast all the all of me.

XXXII

If thou survive my well-contented day,
When that churl Death my bones with dust shall cover,
And shalt by fortune once more re-survey
These poor rude lines of thy deceased lover,
Compare them with the bettering of the time,
And though they be outstripp'd by every pen, 6
Reserve them for my love, not for their rime,
Exceeded by the height of happier men.
O ! then vouchsafe me but this loving thought :
' Had my friend's Muse grown with this growing age,
A dearer birth than this his love had brought,
To march in ranks of better equipage : 12
   But since he died, and poets better prove,
   Theirs for their style I'll read, his for his love.'

XXXIII

Full many a glorious morning have I seen
Flatter the mountain-tops with sovereign eye,
Kissing with golden face the meadows green,
Gilding pale streams with heavenly alchemy ;
Anon permit the basest clouds to ride
With ugly rack on his celestial face, 6
And from the forlorn world his visage hide,
Stealing unseen to west with this disgrace :
Even so my sun one early morn did shine,
With all-triumphant splendour on my brow ;
But out ! alack ! he was but one hour mine,
The region cloud hath mask'd him from me now. 12
   Yet him for this my love no whit disdaineth ;
   Suns of the world may stain when heaven's sun
    staineth.

XXXIV

Why didst thou promise such a beauteous day,
And make me travel forth without my cloak,
To let base clouds o'ertake me in my way,
Hiding thy bravery in their rotten smoke ?
'Tis not enough that through the cloud thou break,
To dry the rain on my storm-beaten face, 6

For no man well of such a salve can speak
That heals the wound and cures not the disgrace :
Nor can thy shame give physic to my grief ;
Though thou repent, yet I have still the loss :
The offender's sorrow lends but weak relief
To him that bears the strong offence's cross.　　　12
　　Ah ! but those tears are pearl which thy love sheds,
　　And they are rich and ransom all ill deeds.

XXXV

No more be griev'd at that which thou hast done :
Poses have thorns, and silver fountains mud ;
Clouds and eclipses stain both moon and sun,
And loathsome canker lives in sweetest bud.
All men make faults, and even I in this,
Authorizing thy trespass with compare,　　　6
Myself corrupting, salving thy amiss,
Excusing thy sins more than thy sins are ;
For to thy sensual fault I bring in sense,—
Thy adverse party is thy advocate,—
And 'gainst myself a lawful plea commence :
Such civil war is in my love and hate,　　　12
　　That I an accessary needs must be
　　To that sweet thief which sourly robs from me.

XXXVI

Let me confess that we two must be twain,
Although our undivided loves are one :
So shall those blots that do with me remain,
Without thy help, by me be borne alone.
In our two loves there is but one respect,
Though in our lives a separable spite,　　　6
Which, though it alter not love's sole effect,
Yet doth it steal sweet hours from love's delight.
I may not evermore acknowledge thee,
Lest my bewailed guilt should do thee shame,
Nor thou with public kindness honour me,
Unless thou take that honour from thy name :　　　12
　　But do not so ; I love thee in such sort
　　As thou being mine, mine is thy good report.

XXXVII

As a decrepit father takes delight
To see his active child do deeds of youth,
So I, made lame by fortune's dearest spite,
Take all my comfort of thy worth and truth ;
For whether beauty, birth, or wealth, or wit,
Or any of these all, or all, or more,   6
Entitled in thy parts do crowned sit,
I make my love engrafted to this store :
So then I am not lame, poor, nor despis'd,
Whilst that this shadow doth such substance give
That I in thy abundance am suffic'd
And by a part of all thy glory live.   12
   Look what is best, that best I wish in thee :
   This wish I have ; then ten times happy me !

XXXVIII

How can my Muse want subject to invent,
While thou dost breathe, that pour'st into my verse
Thine own sweet argument, too excellent
For every vulgar paper to rehearse ?
O ! give thyself the thanks, if aught in me
Worthy perusal stand against thy sight ;   6
For who 's so dumb that cannot write to thee,
When thou thyself dost give invention light ?
Be thou the tenth Muse, ten times more in worth
Than those old nine which rimers invocate ;
And he that calls on thee, let him bring forth
Eternal numbers to outlive long date.   12
   If my slight Muse do please these curious days,
   The pain be mine, but thine shall be the praise.

XXXIX

O ! how thy worth with manners may I sing,
When thou art all the better part of me ?
What can mine own praise to mine own self bring ?
And what is 't but mine own when I praise thee ?
Even for this let us divided live,
And our dear love lose name of single one,   6

That by this separation I may give
That due to thee, which thou deserv'st alone.
O absence ! what a torment wouldst thou prove,
Were it not thy sour leisure gave sweet leave
To entertain the time with thoughts of love,
Which time and thoughts so sweetly doth deceive, 12
  And that thou teachest how to make one twain,
  By praising him here who doth hence remain.

XL

Take all my loves, my love, yea, take them all ;
What hast thou then more than thou hadst before ?
No love, my love, that thou mayst true love call ;
All mine was thine before thou hadst this more.
Then, if for my love thou my love receivest,
I cannot blame thee for my love thou usest ; 6
But yet be blam'd, if thou thyself deceivest
By wilful taste of what thyself refusest
I do forgive thy robbery, gentle thief,
Although thou steal thee all my poverty :
And yet, love knows it is a greater grief
To bear love's wrong than hate's known injury. 12
  Lascivious grace, in whom all ill well shows,
  Kill me with spites ; yet we must not be foes.

XLI

Those pretty wrongs that liberty commits,
When I am sometime absent from thy heart,
Thy beauty and thy years full well befits,
For still temptation follows where thou art
Gentle thou art, and therefore to be won,
Beauteous thou art, therefore to be assail'd ; 6
And when a woman woos, what woman's son
Will sourly leave her till she have prevail'd ?
Ay me ! but yet thou mightst my seat forbear,
And chide thy beauty and thy straying youth,
Who lead thee in their riot even there
Where thou art forc'd to break a twofold truth ;— 13
  Hers, by thy beauty tempting her to thee,
  Thine, by thy beauty being false to me.

XLII

That thou hast her, it is not all my grief,
And yet it may be said I lov'd her dearly ;
That she hath thee, is of my wailing chief,
A loss in love that touches me more nearly.
Loving offenders, thus I will excuse ye :
Thou dost love her, because thou know'st I love her ;
And for my sake even so doth she abuse me,   7
Suffering my friend for my sake to approve her.
If I lose thee, my loss is my love's gain,
And losing her, my friend hath found that loss ;
Both find each other, and I lose both twain,
And both for my sake lay on me this cross :   12
   But here 's the joy ; my friend and I are one ;
   Sweet flattery ! then she loves but me alone.

XLIII

When most I wink, then do mine eyes best see,
For all the day they view things unrespected ;
But when I sleep, in dreams they look on thee,
And darkly bright, are bright in dark directed.
Then thou, whose shadow shadows doth make bright,
How would thy shadow's form form happy show   6
To the clear day with thy much clearer light,
When to unseeing eyes thy shade shines so !
How would, I say, mine eyes be blessed made
By looking on thee in the living day,
When in dead night thy fair imperfect shade
Through heavy sleep on sightless eyes doth stay !   12
   All days are nights to see till I see thee,
   And nights bright days when dreams do show thee me.

XLIV

If the dull substance of my flesh were thought,
Injurious distance should not stop my way ;
For then, despite of space, I would be brought,
From limits far remote, where thou dost stay.
No matter then although my foot did stand
Upon the farthest earth remov'd from thee ;   6

For nimble thought can jump both sea and land,
As soon as think the place where he would be.
But, ah! thought kills me that I am not thought,
To leap large lengths of miles when thou art gone,
But that, so much of earth and water wrought,
I must attend time's leisure with my moan; 12
   Receiving nought by elements so slow
   But heavy tears, badges of either's woe.

XLV

The other two, slight air and purging fire
Are both with thee, wherever I abide;
The first my thought, the other my desire
These present-absent with swift motion slide.
For when these quicker elements are gone
In tender embassy of love to thee, 6
My life, being made of four, with two alone
Sinks down to death, oppress'd with melancholy;
Until life's composition be recur'd
By those swift messengers return'd from thee,
Who even but now come back again, assur'd
Of thy fair health, recounting it to me: 12
   This told, I joy; but then no longer glad,
   I send them back again, and straight grow sad.

XLVI

Mine eye and heart are at a mortal war,
How to divide the conquest of thy sight;
Mine eye my heart thy picture's sight would bar,
My heart mine eye the freedom of that right.
My heart doth plead that thou in him dost lie,—
A closet never pierc'd with crystal eyes,— 6
But the defendant doth that plea deny,
And says in him thy fair appearance lies.
To 'cide this title is impannelled
A quest of thoughts, all tenants to the heart;
And by their verdict is determined
The clear eye's moiety and the dear heart's part: 12
   As thus; mine eye's due is thine outward part,
   And my heart's right thine inward love of heart.

XLVII

Betwixt mine eye and heart a league is took,
And each doth good turns now unto the other :
When that mine eye is famish'd for a look,
Or heart in love with sighs himself doth smother,
With my love's picture then my eye doth feast,
And to the painted banquet bids my heart ;　　　　6
Another time mine eye is my heart's guest,
And in his thoughts of love doth share a part :
So, either by thy picture or my love,
Thyself away art present still with me ;
For thou not farther than my thoughts canst move,
And I am still with them and they with thee ;　　　12
　Or, if they sleep, thy picture in my sight
　Awakes my heart to heart's and eye's delight.

XLVIII

How careful was I when I took my way,
Each trifle under truest bars to thrust,
That to my use it might unused stay
From hands of falsehood, in sure wards of trust !
But thou, to whom my jewels trifles are,
Most worthy comfort, now my greatest grief,　　　6
Thou, best of dearest and mine only care,
Art left the prey of every vulgar thief.
Thee have I not lock'd up in any chest,
Save where thou art not, though I feel thou art,
Within the gentle closure of my breast,　　　　11
From whence at pleasure thou mayst come and part ;
　And even thence thou wilt be stol'n, I fear,
　For truth proves thievish for a prize so dear.

XLIX

Against that time, if ever that time come,
When I shall see thee frown on my defects,
When as thy love hath cast his utmost sum,
Call'd to that audit by advis'd respects ;
Against that time when thou shalt strangely pass,
And scarcely greet me with that sun, thine eye,　　　6

When love, converted from the thing it was,
Shall reasons find of settled gravity ;
Against that time do I ensconce me here
Within the knowledge of mine own desert,
And this my hand against myself uprear,
To guard the lawful reasons on thy part :   12
   To leave poor me thou hast the strength of laws,
   Since why to love I can allege no cause.

L

How heavy do I journey on the way,
When what I seek, my weary travel's end,
Doth teach that ease and that repose to say,
' Thus far the miles are measur'd from thy friend ! '
The beast that bears me, tired with my woe,
Plods dully on, to bear that weight in me,   6
As if by some instinct the wretch did know
His rider lov'd not speed, being made from thee :
The bloody spur cannot provoke him on
That sometimes anger thrusts into his hide,
Which heavily he answers with a groan,
More sharp to me than spurring to his side ;   12
   For that same groan doth put this in my mind :
   My grief lies onward, and my joy behind.

LI

Thus can my love excuse the slow offence
Of my dull bearer when from thee I speed :
From where thou art why should I haste me thence ?
Till I return, of posting is no need.
O ! what excuse will my poor beast then find,
When swift extremity can seem but slow ?   6
Then should I spur, though mounted on the wind,
In winged speed no motion shall I know :
Then can no horse with my desire keep pace ;
Therefore desire, of perfect'st love being made,
Shall neigh—no dull flesh—in his fiery race ;
But love, for love, thus shall excuse my jade,—   12
   ' Since from thee going he went wilful-slow,
   Towards thee I'll run and give him leave to go.'

LII

So am I as the rich, whose blessed key
Can bring him to his sweet up-locked treasure,
The which he will not every hour survey,
For blunting the fine point of seldom pleasure.
Therefore are feasts so solemn and so rare,
Since, seldom coming, in the long year set,   6
Like stones of worth they thinly placed are,
Or captain jewels in the carconet.
So is the time that keeps you as my chest,
Or as the wardrobe which the robe doth hide,
To make some special instant special blest,
By new unfolding his imprison'd pride.   12
   Blessed are you, whose worthiness gives scope,
   Being had, to triumph ; being lack'd, to hope.

LIII

What is your substance, whereof are you made,
That millions of strange shadows on you tend ?
Since every one hath, every one, one shade,
And you, but one, can every shadow lend.
Describe Adonis, and the counterfeit
Is poorly imitated after you ;   6
On Helen's cheek all art of beauty set,
And you in Grecian tires are painted new :
Speak of the spring and foison of the year,
The one doth shadow of your beauty show,
The other as your bounty doth appear ;
And you in every blessed shape we know.   12
   In all external grace you have some part,
   But you like none, none you, for constant heart.

LIV

O ! how much more doth beauty beauteous seem
By that sweet ornament which truth doth give.
The rose looks fair, but fairer we it deem
For that sweet odour which doth in it live.
The canker-blooms have full as deep a dye
As the perfumed tincture of the roses.   6

Hang on such thorns, and play as wantonly
When summer's breath their masked buds discloses :
But, for their virtue only is their show,
They live unwoo'd, and unrespected fade ;
Die to themselves. Sweet roses do not so ;
Of their sweet deaths are sweetest odours made :　12
    And so of you, beauteous and lovely youth,
    When that shall vade, my verse distils your truth.

LV

Not marble, nor the gilded monuments
Of princes, shall outlive this powerful rime ;
But you shall shine more bright in these contents
Than unswept stone, besmear'd with sluttish time.
When wasteful war shall statues overturn,
And broils root out the work of masonry,　6
Nor Mars his sword nor war's quick fire shall burn
The living record of your memory.
'Gainst death and all-oblivious enmity
Shall you pace forth ; your praise shall still find room
Even in the eyes of all posterity
That wear this world out to the ending doom.　12
    So, till the judgment that yourself arise,
    You live in this, and dwell in lovers' eyes.

LVI

Sweet love, renew thy force ; be it not said
Thy edge should blunter be than appetite,
Which but to-day by feeding is allay'd,
To-morrow sharpen'd in his former might :
So, love, be thou ; although to-day thou fill
Thy hungry eyes, even till they wink with fulness,　6
To-morrow see again, and do not kill
The spirit of love with a perpetual dulness.
Let this sad interim like the ocean be
Which parts the shore, where two contracted new
Come daily to the banks, that, when they see
Return of love, more blest may be the view ;　12
    Or call it winter, which, being full of care,
    Makes summer's welcome thrice more wish'd, more
    rare.

SONNETS

LVII

Being your slave, what should I do but tend
Upon the hours and times of your desire ?
I have no precious time at all to spend,
Nor services to do, till you require.
Nor dare I chide the world-without-end hour
Whilst I, my sovereign, watch the clock for you,   6
Nor think the bitterness of absence sour
When you have bid your servant once adieu ;
Nor dare I question with my jealous thought
Where you may be, or your affairs suppose,
But, like a sad slave, stay and think of nought
Save, where you are how happy you make those.   12
  So true a fool is love that in your will,
  Though you do anything, he thinks no ill.

LVIII

That god forbid that made me first your slave,
I should in thought control your times of pleasure,
Or at your hand the account of hours to crave,
Being your vassal, bound to stay your leisure !
O ! let me suffer, being at your beck,
The imprison'd absence of your liberty ;   6
And patience, tame to sufferance, bide each cheek,
Without accusing you of injury.
Be where you list, your charter is so strong
That you yourself may privilege your time
To what you will ; to you it doth belong
Yourself to pardon of self-doing crime.   12
  I am to wait, though waiting so be hell,
  Not blame your pleasure, be it ill or well.

LIX

If there be nothing new, but that which is
Hath been before, how are our brains beguil'd,
Which, labouring for invention, bear amiss
The second burthen of a former child !
O ! that record could with a backward look,
Even of five hundred courses of the sun,   6

232

Show me your image in some antique book,
Since mind at first in character was done !
That I might see what the old world could say
To this composed wonder of your frame ;
Whe'r we are mended, or whe'r better they,
Or whether revolution be the same.   12
   O ! sure I am, the wits of former days
   To subjects worse have given admiring praise.

LX

Like as the waves make towards the pebbled shore,
So do our minutes hasten to their end ;
Each changing place with that which goes before,
In sequent toil all forwards do contend.
Nativity, once in the main of light,
Crawls to maturity, wherewith being crown'd,   6
Crooked eclipses 'gainst his glory fight,
And Time that gave doth now his gift confound.
Time doth transfix the flourish set on youth
And delves the parallels in beauty's brow,
Feeds on the rarities of nature's truth,
And nothing stands but for his scythe to mow :   12
   And yet to times in hope my verse shall stand,
   Praising thy worth, despite his cruel hand.

LXI

Is it thy will thy image should keep open
My heavy eyelids to the weary night ?
Dost thou desire my slumbers should be broken,
While shadows, like to thee, do mock my sight ?
Is it thy spirit that thou send'st from thee
So far from home, into my deeds to pry,   6
To find out shames and idle hours in me,
The scope and tenour of thy jealousy ?
O, no ! thy love, though much, is not so great :
It is my love that keeps mine eye awake ;
Mine own true love that doth my rest defeat,
To play the watchman ever for thy sake :   12
   For thee watch I whilst thou dost wake elsewhere,
   From me far off, with others all too near.

LXII

Sin of self-love possesseth all mine eye
And all my soul and all my every part ;
And for this sin there is no remedy,
It is so grounded inward in my heart.
Methinks no face so gracious is as mine,
No shape so true, no truth of such account ;   6
And for myself mine own worth do define,
As I all other in all worths surmount.
But when my glass shows me myself indeed,
Beated and chopp'd with tann'd antiquity,
Mine own self-love quite contrary I read ;
Self so self-loving were iniquity.   12
   'Tis thee,—myself,—that for myself I praise,
   Painting my age with beauty of thy days.

LXIII

Against my love shall be, as I am now,
With Time's injurious hand crush'd and o'erworn ;
When hours have drain'd his blood and fill'd his brow
With lines and wrinkles ; when his youthful morn
Hath travell'd on to age's steepy night ;
And all those beauties whereof now he 's king   6
Are vanishing or vanish'd out of sight,
Stealing away the treasure of his spring ;
For such a time do I now fortify
Against confounding age's cruel knife,
That he shall never cut from memory
My sweet love's beauty, though my lover's life :   12
   His beauty shall in these black lines be seen,
   And they shall live, and he in them still green.

LXIV

When I have seen by Time's fell hand defac'd
The rich-proud cost of outworn buried age ;
When sometime lofty towers I see down-raz'd.
And brass eternal slave to mortal rage ;
When I have seen the hungry ocean gain
Advantage on the kingdom of the shore,   6

And the firm soil win of the watery main,
Increasing store with loss, and loss with store ;
When I have seen such interchange of state,
Or state itself confounded to decay;
Ruin hath taught me thus to ruminate—
That time will come and take my love away.　　12
　　This thought is as a death, which cannot choose
　　But weep to have that which it fears to lose.

LXV

Since brass, nor stone, nor earth, nor boundless sea,
But sad mortality o'ersways their power,
How with this rage shall beauty hold a plea,
Whose action is no stronger than a flower ?
O ! how shall summer's honey breath hold out
Against the wrackful siege of battering days,　　6
When rocks impregnable are not so stout,
Nor gates of steel so strong, but Time decays ?
O fearful meditation ! where, alack,
Shall Time's best jewel from Time's chest lie hid ?
Or what strong hand can hold his swift foot back ?
Or who his spoil of beauty can forbid ?　　12
　　O ! none, unless this miracle have might,
　　That in black ink my love may still shine bright.

LXVI

Tir'd with all these, for restful death I cry,
As to behold desert a beggar born,
And needy nothing trimm'd in jollity,
And purest faith unhappily forsworn,
And gilded honour shamefully misplac'd,
And maiden virtue rudely strumpeted,　　6
And right perfection wrongfully disgrac'd,
And strength by limping sway disabled,
And art made tongue-tied by authority,
And folly—doctor-like—controlling skill,
And simple truth miscall'd simplicity,
And captive good attending captain ill :　　12
　　Tir'd with all these, from these would I be gone,
　　Save that, to die, I leave my love alone.

LXVII

Ah ! wherefore with infection should he live,
And with his presence grace impiety,
That sin by him advantage should achieve,
And lace itself with his society ?
Why should false painting imitate his cheek,
And steel dead seeing of his living hue ?   6
Why should poor beauty indirectly seek
Roses of shadow, since his rose is true ?
Why should he live, now Nature bankrupt is,
Beggar'd of blood to blush through lively veins ?
For she hath no exchequer now but his,
And, proud of many, lives upon his gains.   12
 O ! him she stores, to show what wealth she had
 In days long since, before these last so bad.

LXVIII

Thus is his cheek the map of days outworn,
When beauty liv'd and died as flowers do now,
Before these bastard signs of fair were born,
Or durst inhabit on a living brow ;
Before the golden tresses of the dead,
The right of sepulchres, were shorn away,   6
To live a second life on second head ;
Ere beauty's dead fleece made another gay :
In him those holy antique hours are seen,
Without all ornament, itself and true,
Making no summer of another's green,
Robbing no old to dress his beauty new ;   12
 And him as for a map doth Nature store,
 To show false Art what beauty was of yore.

LXIX

Those parts of thee that the world's eye doth view
Want nothing that the thought of hearts can mend ;
All tongues—the voice of souls—give thee that due,
Uttering bare truth, even so as foes commend.
Thy outward thus with outward praise is crown'd ;
But those same tongues, that give thee so thine own,

In other accents do this praise confound   7
By seeing farther than the eye hath shown.
They look into the beauty of thy mind,
And that, in guess, they measure by thy deeds ;
Then,—churls,—their thoughts, although their eyes were
    kind,
To thy fair flower add the rank smell of weeds :   12
  But why thy odour matcheth not thy show,
   The soil is this, that thou dost common grow.

LXX

That thou art blam'd shall not be thy defect,
For slander's mark was ever yet the fair ;
The ornament of beauty is suspect,
A crow that flies in heaven's sweetest air.
So thou be good, slander doth but approve
Thy worth the greater, being woo'd of time ;   6
For canker vice the sweetest buds doth love,
And thou present'st a pure unstained prime.
Thou hast pass'd by the ambush of young days
Either not assail'd, or victor being charg'd ;
Yet this thy praise cannot be so thy praise,
To tie up envy evermore enlarg'd :   12
  If some suspect of ill mask'd not thy show,
   Then thou alone kingdoms of hearts shouldst owe.

LXXI

No longer mourn for me when I am dead
Than you shall hear the surly sullen bell
Give warning to the world that I am fled
From this vile world, with vilest worms to dwell :
Nay, if you read this line, remember not
The hand that writ it ; for I love you so,   6
That I in your sweet thoughts would be forgot,
If thinking on me then should make you woe.
O ! if,—I say, you look upon this verse,
When I perhaps compounded am with clay,
Do not so much as my poor name rehearse,
But let your love even with my life decay ;   12
  Lest the wise world should look into your moan,
   And mock you with me after I am gone.

SONNETS

LXXII

O ! lest the world should task you to recite
What merit lived in me, that you should love
After my death,—dear love, forget me quite,
For you in me can nothing worthy prove ;
Unless you would devise some virtuous lie,
To do more for me than mine own desert,   6
And hang more praise upon deceased I
Than niggard truth would willingly impart :
O ! lest your true love may seem false in this
That you for love speak well of me untrue,
My name be buried where my body is,
And live no more to shame nor me nor you.   12
  For I am sham'd by that which I bring forth,
  And so should you, to love things nothing worth.

LXXIII

That time of year thou mayst in me behold
When yellow leaves, or none, or few, do hang
Upon those boughs which shake against the cold,
Bare ruin'd choirs, where late the sweet birds sang.
In me thou see'st the twilight of such day
As after sunset fadeth in the west ;   6
Which by and by black night doth take away,
Death's second self, that seals up all in rest.
In me thou see'st the glowing of such fire,
That on the ashes of his youth doth lie,
As the death-bed whereon it must expire,
Consum'd with that which it was nourish'd by.   12
  This thou perceiv'st, which makes thy love more strong,
  To love that well which thou must leave ere long.

LXXIV

But be contented : when that fell arrest
Without all bail shall carry me away,
My life hath in this line some interest,
Which for memorial still with thee shall stay.
When thou reviewest this, thou dost review
The very part was consecrate to thee :   6

SONNETS

The earth can have but earth, which is his due ;
My spirit is thine, the better part of me :
So then thou hast but lost the dregs of life,
The prey of worms, my body being dead ;
The coward conquest of a wretch's knife,
Too base of thee to be remembered.   12
  The worth of that is that which it contains,
  And that is this, and this with thee remains.

LXXV

So are you to my thoughts as food to life,
Or as sweet-season'd showers are to the ground ;
And for the peace of you I hold such strife
As 'twixt a miser and his wealth is found ;
Now proud as an enjoyer, and anon
Doubting the filching age will steal his treasure ;   6
Now counting best to be with you alone,
Then better'd that the world may see my pleasure :
Sometime at full with feasting on your sight,
And by and by clean starved for a look ;
Possessing or pursuing no delight,
Save what is had or must from you be took.   12
  Thus do I pine and surfeit day by day,
  Or gluttoning on all, or all away.

LXXVI

Why is my verse so barren of new pride,
So far from variation or quick change ?
Why with the time do I not glance aside
To new-found methods and to compounds strange ?
Why write I still all one, ever the same,
And keep invention in a noted weed,   6
That every word doth almost tell my name,
Showing their birth, and where they did proceed ?
O ! know, sweet love, I always write of you,
And you and love are still my argument ;
So all my best is dressing old words new,
Spending again what is already spent :   12
  For as the sun is daily new and old,
  So is my love still telling what is told.

SH. II   N n

LXXVII

Thy glass will show thee how thy beauties wear,
Thy dial how thy precious minutes waste ;
The vacant leaves thy mind's imprint will bear,
And of this book this learning mayst thou taste.
The wrinkles which thy glass will truly show
Of mouthed graves will give thee memory ;   6
Thou by thy dial's shady stealth mayst know
Time's thievish progress to eternity.
Look ! what thy memory cannot contain,
Commit to these waste blanks, and thou shalt find
Those children nursed, deliver'd from thy brain,
To take a new acquaintance of thy mind.   12
   These offices, so oft as thou wilt look,
   Shall profit thee and much enrich thy book.

LXXVIII

So oft have I invok'd thee for my Muse
And found such fair assistance in my verse
As every alien pen hath got my use
And under thee their poesy disperse.
Thine eyes, that taught the dumb on high to sing
And heavy ignorance aloft to fly,   6
Have added feathers to the learned's wing
And given grace a double majesty.
Yet be most proud of that which I compile,
Whose influence is thine, and born of thee :
In others' works thou dost but mend the style,
And arts with thy sweet graces graced be ;   12
   But thou art all my art, and dost advance
   As high as learning my rude ignorance.

LXXIX

Whilst I alone did call upon thy aid,
My verse alone had all thy gentle grace ;
But now my gracious numbers are decay'd,
And my sick Muse doth give another place.
I grant, sweet love, thy lovely argument
Deserves the travail of a worthier pen ;   6

Yet what of thee thy poet doth invent
He robs thee of, and pays it thee again.
He lends thee virtue, and he stole that word
From thy behaviour ; beauty doth he give,
And found it in thy cheek : he can afford
No praise to thee but what in thee doth live.   12
   Then thank him not for that which he doth say,
   Since what he owes thee thou thyself dost pay.

LXXX

O ! how I faint when I of you do write,
Knowing a better spirit doth use your name,
And in the praise thereof spends all his might,
To make me tongue-tied, speaking of your fame !
But since your worth—wide as the ocean is,—
The humble as the proudest sail doth bear,   6
My saucy bark, inferior far to his,
On your broad main doth wilfully appear.
Your shallowest help will hold me up afloat,
Whilst he upon your soundless deep doth ride ;
Or, being wrack'd, I am a worthless boat,
He of tall building and of goodly pride :   12
   Then if he thrive and I be cast away,
   The worst was this,—my love was my decay.

LXXXI

Or I shall live your epitaph to make,
Or you survive when I in earth am rotten ;
From hence your memory death cannot take,
Although in me each part will be forgotten.
Your name from hence immortal life shall have,
Though I, once gone, to all the world must die :   6
The earth can yield me but a common grave,
When you entombed in men's eyes shall lie.
Your monument shall be my gentle verse,
Which eyes not yet created shall o'er-read ;
And tongues to be your being shall rehearse,
When all the breathers of this world are dead ;   12
   You still shall live,—such virtue hath my pen,—
   Where breath most breathes, even in the mouths of
     men.

LXXXII

I grant thou wert not married to my Muse,
And therefore mayst without attaint o'erlook
The dedicated words which writers use
Of their fair subject, blessing every book.
Thou art as fair in knowledge as in hue,
Finding thy worth a limit past my praise ;   6
And therefore art enforc'd to seek anew
Some fresher stamp of the time-bettering days.
And do so, love ; yet when they have devis'd
What strained touches rhetoric can lend,
Thou truly fair wert truly sympathiz'd
In true plain words by thy true-telling friend ;   12
    And their gross painting might be better us'd
    Where cheeks need blood ; in thee it is abus'd.

LXXXIII

I never saw that you did painting need,
And therefore to your fair no painting set ;
I found, or thought I found, you did exceed
The barren tender of a poet's debt :
And therefore have I slept in your report,
That you yourself, being extant, well might show   6
How far a modern quill doth come too short,
Speaking of worth, what worth in you doth grow.
This silence for my sin you did impute,
Which shall be most my glory, being dumb ;
For I impair not beauty being mute,
When others would give life, and bring a tomb.   12
    There lives more life in one of your fair eyes
    Than both your poets can in praise devise.

LXXXIV

Who is it that says most ? which can say more
Than this rich praise,—that you alone are you ?
In whose confine immured is the store
Which should example where your equal grew.
Lean penury within that pen doth dwell
That to his subject lends not some small glory ;   6

But he that writes of you, if he can tell
That you are you, so dignifies his story,
Let him but copy what in you is writ,
Not making worse what nature made so clear,
And such a counterpart shall fame his wit,
Making his style admired every where.   12
    You to your beauteous blessings add a curse,
    Being fond on praise, which makes your praises worse.

LXXXV

My tongue-tied Muse in manners holds her still,
While comments of your praise, richly compil'd,
Reserve their character with golden quill,
And precious phrase by all the Muses fil'd.
I think good thoughts, whilst others write good words,
And, like unletter'd clerk, still cry ' Amen '   6
To every hymn that able spirit affords,
In polish'd form of well-refined pen.
Hearing you prais'd, I say, ' 'Tis so, 'tis true,'
And to the most of praise add something more ;
But that is in my thought, whose love to you,
Though words come hindmost, holds his rank before.
    Then others for the breath of words respect,   13
    Me for my dumb thoughts, speaking in effect.

LXXXVI

Was it the proud full sail of his great verse,
Bound for the prize of all too precious you,
That did my ripe thoughts in my brain inhearse,
Making their tomb the womb wherein they grew ?
Was it his spirit, by spirits taught to write
Above a mortal pitch, that struck me dead ?   6
No, neither he, nor his compeers by night
Giving him aid, my verse astonished.
He, nor that affable familiar ghost
Which nightly gulls him with intelligence,
As victors of my silence cannot boast ;
I was not sick of any fear from thence :   12
    But when your countenance fill'd up his line,
    Then lack'd I matter ; that enfeebled mine.

LXXXVII

Farewell ! thou art too dear for my possessing,
And like enough thou know'st thy estimate :
The charter of thy worth gives thee releasing ;
My bonds in thee are all determinate.
For how do I hold thee but by thy granting ?
And for that riches where is my deserving ?   6
The cause of this fair gift in me is wanting,
And so my patent back again is swerving.
Thyself thou gav'st, thy own worth then not knowing,
Or me, to whom thou gav'st it, else mistaking ;
So thy great gift, upon misprision growing,
Comes home again, on better judgment making.   12
  Thus have I had thee, as a dream doth flatter,
  In sleep a king, but, waking, no such matter.

LXXXVIII

When thou shalt be dispos'd to set me light,
And place my merit in the eye of scorn,
Upon thy side against myself I'll fight,
And prove thee virtuous, though thou art forsworn.
With mine own weakness, being best acquainted,
Upon thy part I can set down a story   6
Of faults conceal'd, wherein I am attainted ;
That thou in losing me shalt win much glory :
And I by this will be a gainer too ;
For bending all my loving thoughts on thee,
The injuries that to myself I do,
Doing thee vantage, double-vantage me.   12
  Such is my love, to thee I so belong,
  That for thy right myself will bear all wrong.

LXXXIX

Say that thou didst forsake me for some fault,
And I will comment upon that offence :
Speak of my lameness, and I straight will halt.
Against thy reasons making no defence.
Thou canst not, love, disgrace me half so ill,
To set a form upon desired change,   6

As I'll myself disgrace ; knowing thy will,
I will acquaintance strangle, and look strange ;
Be absent from thy walks ; and in my tongue
Thy sweet beloved name no more shall dwell,
Lest I, too much profane, should do it wrong,
And haply of our old acquaintance tell.   12
   For thee, against myself I'll vow debate,
   For I must ne'er love him whom thou dost hate.

XC

Then hate me wnen thou wilt ; if ever, now ;
Now, while the world is bent my deeds to cross,
Join with the spite of fortune, make me bow,
And do not drop in for an after-loss :
Ah ! do not, when my heart hath 'scap'd this sorrow,
Come in the rearward of a conquer'd woe ;   6
Give not a windy night a rainy morrow,
To linger out a purpos'd overthrow.
If thou wilt leave me, do not leave me last,
When other petty griefs have done their spite,
But in the onset come : so shall I taste
At first the very worst of fortune's might ;   12
   And other strains of woe, which now seem woe,
   Compar'd with loss of thee will not seem so.

XCI

Some glory in their birth, some in their skill,
Some in their wealth, some in their body's force,
Some in their garments, though new-fangled ill ;
Some in their hawks and hounds, some in their horse ;
And every humour hath his adjunct pleasure,
Wherein it finds a joy above the rest :   6
But these particulars are not my measure ·
All these I better in one general best.
Thy love is better than high birth to me,
Richer than wealth, prouder than garments' cost,
Of more delight than hawks or horses be ;
And having thee, of all men's pride I boast :   12
   Wretched in this alone, that thou mayst take
   All this away, and me most wretched make.

XCII

But do thy worst to steal thyself away,
For term of life thou art assured mine ;
And life no longer than thy love will stay,
For it depends upon that love of thine.
Then need I not to fear the worst of wrongs,
When in the least of them my life hath end.　　　6
I see a better state to me belongs
Than that which on thy humour doth depend :
Thou canst not vex me with inconstant mind,
Since that my life on thy revolt doth lie.
O ! what a happy title do I find,
Happy to have thy love, happy to die !　　　12
　　But what 's so blessed-fair that fears no blot ?
　　Thou mayst be false, and yet I know it not.

XCIII

So shall I live, supposing thou art true,
Like a deceived husband ; so love's face
May still seem love to me, though alter'd new ;
Thy looks with me, thy heart in other place :
For there can live no hatred in thine eye,
Therefore in that I cannot know thy change.　　　6
In many's looks the false heart's history
Is writ in moods, and frowns, and wrinkles strange,
But heaven in thy creation did decree
That in thy face sweet love should ever dwell ;
Whate'er thy thoughts or thy heart's workings be,
Thy looks should nothing thence but sweetness tell.
　　How like Eve's apple doth thy beauty grow,　　　13
　　If thy sweet virtue answer not thy show !

XCIV

They that have power to hurt and will do none,
That do not do the thing they most do show,
Who, moving others, are themselves as stone,
Unmoved, cold, and to temptation slow ;
They rightly do inherit heaven's graces,
And husband nature's riches from expense ;　　　6

They are the lords and owners of their faces,
Others but stewards of their excellence.
The summer's flower is to the summer sweet,
Though to itself it only live and die,
But if that flower with base infection meet,
The basest weed outbraves his dignity :   12
    For sweetest things turn sourest by their deeds ;
    Lilies that fester smell far worse than weeds.

XCV

How sweet and lovely dost thou make the shame
Which, like a canker in the fragrant rose,
Doth spot the beauty of thy budding name !
O ! in what sweets dost thou thy sins enclose.
That tongue that tells the story of thy days,
Making lascivious comments on thy sport,   6
Cannot dispraise but in a kind of praise ;
Naming thy name blesses an ill report.
O ! what a mansion have those vices got
Which for their habitation chose out thee,
Where beauty's veil doth cover every blot
And all things turn to fair that eyes can see !   12
    Take heed, dear heart, of this large privilege ;
    The hardest knife ill-us'd doth lose his edge.

XCVI

Some say thy fault is youth, some wantonness ;
Some say thy grace is youth and gentle sport ;
Both grace and faults are lov'd of more and less :
Thou makest faults graces that to thee resort.
As on the finger of a throned queen
The basest jewel will be well esteem'd,   6
So are those errors that in thee are seen
To truths translated and for true things deem'd.
How many lambs might the stern wolf betray,
If like a lamb he could his looks translate !
How many gazers mightst thou lead away,
If thou wouldst use the strength of all thy state !
    But do not so ; I love thee in such sort,   13
    As, thou being mine, mine is thy good report.

XCVII

How like a winter hath my absence been
From thee, the pleasure of the fleeting year !
What freezings have I felt, what dark days seen !
What old December's bareness every where !
And yet this time remov'd was summer's time ;
The teeming autumn, big with rich increase,   6
Bearing the wanton burthen of the prime,
Like widow'd wombs after their lords' decease :
Yet this abundant issue seem'd to me
But hope of orphans and unfather'd fruit ;
For summer and his pleasures wait on thee,
And, thou away, the very birds are mute :   12
  Or, if they sing, 'tis with so dull a cheer,
  That leaves look pale, dreading the winter 's near.

XCVIII

From you have I been absent in the spring,
When proud-pied April, dress'd in all his trim,
Hath put a spirit of youth in every thing,
That heavy Saturn laugh'd and leap'd with him.
Yet nor the lays of birds, nor the sweet smell
Of different flowers in odour and in hue,   6
Could make me any summer's story tell,
Or from their proud lap pluck them where they grew :
Nor did I wonder at the lily's white,
Nor praise the deep vermilion in the rose ;
They were but sweet, but figures of delight,
Drawn after you, you pattern of all those.   12
  Yet seem'd it winter still, and, you away,
  As with your shadow I with these did play.

XCIX

The forward violet thus did I chide :
Sweet thief, whence didst thou steal thy sweet that
    smells,
If not from my love's breath ? The purple pride
Which on thy soft cheek for complexion dwells
In my love's veins thou hast too grossly dy'd.
The lily I condemned for thy hand,   6

248

And buds of marjoram had stol'n thy hair ;
The roses fearfully on thorns did stand,
One blushing shame, another white despair ;
A third, nor red nor white, had stol'n of both,
And to his robbery had annex'd thy breath ;
But, for his theft, in pride of all his growth   12
A vengeful canker eat him up to death.
  More flowers I noted, yet I none could see
  But sweet or colour it had stol'n from thee.

C

Where art thou, Muse, that thou forget'st so long
To speak of that which gives thee all thy might ?
Spend'st thou thy fury on some worthless song,
Darkening thy power to lend base subjects light ?
Return, forgetful Muse, and straight redeem
In gentle numbers time so idly spent ;   6
Sing to the ear that doth thy lays esteem
And gives thy pen both skill and argument.
Rise, resty Muse, my love's sweet face survey,
If Time have any wrinkle graven there ;
If any, be a satire to decay,
And make Time's spoils despised every where.   12
  Give my love fame faster than Time wastes life ;
  So thou prevent'st his scythe and crooked knife.

CI

O truant Muse, what shall be thy amends
For thy neglect of truth in beauty dy'd ?
Both truth and beauty on my love depends ;
So dost thou too, and therein dignified.
Make answer, Muse : wilt thou not haply say,
' Truth needs no colour, with his colour fix'd ;   6
Beauty no pencil, beauty's truth to lay ;
But best is best, if never intermix'd ' ?
Because he needs no praise, wilt thou be dumb ?
Excuse not silence so, for 't lies in thee
To make him much outlive a gilded tomb
And to be prais'd of ages yet to be.   12
  Then do thy office, Muse ; I teach thee how
  To make him seem long hence as he shows now.

CII

My love is strengthen'd, though more weak in seeming;
I love not less, though less the show appear:
That love is merchandiz'd whose rich esteeming
The owner's tongue doth publish every where.
Our love was new, and then but in the spring,
When I was wont to greet it with my lays;   6
As Philomel in summer's front doth sing,
And stops her pipe in growth of riper days:
Not that the summer is less pleasant now
Than when her mournful hymns did hush the night,
But that wild music burthens every bough,   11
And sweets grown common lose their dear delight.
    Therefore, like her, I sometime hold my tongue,
    Because I would not dull you with my song.

CIII

Alack! what poverty my Muse brings forth,
That having such a scope to show her pride,
The argument, all bare, is of more worth
Than when it hath my added praise beside!
O! blame me not, if I no more can write!
Look in your glass, and there appears a face   6
That over-goes my blunt invention quite,
Dulling my lines and doing me disgrace.
Were it not sinful then, striving to mend,
To mar the subject that before was well?
For to no other pass my verses tend
Than of your graces and your gifts to tell;   12
    And more, much more, than in my verse can sit,
    Your own glass shows you when you look in it.

CIV

To me, fair friend, you never can be old,
For as you were when first your eye I ey'd,
Such seems your beauty still. Three winters cold
Have from the forests shook three summers' pride,
Three beauteous springs to yellow autumn turn'd
In process of the seasons have I seen,   6

Three April perfumes in three hot Junes burn'd,
Since first I saw you fresh, which yet are green.
Ah ! yet doth beauty, like a dial-hand,
Steal from his figure, and no pace perceiv'd ;
So your sweet hue, which methinks still doth stand,
Hath motion, and mine eye may be deceiv'd :   12
  For fear of which, hear this, thou age unbred :
  Ere you were born was beauty's summer dead.

CV

Let not my love be call'd idolatry,
Nor my beloved as an idol show,
Since all alike my songs and praises be
To one, of one, still such, and ever so.
Kind is my love to-day, to-morrow kind,
Still constant in a wondrous excellence ;   6
Therefore my verse, to constancy confin'd,
One thing expressing, leaves out difference.
' Fair, kind, and true,' is all my argument,
' Fair, kind, and true,' varying to other words ;
And in this change is my invention spent,   11
Three themes in one, which wondrous scope affords.
  ' Fair, kind, and true,' have often liv'd alone,
  Which three till now never kept seat in one.

CVI

When in the chronicle of wasted time
I see descriptions of the fairest wights,
And beauty making beautiful old rime,
In praise of ladies dead and lovely knights,
Then, in the blazon of sweet beauty's best,
Of hand, of foot, of lip, of eye, of brow,   6
I see their antique pen would have express'd
Even such a beauty as you master now.
So all their praises are but prophecies
Of this our time, all you prefiguring ;
And, for they look'd but with divining eyes,
They had not skill enough your worth to sing :   12
  For we, which now behold these present days,
  Have eyes to wonder, but lack tongues to praise

CVII

Not mine own fears, nor the prophetic soul
Of the wide world dreaming on things to come,
Can yet the lease of my true love control,
Suppos'd as forfeit to a confin'd doom.
The mortal moon hath her eclipse endur'd,
And the sad augurs mock their own presage ;   6
Incertainties now crown themselves assur'd,
And peace proclaims olives of endless age.
Now with the drops of this most balmy time
My love looks fresh, and Death to me subscribes,
Since, spite of him, I'll live in this poor rime,
While he insults o'er dull and speechless tribes :   12
  And thou in this shalt find thy monument,
  When tyrants' crests and tombs of brass are spent.

CVIII

What 's in the brain, that ink may character,
Which hath not figur'd to thee my true spirit ?
What 's new to speak, what new to register,
That may express my love, or thy dear merit ?
Nothing, sweet boy ; but yet, like prayers divine,
I must each day say o'er the very same ;   6
Counting no old thing old, thou mine, I thine,
Even as when first I hallow'd thy fair name.
So that eternal love in love's fresh case
Weighs not the dust and injury of age,
Nor gives to necessary wrinkles place,
But makes antiquity for aye his page ;   12
  Finding the first conceit of love there bred,
  Where time and outward form would show it dead

CIX

O ! never say that I was false of heart,
Though absence seem'd my flame to qualify.
As easy might I from myself depart
As from my soul, which in thy breast doth lie :
That is my home of love : if I have rang'd,
Like him that travels, I return again ;   6

Just to the time, not with the time exchang'd,
So that myself bring water for my stain.
Never believe, though in my nature reign'd
All frailties that besiege all kinds of blood,
That it could so preposterously be stain'd,
To leave for nothing all thy sum of good ;   12
   For nothing this wide universe I call,
    Save thou, my rose ; in it thou art my all.

CX

Alas ! 'tis true I have gone here and there,
And made myself a motley to the view,
Gor'd mine own thoughts, sold cheap what is most dear.
Made old offences of affections new ;
Most true it is that I have look'd on truth
Askance and strangely ; but, by all above,   6
These blenches gave my heart another youth,
And worse essays prov'd thee my best of love.
Now all is done, save what shall have no end :
Mine appetite I never more will grind
On newer proof, to try an older friend,
A god in love, to whom I am confin'd.   12
   Then give me welcome, next my heaven the best,
    Even to thy pure and most loving breast.

CXI

O ! for my sake do you with Fortune chide,
The guilty goddess of my harmful deeds,
That did not better for my life provide
Than public means which public manners breeds.
Thence comes it that my name receives a brand,
And almost thence my nature is subdu'd   6
To what it works in, like the dyer's hand :
Pity me, then, and wish I were renew'd ;
Whilst, like a willing patient, I will drink
Potions of eisel 'gainst my strong infection ;
No bitterness that I will bitter think,
Nor double penance, to correct correction.   12
   Pity me, then, dear friend, and I assure ye
    Even that your pity is enough to cure me.

CXII

Your love and pity doth the impression fill
Which vulgar scandal stamp'd upon my brow;
For what care I who calls me well or ill,
So you o'er-green my bad, my good allow?
You are my all-the-world, and I must strive
To know my shames and praises from your tongue;   6
None else to me, nor I to none alive,
That my steel'd sense or changes right or wrong.
In so profound abysm I throw all care
Of others' voices, that my adder's sense
To critic and to flatterer stopped are.
Mark how with my neglect I do dispense: 12
   You are so strongly in my purpose bred,
   That all the world besides methinks are dead.

CXIII

Since I left you, mine eye is in my mind;
And that which governs me to go about
Doth part his function and is partly blind,
Seems seeing, but effectually is out;
For it no form delivers to the heart
Of bird, of flower, or shape, which it doth latch: 6
Of his quick objects hath the mind no part,
Nor his own vision holds what it doth catch;
For if it see the rud'st or gentlest sight,
The most sweet favour or deformed'st creature,
The mountain or the sea, the day or night,
The crow or dove, it shapes them to your feature
   Incapable of more, replete with you,   13
   My most true mind thus maketh mine untrue.

CXIV

Or whether doth my mind, being crown'd with you,
Drink up the monarch's plague, this flattery?
Or whether shall I say, mine eye saith true,
And that your love taught it this alchemy,
To make of monsters and things indigest
Such cherubins as your sweet self resemble,   6

Creating every bad a perfect best,
As fast as objects to his beams assemble ?
O ! 'tis the first, 'tis flattery in my seeing,
And my great mind most kingly drinks it up :
Mine eye well knows what with his gust is 'greeing,
And to his palate doth prepare the cup :   12
    If it be poison'd, 'tis the lesser sin
    That mine eye loves it and doth first begin.

CXV

Those lines that I before have writ do lie,
Even those that said I could not love you dearer :
Yet then my judgment knew no reason why
My most full flame should afterwards burn clearer.
But reckoning Time, whose million'd accidents
Creep in 'twixt vows, and change decrees of kings,   6
Tan sacred beauty, blunt the sharp'st intents,
Divert strong minds to the course of altering things ;
Alas ! why, fearing of Time's tyranny,
Might I not then say, ' Now I love you best,'
When I was certain o'er incertainty,
Crowning the present, doubting of the rest ?   12
    Love is a babe ; then might I not say so,
    To give full growth to that which still doth grow ?

CXVI

Let me not to the marriage of true minds
Admit impediments. Love is not love
Which alters when it alteration finds,
Or bends with the remover to remove :
O, no ! it is an ever-fixed mark,
That looks on tempests and is never shaken ;   6
It is the star to every wandering bark,
Whose worth 's unknown, although his height be taken.
Love 's not Time's fool, though rosy lips and cheeks
Within his bending sickle's compass come ;
Love alters not with his brief hours and weeks,
But bears it out even to the edge of doom.   12
    If this be error, and upon me prov'd,
    I never writ, nor no man ever lov'd.

CXVII

Accuse me thus : that I have scanted all
Wherein I should your great deserts repay,
Forgot upon your dearest love to call,
Whereto all bonds do tie me day by day ;
That I have frequent been with unknown minds,
And given to time your own dear-purchas'd right ;   6
That I have hoisted sail to all the winds
Which should transport me farthest from your sight.
Book both my wilfulness and errors down,
And on just proof surmise accumulate ;
Bring me within the level of your frown,
But shoot not at me in your waken'd hate ;   12
   Since my appeal says I did strive to prove
   The constancy and virtue of your love.

CXVIII

Like as, to make our appetites more keen,
With eager compounds we our palate urge ;
As, to prevent our maladies unseen,
We sicken to shun sickness when we purge ;
Even so, being full of your ne'er-cloying sweetness,
To bitter sauces did I frame my feeding ;   6
And, sick of welfare, found a kind of meetness
To be diseas'd, ere that there was true needing.
Thus policy in love, to anticipate
The ills that were not, grew to faults assur'd,
And brought to medicine a healthful state,
Which, rank of goodness, would by ill be cur'd ;   12
   But thence I learn, and find the lesson true,
   Drugs poison him that so fell sick of you.

CXIX

What potions have I drunk of Siren tears,
Distill'd from limbecks foul as hell within,
Applying fears to hopes, and hopes to fears,
Still losing when I saw myself to win !
What wretched errors hath my heart committed,
Whilst it hath thought itself so blessed never !   6

How have mine eyes out of their spheres been fitted,
In the distraction of this madding fever !
O benefit of ill ! now I find true
That better is by evil still made better ;
And ruin'd love, when it is built anew,
Grows fairer than at first, more strong, far greater.
   So I return rebuk'd to my content,   13
     And gain by ill thrice more than I have spent.

CXX

That you were once unkind befriends me now,
And for that sorrow, which I then did feel,
Needs must I under my transgression bow,
Unless my nerves were brass or hammer'd steel.
For if you were by my unkindness shaken,
As I by yours, you 've pass'd a hell of time ;   6
And I, a tyrant, have no leisure taken
To weigh how once I suffer'd in your crime.
O ! that our night of woe might have remember'd
My deepest sense, how hard true sorrow hits,
And soon to you, as you to me, then tender'd
The humble salve which wounded bosoms fits !   12
   But that your trespass now becomes a fee ;
     Mine ransoms yours, and yours must ransom me.

CXXI

'Tis better to be vile than vile esteem'd,
When not to be receives reproach of being ;
And the just pleasure lost, which is so deem'd
Not by our feeling, but by others' seeing :
For why should others' false adulterate eyes
Give salutation to my sportive blood ?   6
Or on my frailties why are frailer spies,
Which in their wills count bad what I think good ?
No, I am that I am, and they that level
At my abuses reckon up their own :
I may be straight though they themselves be bevel ;
By their rank thoughts my deeds must not be shown ;   13
   Unless this general evil they maintain,
     All men are bad and in their badness reign.

CXXII

Thy gift, thy tables, are within my brain
Full character'd with lasting memory,
Which shall above that idle rank remain,
Beyond all date, even to eternity :
Or, at the least, so long as brain and heart
Have faculty by nature to subsist ;   6
Till each to raz'd oblivion yield his part
Of thee, thy record never can be miss'd.
That poor retention could not so much hold,
Nor need I tallies thy dear love to score ;
Therefore to give them from me was I bold,
To trust those tables that receive thee more :   12
   To keep an adjunct to remember thee
   Were to import forgetfulness in me.

CXXIII

No, Time, thou shalt not boast that I do change :
Thy pyramids built up with newer might
To me are nothing novel, nothing strange ;
They are but dressings of a former sight.
Our dates are brief, and therefore we admire
What thou dost foist upon us that is old ;   6
And rather make them born to our desire
Than think that we before have heard them told.
Thy registers and thee I both defy,
Not wondering at the present nor the past,
For thy records and what we see doth lie,
Made more or less by thy continual haste.   12
   This I do vow, and this shall ever be ;
   I will be true, despite thy scythe and thee.

CXXIV

If my dear love were but the child of state,
It might for Fortune's bastard be unfather'd,
As subject to Time's love or to Time's hate,
Weeds among weeds, or flowers with flowers gather'd
No, it was builded far from accident ;
It suffers not in smiling pomp, nor falls   6

Under the blow of thralled discontent,
Whereto th' inviting time our fashion calls :
If fears not policy, that heretic,
Which works on leases of short number'd hours,
But all alone stands hugely politic,
That it nor grows with heat, nor drowns with showers.
   To this I witness call the fools of time,   13
    Which die for goodness, who have liv'd for crime.

CXXV

Were 't aught to me I bore the canopy,
With my extern the outward honouring,
Or laid great bases for eternity,
Which proves more short than waste or ruining ?
Have I not seen dwellers on form and favour
Lose all and more by paying too much rent,   6
For compound sweet foregoing simple savour,
Pitiful thrivers, in their gazing spent ?
No ; let me be obsequious in thy heart,
And take thou my oblation, poor but free,
Which is not mix'd with seconds, knows no art,
But mutual render, only me for thee.   12
   Hence, thou suborn'd informer ! a true soul
    When most impeach'd stands least in thy control.

CXXVI

O thou, my lovely boy, who in thy power
Dost hold Time's fickle glass, his sickle hour ;
Who hast by waning grown, and therein show'st
Thy lovers withering as thy sweet self grow'st ;
If Nature, sovereign mistress over wrack,
As thou goest onwards, still will pluck thee back,   6
She keeps thee to this purpose, that her skill
May time disgrace and wretched minutes kill.
Yet fear her, O thou minion of her pleasure !
She may detain, but not still keep, her treasure :
   Her audit, though delay'd, answer'd must be,
    And her quietus is to render thee.   12

CXXVII

In the old age black was not counted fair,
Or if it were, it bore not beauty's name ;
But now is black beauty's successive heir,
And beauty slander'd with a bastard's shame :
For since each hand hath put on Nature's power,
Fairing the foul with Art's false borrow'd face,   6
Sweet beauty hath no name, no holy bower,
But is profan'd, if not lives in disgrace.
Therefore my mistress' brows are raven black,
Her eyes so suited, and they mourners seem
At such who, not born fair, no beauty lack,
Sland'ring creation with a false esteem :   12
    Yet so they mourn, becoming of their woe,
    That every tongue says beauty should look so.

CXXVIII

How oft, when thou, my music, music play'st,
Upon that blessed wood whose motion sounds
With thy sweet fingers, when thou gently sway'st
The wiry concord that mine ear confounds,
Do I envy those jacks that nimble leap
To kiss the tender inward of thy hand,   6
Whilst my poor lips, which should that harvest reap,
At the wood's boldness by thee blushing stand !
To be so tickled, they would change their state
And situation with those dancing chips,
O'er whom thy fingers walk with gentle gait,
Making dead wood more bless'd than living lips.
    Since saucy jacks so happy are in this,   13
    Give them thy fingers, me thy lips to kiss.

CXXIX

The expense of spirit in a waste of shame
Is lust in action ; and till action, lust
Is perjur'd, murderous, bloody, full of blame,
Savage, extreme, rude, cruel, not to trust ;
Enjoy'd no sooner but despised straight ;
Past reason hunted ; and no sooner had,   6

Past reason hated, as a swallow'd bait,
On purpose laid to make the taker mad :
Mad in pursuit, and in possession so ;
Had, having, and in quest to have, extreme ;
A bliss in proof,—and prov'd, a very woe ;
Before, a joy propos'd ; behind, a dream.   12
   All this the world well knows ; yet none knows well
   To shun the heaven that leads men to this hell.

CXXX

My mistress' eyes are nothing like the sun ;
Coral is far more red than her lips' red :
If snow be white, why then her breasts are dun ;
If hairs be wires, black wires grow on her head.
I have seen roses damask'd, red and white,
But no such roses see I in her cheeks ;   6
And in some perfumes is there more delight
Than in the breath that from my mistress reeks.
I love to hear her speak, yet well I know
That music hath a far more pleasing sound :
I grant I never saw a goddess go,—
My mistress, when she walks, treads on the ground :
   And yet, by heaven, I think my love as rare   13
   As any she belied with false compare.

CXXXI

Thou art as tyrannous, so as thou art,
As those whose beauties proudly make them cruel ;
For well thou know'st to my dear doting heart
Thou art the fairest and most precious jewel.
Yet, in good faith, some say that thee behold,
Thy face hath not the power to make love groan :
To say they err I dare not be so bold,   7
Although I swear it to myself alone.
And to be sure that is not false I swear,
A thousand groans, but thinking on thy face,
One on another's neck, do witness bear
Thy black is fairest in my judgment's place.   12
   In nothing art thou black save in thy deeds,
   And thence this slander, as I think, proceeds.

CXXXII

Thine eyes I love, and they, as pitying me,
Knowing thy heart torments me with disdain,
Have put on black and loving mourners be,
Looking with pretty ruth upon my pain.
And truly not the morning sun of heaven
Better becomes the grey cheeks of the east,   6
Nor that full star that ushers in the even,
Doth half that glory to the sober west,
As those two mourning eyes become thy face :
O ! let it then as well beseem thy heart
To mourn for me, since mourning doth thee grace,
And suit thy pity like in every part.   12
   Then will I swear beauty herself is black,
   And all they foul that thy complexion lack.

CXXXIII

Beshrew that heart that makes my heart to groan
For that deep wound it gives my friend and me !
Is 't not enough to torture me alone,
But slave to slavery my sweet'st friend must be ?
Me from myself thy cruel eye hath taken,
And my next self thou harder hast engross'd :   6
Of him, myself, and thee, I am forsaken ;
A torment thrice threefold thus to be cross'd.
Prison my heart in thy steel bosom's ward,
But then my friend's heart let my poor heart bail ;
Whoe'er keeps me, let my heart be his guard ;
Thou canst not then use rigour in my jail :   12
   And yet thou wilt ; for I, being pent in thee,
   Perforce am thine, and all that is in me.

CXXXIV

So, now I have confess'd that he is thine,
And I myself am mortgag'd to thy will,
Myself I'll forfeit, so that other mine
Thou wilt restore, to be my comfort still :
But thou wilt not, nor he will not be free,
For thou art covetous and he is kind ;   6

He learn'd but surety-like to write for me,
Under that bond that him as fast doth bind.
The statute of thy beauty thou wilt take,
Thou usurer, that putt'st forth all to use,
And sue a friend came debtor for my sake ;
So him I lose through my unkind abuse.   12
    Him have I lost ; thou hast both him and me :
    He pays the whole, and yet am I not free.

CXXXV

Whoever hath her wish, thou hast thy ' Will,'
And ' Will ! to boot, and ' Will ' in over-plus ;
More than enough am I that vex'd thee still,
To thy sweet will making addition thus.
Wilt thou, whose will is large and spacious,
Not once vouchsafe to hide my will in thine ?   6
Shall will in others seem right gracious,
And in my will no fair acceptance shine ?
The sea, all water, yet receives rain still,
And in abundance addeth to his store ;
So thou, being rich in ' Will,' add to thy ' Will '
One will of mine, to make thy large ' Will ' more.   12
    Let no unkind ' No ' fair beseechers kill ;
    Think all but one, and me in that one ' Will.'

CXXXVI

If thy soul check thee that I come so near,
Swear to thy blind soul that I was thy ' Will,'
And will, thy soul knows, is admitted there ;
Thus far for love, my love-suit, sweet, fulfil.
' Will ' will fulfil the treasure of thy love,
Ay, fill it full with wills, and my will one.
In things of great receipt with ease we prove
Among a number one is reckon'd none :
Then in the number let me pass untold,
Though in thy stores' account I one must be ;
For nothing hold me, so it please thee hold
That nothing me, a something sweet to thee :   12
    Make but my name thy love, and love that still,
    And then thou lovest me, for my name is ' Will.'

CXXXVII

Thou blind fool, Love, what dost thou to mine eyes,
That they behold, and see not what they see ?
They know what beauty is, see where it lies,
Yet what the best is take the worst to be.
If eyes, corrupt by over-partial looks,
Be anchor'd in the bay where all men ride,   6
Why of eyes' falsehood hast thou forged hooks,
Whereto the judgment of my heart is tied ?
Why should my heart think that a several plot
Which my heart knows the wide world's common place ?
Or mine eyes, seeing this, say this is not,
To put fair truth upon so foul a face ?   12
   In things right true my heart and eyes have err'd,
   And to this false plague are they now transferr'd.

CXXXVIII

When my love swears that she is made of truth,
I do believe her, though I know she lies,
That she might think me some untutor'd youth,
Unlearned in the world's false subtleties.
Thus vainly thinking that she thinks me young,
Although she knows my days are past the best,   6
Simply I credit her false-speaking tongue :
On both sides thus is simple truth supprest.
But wherefore says she not she is unjust ?
And wherefore say not I that I am old ?
O ! love's best habit is in seeming trust,
And age in love loves not to have years told :   12
   Therefore I lie with her, and she with me,
   And in our faults by lies we flatter'd be.

CXXXIX

O ! call not me to justify the wrong
That thy unkindness lays upon my heart ;
Wound me not with thine eye, but with thy tongue :
Use power with power, and slay me not by art.
Tell me thou lovest elsewhere ; but in my sight,
Dear heart, forbear to glance thine eye aside :   6

What need'st thou wound with cunning, when thy might
Is more than my o'erpress'd defence can bide ?
Let me excuse thee : ah ! my love well knows
Her pretty looks have been mine enemies ;
And therefore from my face she turns my foes,
That they elsewhere might dart their injuries :   12
   Yet do not so ; but since I am near slain,
   Kill me outright with looks, and rid my pain.

CXL

Be wise as thou art cruel ; do not press
My tongue-tied patience with too much disdain ;
Lest sorrow lend me words, and words express
The manner of my pity-wanting pain.
If I might teach thee wit, better it were,
Though not to love, yet, love, to tell me so ;—   6
As testy sick men, when their deaths be near,
No news but health from their physicians know ;—
For, if I should despair, I should grow mad,
And in my madness might speak ill of thee :
Now this ill-wresting world is grown so bad,
Mad slanderers by mad ears believed be.   12
   That I may not be so, nor thou belied,
   Bear thine eyes straight, though thy proud heart
     go wide.

CXLI

In faith, I do not love thee with mine eyes,
For they in thee a thousand errors note ;
But 'tis my heart that loves what they despise,
Who, in despite of view, is pleas'd to dote.
Nor are mine ears with thy tongue's tune delighted ;
Nor tender feeling, to base touches prone,   6
Nor taste, nor smell, desire to be invited
To any sensual feast with thee alone :
But my five wits nor my five senses can
Dissuade one foolish heart from serving thee,
Who leaves unsway'd the likeness of a man,
Thy proud heart's slave and vassal wretch to be :   12
   Only my plague thus far I count my gain,   13
   That she that makes me sin awards me pain.

CXLII

Love is my sin, and thy dear virtue hate,
Hate of my sin, grounded on sinful loving :
O ! but with mine compare thou thine own state,
And thou shalt find it merits not reproving ;
Or, if it do, not from those lips of thine,
That have profan'd their scarlet ornaments   6
And seal'd false bonds of love as oft as mine,
Robb'd others' beds' revenues of their rents.
Be it lawful I love thee, as thou lov'st those
Whom thine eyes woo as mine importune thee :
Root pity in thy heart, that, when it grows,
Thy pity may deserve to pitied be.   12
   If thou dost seek to have what thou dost hide,
   By self-example mayst thou be denied !

CXLIII

Lo, as a careful housewife runs to catch
One of her feather'd creatures broke away,
Sets down her babe, and makes all swift dispatch
In pursuit of the thing she would have stay ;
Whilst her neglected child holds her in chase,
Cries to catch her whose busy care is bent   6
To follow that which flies before her face,
Not prizing her poor infant's discontent :
So runn'st thou after that which flies from thee,
Whilst I thy babe chase thee afar behind ;
But if thou catch thy hope, turn back to me,
And play the mother's part, kiss me, be kind ;   12
   So will I pray that thou mayst have thy ' Will,'
   If thou turn back and my loud crying still.

CXLIV

Two loves I have of comfort and despair,
Which like two spirits do suggest me still :
The better angel is a man right fair,
The worser spirit a woman colour'd ill.
To win me soon to hell, my female evil
Tempteth my better angel from my side,   6

And would corrupt my saint to be a devil,
Wooing his purity with her foul pride.
And whether that my angel be turn'd fiend
Suspect I may, yet not directly tell ;
But being both from me, both to each friend,
I guess one angel in another's hell :   12
    Yet this shall I ne'er know, but live in doubt,
    Till my bad angel fire my good one out.

CXLV

Those lips that Love's own hand did make,
Breath'd forth the sound that said ' I hate,'
To me that languish'd for her sake :
But when she saw my woeful state,
Straight in her heart did mercy come,
Chiding that tongue that ever sweet   6
Was us'd in giving gentle doom ;
And taught it thus anew to greet ;
' I hate,' she alter'd with an end,
That follow'd it as gentle day
Doth follow night, who like a fiend
From heaven to hell is flown away.   12
    ' I hate ' from hate away she threw,
    And sav'd my life, saying ' Not you.'

CXLVI

Poor soul, the centre of my sinful earth,
Fool'd by these rebel powers that thee array,
Why dost thou pine within and suffer dearth,
Painting thy outward walls so costly gay ?
Why so large cost, having so short a lease,
Dost thou upon thy fading mansion spend ?   6
Shall worms, inheritors of this excess,
Eat up thy charge ?   Is this thy body's end ?
Then, soul, live thou upon thy servant's loss,
And let that pine to aggravate thy store ;
Buy terms divine in selling hours of dross ;
Within be fed, without be rich no more :   12
    So shalt thou feed on Death, that feeds on men,
    And Death once dead, there 's no more dying then.

CXLVII

My love is as a fever, longing still
For that which longer nurseth the disease ;
Feeding on that which doth preserve the ill,
The uncertain sickly appetite to please.
My reason, the physician to my love,
Angry that his prescriptions are not kept,   6
Hath left me, and I desperate now approve
Desire is death, which physic did except.
Past cure I am, now Reason is past care,
And frantic-mad with evermore unrest ;
My thoughts and my discourse as madmen's are,
As random from the truth vainly express'd ;   12
    For I have sworn thee fair, and thought thee bright,
    Who art as black as hell, as dark as night.

CXLVIII

O me ! what eyes hath Love put in my head,
Which have no correspondence with true sight ;
Or, if they have, where is my judgment fled,
That censures falsely what they see aright ?
If that be fair whereon my false eyes dote,
What means the world to say it is not so ?   6
If it be not, then love doth well denote
Love's eye is not so true as all men's : no,
How can it ? O ! how can Love's eye be true,
That is so vex'd with watching and with tears ?
No marvel then, though I mistake my view ;
The sun itself sees not till heaven clears.   12
    O cunning Love ! with tears thou keep'st me blind,
    Lest eyes well-seeing thy foul faults should find.

CXLIX

Canst thou, O cruel ! say I love thee not,
When I against myself with thee partake ?
Do I not think on thee, when I forgot
Am of myself, all tyrant, for thy sake ?
Who hateth thee that I do call my friend ?
On whom frown'st thou that I do fawn upon ?   6

Nay, if thou lour'st on me, do I not spend
Revenge upon myself with present moan ?
What merit do I in myself respect,
That is so proud thy service to despise,
When all my best doth worship thy defect,
Commanded by the motion of thine eyes ?   12
   But, love, hate on, for now I know thy mind ;
    Those that can see thou lov'st, and I am blind.

CL

O ! from what power hast thou this powerful might,
With insufficiency my heart to sway ?
To make me give the lie to my true sight,
And swear that brightness doth not grace the day ?
Whence hast thou this becoming of things ill,
That in the very refuse of thy deeds   6
There is such strength and warrantise of skill,
That, in my mind, thy worst all best exceeds ?
Who taught thee how to make me love thee more,
The more I hear and see just cause of hate ?
O ! though I love what others do abhor,
With others thou shouldst not abhor my state :   12
   If thy unworthiness rais'd love in me,
    More worthy I to be belov'd of thee.

CLI

Love is too young to know what conscience is ;
Yet who knows not conscience is born of love ?
Then, gentle cheater, urge not my amiss,
Lest guilty of my faults thy sweet self prove :
For, thou betraying me, I do betray
My nobler part to my gross body's treason ;   6
My soul doth tell my body that he may
Triumph in love ; flesh stays no farther reason,
But rising at thy name doth point out thee
As his triumphant prize. Proud of this pride,
He is contented thy poor drudge to be,
To stand in thy affairs, fall by thy side.   12
   No want of conscience hold it that I call
    Her ' love ' for whose dear love I rise and fall.

CLII

In loving thee thou know'st I am forsworn,
But thou art twice forsworn, to me love swearing ;
In act thy bed-vow broke, and new faith torn,
In vowing new hate after new love bearing.
But why of two oaths' breach do I accuse thee,
When I break twenty ? I am perjur'd most ;　　　6
For all my vows are oaths but to misuse thee,
And all my honest faith in thee is lost :
For I have sworn deep oaths of thy deep kindness,
Oaths of thy love, thy truth, thy constancy ;
And, to enlighten thee, gave eyes to blindness,
Or made them swear against the thing they see ;　　12
　For I have sworn thee fair ; more perjur'd I,
　To swear against the truth so foul a lie !

CLIII

Cupid laid by his brand and fell asleep :
A maid of Dian's this advantage found,
And his love-kindling fire did quickly steep
In a cold valley-fountain of that ground ;
Which borrow'd from this holy fire of Love
A dateless lively heat, still to endure,　　　6
And grew a seething bath, which yet men prove
Against strange maladies a sovereign cure.
But at my mistress' eye Love's brand new-fired,
The boy for trial needs would touch my breast ;
I, sick withal, the help of bath desired,
And thither hied, a sad distemper'd guest,　　12
　But found no cure : the bath for my help lies
　Where Cupid got new fire, my mistress' eyes.

CLIV

The little Love-god lying once asleep
Laid by his side his heart-inflaming brand,
Whilst many nymphs that vow'd chaste life to keep
Came tripping by ; but in her maiden hand
The fairest votary took up that fire
Which many legions of true hearts had warm'd ;　　6

SONNETS

And so the general of hot desire
Was, sleeping, by a virgin hand disarm'd.
This brand she quenched in a cool well by,
Which from Love's fire took heat perpetual,
Growing a bath and healthful remedy
For men diseas'd; but I, my mistress' thrall,   12
  Came there for cure, and this by that I prove,
  Love's fire heats water, water cools not love.

THE PEEBLES CLASSIC LIBRARY